Capturing The Pagan Mind

Capturing The Pagan Mind

Paul's Blueprint for Thinking and Living in the New Global Culture

Peter Jones

BROADMAN
&HOLMAN
PUBLISHERS

Nashville, Tennessee

0–8054–2589–6

Published by Broadman & Holman Publishers,
Nashville, Tennessee

Dewey Decimal Classification: 261
Subject Heading: PAGANISM \ CHRISTIANITY AND
CULTURE—UNITED STATES

Unless otherwise noted, Scripture is quoted from the Holy Bible,
New International Version, copyright © 1973, 1978, 1984 by
International Bible Society. Scripture quotations marked NASB are
from the New American Standard Bible, © the Lockman
Foundation, 1960, 1962, 1963, 1968, 1971, 1972, 1973, 1975, 1977;
used by permission. Scripture quotations marked NKJV are from
the New King James Version, copyright © 1979, 1980, 1982,
Thomas Nelson, Inc., Publishers.

1 2 3 4 5 6 7 8 9 10 08 07 06 05 04 03

Dedication

I dedicate this work to my grandchildren, Jesse, Liam, and Alethea Stoddard and to those whom God may yet give us, all of whom will doubtless face firsthand the reality of a pagan planet. I trust you will have the courage to live and speak the truth of Paul's timeless, Spirit-inspired message, to the glory of God, Creator and Redeemer, Father, Son, and Holy Spirit. To my grandson, Jonathan David Jones, to whom I can no longer speak in this earthly life. He has been spared the suffering and struggle and has tasted the "already," while we still live partly in the "not yet."

Contents

The Beast and the Prostitute

Simon Peter at last sees it all as Jesus saw it all from the beginning. Even then, Simon sees it from a topsy-turvy angle. He and some two thousand other Christians have been tied to crosses stuck upside down on the grassy embankment around the Imperial Gardens on Vatican Hill. They have been daubed with pitch. Tonight they are to be living, screaming, dying torches. Emperor Nero, his lovely concubine Poppaea, and their guests will have light to eat by and sights to joke about. Each Christian will die in the classic sign of Satan—the upside-down cross.[1]

This moving paragraph from a modern novel about the death of the apostle Peter captures a moment in the cruel history of the Roman persecution of Christians.[2] A similar fate had overtaken Jesus and would soon overwhelm the apostle Paul. How could such cruelty occur in the tolerant, fun-loving culture of first-century Rome? Why would the three great founding figures of early Christianity all die as bloodied victims of sophisticated Roman "justice"? Why would "the Beast" devour unarmed prey?

You are puzzled that I call glorious Rome "the Beast." I have read some Roman history and traveled extensively in Europe, abundant in Roman architectural gems such as the towering stadium tucked in the quaint city of Orange. Who would not be impressed with Roman culture? So solidly did the Romans build that the Europeans still use some of the Roman arenas for bullfights or professional sporting competitions!

I call Rome "the Beast" because the early church described the Roman Empire that way—as "the Beast and the Prostitute." In the X-rated language of the Bible, the risen Lord gives John a vision of "the great Prostitute" with whom "the kings of the earth committed adultery" and by whom "the inhabitants of the earth were intoxicated with the wine of her adulteries" (Rev. 17:1–2).

This "loose woman" rides on the back of the beast.[3] The picture is vivid: (a) powerful religious deception allied to and enforced by (b) totalitarian political power. A more dynamic duo one could hardly imagine. As John wrote to the churches of the Empire in the Roman province of Asia, his readers already knew what he meant. Roman government officials were arresting notable Christian leaders and putting them before the equivalent of a firing squad.[4] In addition, false teachers had infiltrated the church and were leading many into occult paganism.[5] In the context of persecution and heresy, Jesus Christ through John "challenges his people to look past appearances and perceive the horrendous spiritual core of Rome's impressive culture," to ask, "how could Rome be so bad when she looks so good?"[6]

Calling Rome the Beast and the Prostitute was not politically correct speech back then, and it certainly is not now. But Scripture is disarmingly direct when issues of life are at stake. Human empires often begin with beguiling promises and noble dreams, only to end in the nightmare of horrendous human cruelty. In the sad tale recounted by Edward Gibbon,[7] the Roman Empire—with its triumphs and tragedies, with its glory and shame—is but an expression of the general human condition.[8] What happens at the level of empires and nations also happens to individuals. We begin with great hopes, often to finish with deep disappointment and bitterness. The angel becomes a demon. Mankind, desiring the knowledge *of* good and evil,[9] uses that knowledge *for* good and evil. This is why the Bible—and we will follow its lead—speaks of the Roman Empire as the Beast and the Prostitute: because, going to the heart of the matter, Scripture points out the ultimate and inevitable end of autonomous human power and man-made religion as social and spiritual ruin.

I raise the example of the Roman Empire because in our time we are faced by perplexing questions. What does our rapidly globalizing world look like now, and what kind of planetary community awaits us? Can we get a perspective on these confusing times by looking back? How can Christians speak the gospel in a post-modern, post-Christian, and post-national situation? Does the Christian message remain the same? Will a new global situation require a new unifying religion?

The following pages seek to answer these questions that concern our generation, our children, and our grandchildren. I hope in this book to provide perspective on the times in which we live by looking to the early days of the Christian movement. The birth of Christianity coincided with the world dominance of the Roman Empire. The early Christians witnessed to their faith as a minuscule minority in a largely antagonistic, despotic, and pagan theocratic culture. In our day, though numerically powerful,[10] modern Christians often feel socially and politically impotent. Without a recognized voice, the true church finds itself marginalized in a global culture that is progressively more pagan. In some ways our present world culture, in spite of the great claims of democratic freedom, looks more and more like that of ancient Rome. As the West shakes off its Christian mantle and a unified global community begins to take shape, we can see instructive parallels with the past. Contemporary believers begin to relate more easily to their ancestors in the faith. The New Testament becomes obviously relevant, because it addressed situations like those we now face.

The interest now shown for ancient Rome, and Hollywood's plans to exploit it,[11] may mean that the lifestyle of ancient Rome resembles the present "party" lifestyle of the West. Does the next generation see in Rome's sensuality, glitz, and glorification of violence an appealing paradigm and historical justification for its own excesses? If so, can the church keep silent?

In such a project, there are dangers. It is ever so easy to draw superficial parallels and grand conclusions that mask genuine differences. Facile historical generalizations that fail to take into account the many particularities and endless complexities of life in other times may be advanced. It is perhaps a little easy to stack the evidence one way, since the witnesses of the era are long since dead and gone and can raise no protest.

Nevertheless, those who ignore history are condemned to repeat it, and a failure to look back and learn from the past is a form of cultural narcissism. Looking at the past, however, will not help us if we do not make astute comparisons between events from the past and events in our present situation. Without such comparisons, we will stare into the mirror of the past, stand horrified at the image, and then walk away without changing. Christians realize that the Bible is full of lessons from its own past and that God runs history. We are perhaps a little more courageous than some to take the risk of examining history. So let us look boldly at the past, and even more frankly at our present, asking the God of history to preserve us for his own purposes.

Acknowledgments

This book has been a long time in the making. It began in 1970 at Princeton Seminary, as a Ph.D. thesis examining Paul's view of the apostolic office as a fulfillment of the foundation-laying ministry of Moses. It was broadened in 1974 as *La théologie de Paul*, the first course I ever taught as a founding professor of the Free Reformed Seminary in Aix-en-Provence, France. Eighteen years of intellectual and theological stimulation from colleagues and students, my battle with Greek, French, and English all at once, my commentary in French on 2 Corinthians, and interaction with the writings of scholars such as Gerhardus Vos, Hermann Ridderbos and Richard Gaffin—all these sharpened and enriched my thinking about the monumental message of Paul, the "last" apostle.

When I returned to the United States in 1991 to teach at Westminster Theological Seminary, I rejoiced to teach in my mother tongue, but a great surprise awaited me. I found myself driven to understand Paul in the light of the startling reality that "Christian" America had gone pagan. Paul's thought was no longer merely an interesting but closed system. His interaction with the paganism of his day forced me to see his message as a sharp counterpoint to the pagan agenda of our own day.

Many colleagues and students at Westminster encouraged me in this endeavor, for which I am most grateful. I would especially like to thank my colleague Dennis Johnson, New Testament scholar and chairman of the practical theology department, for reading this manuscript and making many insightful comments.

Thanks to the imagination and boldness of Broadman & Holman, and specifically of my friend and editor, Leonard G. Goss, this long-developing, sometimes daunting, project now becomes reality. My deep desire is that the full-orbed revelation of God, communicated through the brilliant, Christ-exalting mind of Paul, will inform our often nar-row and individualistic thinking about the Christian faith, so that in the coming days of certain conflict the church's witness, buoyed by gen-uine hope, will do full justice to God's work of cosmic creation and recreation.

Even the biblical words "suitable helper" sometimes seem inade-quate to describe my wife's participation in bringing this book to term. Her help has been not merely suitable, but overwhelmingly gracious. In addition to all she does for me and our seven children and for count-less friends in need, she has dedicated endless hours to editing, check-ing footnote references, and insisting on style consistency, with a commitment to detail that amazes and honors me. We all rise up and call her blessed. Though the Gnostics believed that Adam's need for a helper was the sign of his fall from autonomous "spiritual" existence, I believe such help is part of God's good design. Scripture has a word for this: "He who finds a wife finds what is good, and receives favor from the Lord" (Prov. 18:22). Rebecca, you bring to me in so many ways the Lord's good favor. Thank you.

Part One

At the beginning of the first century, Rome held sway over the known earth, and neither knew nor cared about the fledgling "Christian" cult from Palestine. The past and future glory and power of Rome determined how people read history.

The coming global village reads history in a similar way—as the triumph of human ingenuity and the forces of nature bringing about a unified and peaceful planet. In spite of two thousand years of Christian civilization, the Christian message no longer determines our expectations. The proof? In the academic circles of the once-Christian West, B.C. (before Christ) and A.D. (in the year of our Lord) has been removed as the means of identifying dates in history.[1] One apostate Christian theologian argues that the demise of Christianity is so obvious that "some future generation may well be moved to discard the Christian calendar entirely, and rename the year A.D. 2000 as 1 G.E., the first year of the global era."[2]

The New Testament writers saw things differently. Christ was the center of history, both as the fulfillment of Israel's hopes and as the future judge and savior of the cosmos. Thus, the Bible reveals the victorious end of the story, and Christians see history from two perspectives, both from a sky box in the heavenlies and from the playing field on which the contest is raging.[3]

From this biblical vantage point, history is not seen as the inevitable progress of mankind in the realization of a this-worldly utopia, but the constant interplay between *the seed of the woman* and *the seed of the serpent* for the ultimate victory of the glory of God, Creator and Redeemer.[4] The apostle John describes this struggle in history against the backdrop of the struggle with Rome. Rome is not only the immediate threat to Christian survival but also the symbol of a final world power with seemingly absolute control. His message is that the slain lamb of God will be the great victor, and "Babylon" will eventually fall.[5]

If ancient Rome is the biblical paradigm for the coming planetary empire, then the Bible hardly leaves us in the dark as to what the future holds. In understanding Rome, we can understand the essential nature of the global village. It is over against Rome, both past and future, that we also understand with informed biblical realism the nature of the Christian message and the character of Christian witness.

Such an undertaking is urgent. The apostle John's apocalyptic read of history is about to become history, making Paul's message to pagans of absolute importance.

Chapter 1

Pax Romana
or Roman Beast?

The Roman Empire was one of the greatest achievements of human civilization. Through its brilliant organization and pragmatic approach to everyday problems, Rome offered its citizens a level of peace and prosperity superior to any the ancient world had ever known. But the benefits had a price tag. In the animal kingdom, the most powerful beast rules. In the human kingdom, as the biblical Book of Revelation declares, the most powerful beast is an international totalitarian political power. That power rules a diverse but pacified population, and offers them no place to hide. Such was the power of the beast that was Rome.

The Coming of Peace and the Birth of the Beast

On September 11, 2001, I watched on live television as a fully-loaded jetliner exploded with hellish ferocity into the Twin Towers in lower Manhattan. Such a catastrophe will forever mark the generations that witnessed it. Reality is stranger than fiction, the daily news more bizarre than a Hollywood script. From a primitive cave on the other side of the world, a wild-eyed Muslim fanatic choreographed the execution of three thousand souls in the bustling business district of sophisticated lower Manhattan. Afghanistan was front page for months, while we learned of the bombing of faraway places like Kabul, Jalalabad, and Kandahar. The world suddenly got smaller.

But that world had become smaller a long time ago. Kandahar is a form of the name "Alexander." In the fourth century B.C., the twenty-five-year-old Alexander the Great—perhaps the original Western hippie

3

to take the road east to Katmandu in search of a spiritual holy grail—
founded this town in Afghanistan and gave it his name. What was a
Western Greek doing so far from home? He was setting up what would
become the Greco-Roman Empire, which stretched from western
Macedonia to Hindu India.

Alexander's Ragged Band

The Roman Beast seemed tame enough when it was defined as
Alexander's dream of taking Western culture to the whole world. In just
eleven years, this brilliant young soldier/statesman defeated the entire
Persian Empire and marched his men east as far as India. Disappointed
to discover that this was not the end of the world, he determined to slog
on; but his exhausted, ragged men would go no farther. But Alexander
had already spread his Greek, Hellenistic Western culture throughout
the known world, an achievement hailed as one of the great events of
human history. Historians contend that his "appearance forms a turning point in the history of the race," an event greater than the
Renaissance or the Reformation.[1] He is believed to be "the inaugurator
of that comprehensive cosmopolitanism . . . (a unified world) . . . that
reached its apogee in the Roman Empire . . . his [great] aim was to
accomplish 'the marriage of the East and the West.'"[2]

This view of modern scholarship mirrors that of ancient writers
who make a similar claim about Alexander: "Considering himself
appointed by God as a universal ruler and reconciler, . . . he brought
together everything from every quarter. . . . He commanded all to
regard the world as their fatherland."[3]

A modern scholar says of the final product, Rome, that it was "the
heart of the world's first and only unified global civilization."[4] This
massive pagan empire spanned the East and the West over a period of
six centuries, from 333 B.C., to the conversion of Constantine in
A.D. 312.[5] It is here that we locate the birth of Rome.

It is not my intention in the pages that follow to give an exhaustive
description of Roman life and culture, which would include the glorious and the inglorious, the beautiful and the ugly, or what theologians
call "common grace" and "common curse." My goal is to highlight the
features of the Roman Empire that brought about global peace and to

explain why Rome can at the same time be called a "beast." To this end,
I will describe first the international and generally pacified character of
the Empire, with its economic successes and its elements of police control. Chapter 2 will attempt to show the place of religion within that
political structure.

The Roman Empire: Global and Pacified

When Rome defeated the last royal descendent of Alexander in 176 B.C.,
she inherited and immediately assumed the full extent and the many
achievements of the Greek Empire. In the fourth century B.C.,
Alexander had destroyed the long-standing political organization of
fiercely independent Greek city-states and had set up imperial, central
control. Under Alexander's rule emerged "a new sense of the inhabited
world, as the international stage for human action."[6]

The pragmatic Romans increased the efficiency of the system they
inherited. Rome became the center of the world and an ethnic melting
pot. At the time of the New Testament, its population had grown to
about a million and a half people, a megalopolis the likes of which the
ancient world had never seen.[7] People flocked to Rome, the unique
city—the only city in the world[8]—a definition Italians still seem to
favor! "The two main poles of the Romans' mental universe were the
city and the world."[9] The pope begins his annual Easter message with
the phrase *ad urbi et orbi*—"to the City and the World." It is the old
Roman imperial, "Romanocentric" way of describing the globe. For the
ancient Romans, "everything that happened began in Rome and to
Rome everything returned."[10] Rome was the center of the universe.
From *la città eterna*, the eternal city, the representatives of power—gov-
ernors, magistrates, and tax collectors—would leave, to levy taxes and
to enforce the pax Romana throughout the Empire.

Rome owed to Alexander the homogeneity of its enormous empire.
Through him, Greek culture, and especially the Greek language, spread
from Greece to India, bringing to East and West a unity that "has never
been achieved since."[11] Some ancient languages and cultures, like the
Phoenician, disappeared for good once Greek ways were adopted.
People dressed like Greeks, undressed and exercised like Greeks (in the
gymnasia),[12] philosophized like Greeks, wrote like Greeks, taught like

Greeks, built buildings like the Greeks, and tried to sound like Greeks. It was cool to be Greek and Western. This was the beginning of the first westernized world culture, a unity that Rome completed and exploited for purposes of empire. Romans were happy to speak Greek well into the first century A.D.[13] Only later did Latin take over.

My sons love Monty Python and sometimes spend a fun evening reciting sections of dialogue from some of the less bawdy skits. Much to our delight, they get all the right accents and intonations. They keep the family in stitches reproducing the hilarious debate among the members of the Judaean Popular People's Front, a radical protest group trying to drum up hatred of the Romans. Revolutionary #1 asks: "What have the Romans ever done for us?" Revolutionary #2, a realist, answers, quite reasonably, "Sanitation." Revolutionary #1, "All right, but apart from that, what have the Romans done for us?" Revolutionary #2 replies, "Education." The debate continues as the realist lists all the advantages brought by the Romans—public order, irrigation, roads, the fresh-water system, public health. Revolutionary #1 replies in frustration: "But apart from sanitation, medicine, education, wine, public order, irrigation, roads, the fresh-water system, and public health, what have the Romans ever done for us?" "Peace!" is one of the helpful answers.

Roman Utopia: Bread and Circuses

Roman citizens doubtless realized that Rome's power and ingenuity had provided an ease of life unequaled in the history of the world. One historian notes that after the triumph of Rome over the Hellenistic empire: "The whole world was weary of war. . . . Hence the rise of the Empire was universally hailed as the dawn of a better era. The *Pax Romana* . . . called forth a chorus of profound thanksgiving. . . . Emperors were hailed as Saviors, sons of the Divine, Protectors of the human race."[14]

These saviors took care of their own. The Roman satirical writer, Juvenal, in around A.D. 100, coined the famous phrase *panem et circences*—"bread and circuses,"[15] to indicate how the Roman state looked after (and controlled) the population through material plenty and endless entertainment. Such economic plenty and social peace must have caused many to believe that life could not be much better.

BREAD

There was an abundance of bread.[16] Alexander's colonization of the ancient world produced the first international mass market, based on ease of travel and transport afforded by the Mediterranean Sea. For the first time, the West gained economic supremacy over the East and a period of unparalleled, sustained prosperity prevailed. Newly minted coins standardized the monetary system so that goods flowed freely. In particular, the granaries of Egypt exported their goods all over the world. Boats loaded with grain left the Egyptian port of Alexandria on the hour to feed the voracious appetite of Roman consumption. There was no problem with the bread side of Juvenal's equation. After the defeat of the last king of Macedonia in 167 B.C., Romans no longer paid taxes. Can you imagine—no IRS? Moreover, constant military conquests meant that unfamiliar and exotic Eastern delicacies from India and Persia now flowed into Rome with untold abundance.[17] The waterways were not the only means of transport. Rome built fifty thousand miles of paved roads to facilitate cultural exchange and political control.

At the time of the formation of the New Testament, Rome attained its highest level of material riches.[18] Conspicuous consumption marked the life of the emperor. Even Nero's fishing nets were made of gold, threaded with meshes of purple and crimson silk. He paid four million sesterces (dollars[19]) for embroidered Babylonian sofa coverlets. His wife, Poppaea, not content with bathing in asses' milk, had her mules decked out in golden shoes;[20] and Caligula kept his favorite horse in a stable made of exquisite marble. It was the horse he planned to make a senator! Approximately twenty thousand slaves were in attendance at the imperial palace to take care of his lordship's every whim. The emperor had as many categories of slaves to arrange and tend his wardrobe as he had separate types of clothes.[21] They had plenty of work, since Nero never wore the same robe twice.[22] Private individuals were only slightly less opulent. Wealthy Roman families often owned up to a thousand slaves. Toward the end of the first century A.D., a successful ex-slave, one C. Caelius Isidorus, owned no less than 4,116 slaves![23]

CIRCUSES—ROME: A SPORTS FAN'S DREAM COME TRUE

Discretionary income was lavished on mass entertainment to a degree never seen in the history of the world and unparalleled until modern times. The emperor, known as the *princeps* (the first citizen), was the number one sports fan. He was also the primary channel surfer—old world style—as well as the number one customer.[24] His lordship's day provided endless pleasures in a personalized home-entertainment center that would put its modern-day multi-channeled, wrap-around stereophonic equivalent to shame. For his majesty's viewing pleasure, an NBA-sized athletic arena stood right next to the imperial palace. Behind and below the palace, which sat on a high bluff, was the Circus Maximus, a stadium three or four times the size of an NFL ball park that could seat anywhere from 250,000 to 380,000.[25] From the palace balcony—a fully-equipped first-century skybox—the emperor could watch chariot races from morning till night, more violent and intense than any Monday Night Football game, complete with *iubilatores*, "cheerleaders," whose duty it was to encourage their racing teams to maximum effort by victory chants.[26]

Life: The Movie

Just as they loved the great spectacles, the Romans loved their bodies. They kept them clean, perfumed, suntanned, and in excellent physical condition, because each Roman pictured himself on stage.[27] Image was everything. To the left of the Circus Maximus were acres of gymnasia and baths that served as an enormous twenty-four-hour imperial fitness center that was a part of the daily life of every able-bodied Roman.[28] It was none other than Juvenal, the Roman author of the first century, who came up with the famous phrase: "a healthy mind in a healthy body."[29] The Romans wanted good bodies to play the part:

One's body could not lie: the image communicated to others was an expression of one's character. Roman culture was without inwardness: a Roman's awareness of himself came from the way others perceived him. His virtues and vices were an open book: they were printed in his movements, style of dress, voice. The Romans were forever on stage but they played themselves. They used their hands, face and gestures as well as words to express themselves. Everything was loudly expressive: even sobriety could be outspoken and flashy. *Gravitas,* the senatorial virtue *par excellence,* meant a careful step, a close-fitting toga, a ponderous delivery, few gestures.[30]

I cannot help thinking of the title of a recent best-seller, *Life: The Movie.*[31]

It's Only a Game

The emperor had other channels to watch. A three-minute chariot ride away from the imperial palace stood the Coliseum, a structure only slightly smaller than the Los Angeles version, built toward the end of the first century A.D., in which his majesty could assuage his thirst for blood, animal or human, throughout the long, hot Roman afternoons. Being there was, doubtless, "twice the fun," for virtually every contest went to the death. It was "fun" for the spectators. For the participants, the next fight could be the last, so it was in their interests to be good. Apparently only two gladiators in a school of twenty thousand were able to train themselves never to blink under any conditions, thereby making themselves invincible, since "they neither missed any of their opponents' moves nor gave anything away themselves."[32] Such intensity of self-control for self-preservation is difficult to imagine. The tension of making a four-foot putt worth a million dollars—without blinking—pales in comparison. What if missing the putt condemned you to death by clubbing with a nine-iron? Such intensity was draining even for the spectators. So in the evening the magnificent dining hall of "Caesar's Palace" doubled as both a five-star restaurant and a relaxing nightclub floor show, worthy of any Las Vegas extravaganza.

In Rome's early history, from around 200 B.C., there were seven days per year devoted to "games" (*ludi,* from which we get "ludicrous," which means frivolous). At the time of the emperor Claudius (10 B.C.–A.D. 54) the Roman calendar contained 159 days celebrated as holidays, of which 93 were devoted to games given at public expense, and this list does not include many non-state sponsored ceremonies.[33] The emperors added official game days the way we add TV channels. For a sports fan, that's progress! With the obsession for sports came an obsession for gambling, the proceeds from which the state used for its own ends.[34]

The Mark of the Beast—Totalitarian Control

Material success and leisure came at a price. From one perspective, Rome was a fabulous social achievement. From another, it was a terrifying success in social manipulation. This geographically vast and ethnically cosmopolitan empire was held together by overt and subtle techniques of control. Material plenty, often ill-gotten[35] and ill-used, dependent on the scandal of slavery, bred complacency. People demanded more and more festive wealth until Rome choked on its own affluence. A contemporary of Jesus, the Roman historian Livy (59 B.C.–A.D. 17), left this telling indictment: "Of late, wealth has made us greedy, and excessive pleasures produce a general desire to carry wantonness and license to the point of personal ruin and universal destruction."[36]

Though state welfare and material excess produced inevitable social decadence, they also worked wonders as an unintended form of state control. Some were not fooled, as Juvenal's "bread and circuses" remark indicates. The general populace was not bothered, as long as food and entertainment abounded. The emperors, eager to maintain power, were happy to oblige.[37] A historian of the period remarks: "Even in lean years, when treasury shortages compelled them to ration their expenditure, [the rulers] exhausted their ingenuity to provide the public with more festivals than any people, in any country, at any time, has ever seen."[38]

A contemporary said of the emperor Trajan at the end of the first century that his "wisdom never failed to pay attention to the stars of the theatre, the circus, or the arena, for he well knew that the excellence of a government is shown no less in its care for the amusements of the people than in serious matters, and that although the distribution of corn and money may satisfy the individual, spectacles are necessary for the contentment of the masses."[39]

Perhaps no culture except our own has been so dominated by entertainment. Back then the emperors consciously used it for social control.

Crumbling Intermediary Social Structures

A balanced society includes intermediary structures that tend to limit state power. In the Roman Empire, those structures included the family and marriage. Critics of patriarchy in any form will often turn to the Roman family as the classical expression of patriarchal authority. The Roman patriarch was an all-powerful father in a hierarchical structure. The Roman family was no idyllic institution, and the Roman *pater* was far from angelic. For various reasons "the Romans proclaimed to any-one prepared to listen that there was nothing worse than marriage, and that, were it not for the necessity of producing children, no one would ever get married."[40] Married couples avoided meeting one another in private, for privacy was a constant source of friction.[41] All this valid criticism notwithstanding, the Roman family constituted a structure of stability for all involved, husbands, wives, and children alike. During the first century A.D., the Roman family, this "unassailable rock," had cracked and crumbled away on every side.[42]

EARLY FEMINISM

During this same period the role of the woman began to change. No longer content to be "housewives," some Roman women, for reasons good or not so good, chose "emancipation" from the duties of maternity and engaged in "male" pursuits like law, politics, public debate, dressing like a man, hunting with men (spear in hand), gladiatorial jousting in full armor, fencing, wrestling in the nude, and other feats of strength and physical prowess.[43] Historian Carcopino speaks of "'emanci pated' . . . wives, who were the various product of the new conditions of Roman marriage. Some evaded the duties of maternity for fear of losing their good looks; some took a pride in being behind their husbands in no sphere of activity, and vied with them in tests of strength which their sex would have seemed to forbid; some were not content to live their lives by their husband's side, but carried on another life without him at the price of betrayals and surrenders for which they did not even trouble to blush."[44] Freedom came with a price.

REDEFINITION OF THE FAMILY

With emancipation came the loosening of family ties. At the beginning of the second century A.D., the family name was no longer exclusively defined by male descent. Now the line could be traced through the female and through illegitimate relationships.[45] By the second century the father's absolute authority over his children and wife, the so-called *Patria Potestas,* had "completely disappeared."[46] Fathers gave up their rights to arrange marriages for their children, thus revolutionizing both marriage and the family—for good and ill.[47]

In this "liberated culture," personal "choice" prevailed, adultery became endemic,[48] and divorce spread unchecked. Men divorced their wives with impunity, and women their husbands. Juvenal illustrates the situation with biting humor: "Thus does she lord it over her husband. But before long she vacates her kingdom; she flits from one home to another wearing out her bridal veil. . . . Thus does the tale of her husbands grow; there will be eight of them in the course of five autumns— a fact worthy of commemoration on her tomb."[49]

Another Roman writer of the period, Martial (A.D. 38–101), comments about a woman marrying her tenth husband: "I am less offended by a more straightforward prostitute."[50] Says the historian Carcopino, "Divorces were so common that—as we learn from the jurists of the time—a series of them not infrequently led to the fair lady and her dowry returning, after many intermediate stages, to her original bridal bed."[51]

ALTERNATE SEXUALITY

Outside the limiting sphere of heterosexual marriage, already disfigured, other more or less accepted forms of sexual activity called for Roman attention. Bisexuality was common among the elite.[52] According to Suetonius, the Roman historian and biographer, the Roman Emperor Caligula (A.D. 12–41), believing himself to be God, once said: "for me anything is licit."[53] He put his religion into practice by living in habitual incest with his sisters,[54] and at the same time having homosexual relations with a number of courtiers.[55] In addition, according to the historian Florence Dupont, paedophilia was a constant and accepted expression of Roman sexual appetite. As in ancient Greece, "Roman boys were pursued relentlessly by adult men. . . . Sooner or later, in fact, every Roman was accused of being effeminate."[56] Dupont goes on to state: "If children were constantly molested, it was because Roman adults found that the deepest-rooted passion and the one that was hardest to overcome was sexual desire for very young boys and girls."[57]

DROP OF THE BIRTH RATE

This liberation movement of the first century inevitably affected the birth rate at the beginning of the second century and beyond. According to the historian Will Durant, the fall of Rome was in great part attributable to the Roman refusal to bear and raise children. A serious decline of population appears in the West after Hadrian (emperor A.D. 117–138): "A law of Septimus Severus speaks of a *penuria hominum*—a shortage of men." In Greece the depopulation had been going on for centuries. In Alexandria, which had boasted of its numbers, Bishop Dionysius calculated that the population had been halved in his time (A.D. 250). He mourned to see "the human race diminishing and constantly wasting away. Only the barbarians and Orientals were increasing, outside the Empire and within."[58] Durant points to the widespread practice of infanticide, abortion, sexual excesses, and the avoidance or deferment of marriage as the likely causes in this plunging population.[59]

With the weakening of these intermediary structures of family and marriage, the socially destabilizing effects of alternate sexual practices, and the depressing, relentless drop in the birth rate, the liberated individual stood face to face and often alone before the enormous power of the police state. What looked like utopia on earth from one perspective seemed dark and foreboding from another.

Police Control

Discipline was absolutely necessary in an empire of police control. Such discipline was evident in the sporting performances of gladiators and charioteers, but these spectacles were merely one facet of dazzling Roman pomp—as any fan of Hollywoodian imperial epics knows. *Ben Hur, Quo Vadis, Spartacus* and *The Robe* give some idea of the impressive pageantry Rome produced so professionally for the admiring throngs. Though American high school grad nights may be getting close, no one did victory processions or "triumphs" better than the Romans. In memory of the defeat of the Palestinian insurrection and the destruction of the Jerusalem temple in the Jewish War of A.D. 68–70, the emperor Titus later built at one end of the Forum (the ancient Roman civic center) a massive stone arch, like the *Arc de*

Triomphe in Paris. Upon returning to Rome, he, his troops, his brother Domitian (another future emperor and ruthless persecutor of Christians), and his father, the newly appointed emperor Vespasian, processed in their many-colored military splendor, as thousands of spectators lining the main street roared in approval. Behind the conquerors were dragged in chains the benighted Israelite prisoners of war. At the lower end of the Forum, in front of the great temple of Jupiter Capitolinus, the procession concluded with an elaborate religious ceremony in praise of imperial divine power. As the crowd cheered, some of the notable prisoners were killed on the spot. The rest were led to the adjacent Mamartine prison where they too were butchered to the glory of the eternal Roman *Reich*.

The message of the Roman *triumph* was unmistakable to foreign enemies and citizens alike—do not mess with Rome. The unbending discipline found among the gladiators was also to be found in the common soldier, and its rigor turned the Roman army into an invincible killing machine.[60] For the Roman soldier, surrender was unthinkable, defeat an unacceptable outcome. "Rome had a way of waging war that was incomprehensible to other nations and which transformed its soldiers into conquerors; it no longer played traditional war games."[61] To this as well, Alexander made a small contribution by introducing to the West the Eastern practice of crucifixion.[62] With this and other gruesome control techniques, an implacably cruel military dictatorship ruled the earth (*orbis*) but also the city (*urbis*).

Give Peace a Chance

The famous pax Romana (generally tranquil conditions made possible by efficient administration and unequaled authority) was clearly a military and political peace, producing an unusually fruitful period of economic "good times." But some paid for peace with their lives. Roman power could put down dissent in the name of civic order whenever it desired. One example must suffice. In A.D. 61 a slave murdered his master, Lucius Pedanius Secundus, either because master Lucius had failed to give the slave his promised freedom or because he had seduced the slave's male lover.[63] The law required the execution not only of the murderer, but of every slave living under Lucius' roof (four hundred men, women, and children). In spite of great opposition from the crowds, and some hesitation even on Nero's part, the four hundred were burned alive. The social order had to be preserved.

Cicero, the famous Roman orator, born in 106 B.C., reminded an exiled political opponent of the Empire: "Remember that [wherever you go] you are equally within the power of the conqueror."[64] For its time, Rome was an overwhelming "global village." Dissidents could find no place to run. In the eighteenth century, Edward Gibbon wrote a two-thousand-page history of the decline and fall of Rome, long before the modern reality of our planetary village. However, he caught something of the "globalist" character of Roman power. Comparing his own time of separate nation-states, and the freedom to change one's ruler for another in order to escape a local tyrant,[65] Gibbon sees the Roman Empire as fearfully totalitarian. "The empire of the Romans filled the world . . . [which] became a safe and dreary prison for [Caesar's] enemies. . . . To resist was fatal, and it was impossible to fly."[66] "Safe and dreary" is one form of peace, I suppose.

The Roman peace was assured by bread and circuses and the iron hand of the police state. Rome promised a lot to its citizens and delivered a lot, but it ultimately collapsed from moral failure. A population fed and entertained to the maximum and kept in check by the exercise of ruthless and often arbitrary physical power was sufficiently docile to see the cruelty of Rome as normal and necessary. That Rome enjoyed watching undesirable human beings ripped apart by wild beasts[67] makes the "beast" an appropriate symbol for what she became before her collapse.

Surprisingly, it was often harmless Christians who served as victims. One was Blandina, a frail young servant girl from a Christian community in Lyons. She was arrested during the persecutions of Marcus Aurelius (A.D. 161–180), the Stoic moral philosopher and white-haired gentle emperor of *Gladiator* fame. Not benefiting from the good emperor's general theories of the grandeur and order of the universe and the providence of the gods, this young lady was tortured from morning till night, with techniques that would have killed more sturdy souls. Indeed, eyewitnesses say she got stronger, buoyed up by the thought she constantly repeated: "I am a Christian woman, and nothing wicked happens to us." Eusebius, the church historian, says "she had put on the great and invincible athlete, Christ."[68] Sometime later she was put in the arena for the viewing pleasure of the blood-thirsty crowd. Here is how the witnesses described the event: "After scourging, after the beasts, after the gridiron (a heated iron chair), she was put into a net and thrown to a bull. She was tossed about a long time by the beast . . . and the pagans themselves confessed that never before among them had a woman suffered so much and so long."[69]

The long-suffering Blandina went to her well-earned heavenly reward. I plan to meet her one day. But this hideous spectacle in the arena is pregnant with larger significance. The Christian virgin ends up in the fangs of the pagan Beast not by accident or simply to fill a vacant spot in the afternoon program. She is devoured by the Beast at the urging of the Harlot.

Rome's intention was to control not just the body but also the soul—for the good of its world utopia.

Chapτer 2

Religious Harmony: The Harlot of Spiritual Deception

The Goddess Comes to Rome

Sated by material plenty and social ease, Rome was ready for spirituality. And, like two guided missiles honing in on a target, two powerful spiritual forces set their sights on Rome—the Goddess Earth Mother of this-worldly paganism and God the Father of our Lord Jesus Christ, Creator of heaven and earth.

Tradition has it that the covetous eye of Isis, the Egyptian goddess of witchcraft and magic, fell on Rome. As divine queen of the cosmos and the underworld, this "Goddess of a Thousand Names," under the name of Cybele, accompanied by her feminized priests, reputedly declared at the moment of an earthquake in the second century B.C.: "Rome is worthy to become the meeting-place of all the gods."[1] The all-knowing Great Mother realized that cosmopolitan Rome—cultural and political center of the ancient world—was ripe for occult spirituality and would give her an enthusiastic welcome. Christianity also headed for Rome, for similar "geo-religious" reasons.[2] These two powers were on a collision course that began in the East and culminated in the Western capital of the world, for one of the great face-offs in human religious history. The first round seems to have gone to the goddess.

17

Goddess from the East

When Paul got to Rome sometime in the fifties of the first century, temples dedicated to the Egyptian goddess of magic already had been erected and had taken their place in a vast array of religious options in a context of open-minded tolerance. The city was already under new management—though the takeover had not been without resistance. The goddess had not always reigned there.

The goddess came from the mists of time, from the Eastern reaches of the ancient planet. When I use the term *goddess*, I realize that I am in some sense making an amalgam of various female deity figures from a variety of religions. However, the goddess figure does represent a common understanding of spirituality. Often known as the Great Mother, she communicated the powers of the occult. The goddess Istar was a spiritual force in the Sumerian age (1800 B.C.), bridging the gap between the living and the dead with her occultic power.[3] The pagan religions of ancient Canaan worshiped the goddess Anat, a divinity resembling Istar.[4] The Syrian goddess Cybele or Atargatis had all the qualities of Anat.[5] The Cybele myth reproduces the cult myth of the Egyptian Isis, the goddess of witchcraft and magic.[6] This Eastern occultic goddess finally came to Rome.

Alexander Again

As in so many areas of Roman life, Alexander played a crucial role in preparing the way for her ladyship. While Alexander took Western culture and commerce to the East, the trade winds blew in the opposite direction when it came to religious matters. Oriental mysticism invaded the pragmatic, rationalistic West, bringing a dynamic of occult spirituality and creating what one scholar calls "the prevalence for half a millennium of the Gnosis conception of religion,"[7] a religious approach typical of the "mystery cults."[8] The rational, sophisticated Greeks, raised on Plato and Aristotle, discovered Eastern occult spirituality, served up in all kinds of mystical practices—"magic, astrology, demonology, theosophy, physico-psychical experiments,"[9] and goddess worship. The French historian, Robert Turcan, speaks of "an overwhelming and irresistible tide of eastern cults," flooding into the West.[10] In other words, when the goddess arrived in Rome, thanks to Alexander, she was already Westernized and spoke fluent Greek.[11]

She got to Rome just in time.

Religion in Rome: Caesar Is God

There were no atheists in Rome. Religion was not relegated, as it is in my local newspaper, to the back pages of the E Section—Food. It was center stage, headline news, an integral part of Roman culture. Roman religion was a tissue of daily, monthly, and yearly rituals, with the social and the religious virtually indistinguishable.[12] Like the games, Rome was a great pageant of the gods.

Official Roman religion was the preserve of the state. There was no church and state separation. Religion was political, and politics was religious.[13] As Cicero (106–43 B.C.), one of the great Roman statesmen/orators, said, a few years before the birth of Christ: "Among the many things . . . that our ancestors created under divine inspiration, nothing is more renowned than their decision to entrust the worship of the gods and the highest interests of the state to *the same men*."[14]

Politicians were pagan priests who ran the state, and the emperor, the *pontifex maximus,* was the highest priest/politician of them all, for he was considered the intermediary between Rome and the gods.[15] Specifically, the emperor was military commander in chief, political head of the government, and spiritual mediator for the Empire's vast religious needs—now that is *real* power! To reinforce the subjugation of religion to the state, the Roman cults were served exclusively by priests taken from the hundred or so elite senatorial families. Their readings of the oracles and omens inevitably confirmed the imperial status quo. Sponsored by the state, these official Roman cults enjoyed many privileges not granted to other religious expressions: their buildings stood on public land;[16] they were granted their festival days on the imperial calendar; and all Roman citizens, both high and low, were expected to participate,[17] which they did in great numbers, especially on the countless civic holidays. Naturally, the gods of the Roman pantheon represented imperial virtues and ideals such as valor, courage, and patriotism, and included, to name just a few, Aphrodite,

Apollo, Athena, Castor, Ceres, Diana, Demeter, Hephaistos, Hera, Hermes, Hestia, Hygieia, Juno, Jupiter, Minerva, Mars, Mercury, Neptune, Ourania, Pan, Pax, Pollux, Roma, Romulus, Rhea Silvia, Quirinus, Saturn, Venus, Vesta, Virgo, and Vulcan.[18] That's a lot of gods, and there were many more. No wonder they called it a "pan *(all)*— theon *(gods)*." Plutarch, an ancient writer and a contemporary of Paul, characterized imperial culture as "a goblet seething with myths."[19]

But they needed one more myth to make the system really work.

The emperor became so important in religious affairs that around the time of the beginning of Christianity some emperors were actually considered gods and worshiped along with Jupiter and Pan. Caesar Augustus (63 B.C.–A.D. 14) was divinized after his death. Caligula (A.D. 12–41), according to the contemporary Jewish historian Josephus, ceased to think of himself as a man . . . and imagined himself a god."[20] Toward the end of his reign Domitian (A.D. 51–96) demanded that public worship be given him as *Dominus et Deus* [Lord and God].[21] Totalitarian power could not be more complete.

FLAWS AND CRACKS

Traditional Roman religion kept pace with the religious-state system, but by the first century A.D., it had lost its *spiritual* power. Like what some would call "territorial spirits," the gods needed placating. This approach to spirituality is found in all pagan societies and can be thought of as a kind of animism; that is, the belief in and the need for control over evil spirits. Though we do not tend to think of the Greco-Roman Empire as animistic in its spirituality, the practical effects of their religious system meant that life was dominated by the perceived caprices of the gods. Life was threatened by the tyranny of fate, the caprice of fortune, the malice of demons, the crushing weight of the stars, the dread of magic, and the mystery of death. "The Romans thus spent their lives moving between one religious space and the next, switching gods and appropriate behavior as they went. This was the form assumed by polytheism in Rome: a proliferation of religious spaces. Each human activity was an act of worship to the deity that watched over it."[22]

There were gods of war, of home life, of cultivated soil, and of the garden. There were forest gods, hunting gods, gods of pasture, and gods of the sea. The Romans would have agreed that it "takes a village" of gods to rear a child: "Vitumnus gave him the breath of life, Sentinus his senses; Opis welcomed him on the ground; Vaticanus opened his mouth for his first scream; Levana lifted him from the ground; Cunina watched over his cradle and Ruminus over his breast-feeding; Paventia allayed his fears; Potina and Educa taught him how to drink and eat; Stativus showed him how to stand upright; and Adeona and Abeona helped him to walk to and fro."[23]

If someone fell ill, those around him would attempt to placate the gods. Life was filled with fear and worry that the gods had not been satisfied. Even state decisions were made with the whims of the gods in mind. Politicians would consult paid "augurs" to know when to engage foreign policy. "The augurs had classified and foretold everything: the various bird species; those whose flight one had to observe; those whose song alone was significant; the favorable and the unfavorable birds. They knew how to interpret the height and manner of flight, the type of perch chosen, the way a bird walked on touching down. Signs possessed their own arithmetic. If a woodpecker gave a sign but an eagle then arrived to take its place, the sign given by the eagle would cancel out that of the woodpecker."[24]

On a more mundane level, the fear of the unknown or the uncontrollable in the spirit world challenged the peace of everyday living. Individuals attempted to control their circumstances by manipulating the gods and one another. "How can I make this woman fall in love with me?" "How can I get even for the injustice my neighbor has inflicted upon me?" Such were the issues of life that frustrated powerless people. The ancient texts indicate that many were bound in crippling fear of the fates, refusing even to "take a bath, go to the barber, change their clothes, or manicure their fingernails without first awaiting the proper moment."[25] Bad fate (one can hardly avoid thinking of "karma") and evils spirits conspired to deny personal happiness. Solutions had to be found.[26] The never-ending struggle for deliverance from the spirits dominated people's lives.[27] It required constant attention, brought incapacitating mental fatigue, and caused great financial drain. Any promise of definitive release or rebirth, or the acquisition of real power, would be seen as a radical, liberating godsend.

That promise was offered by the goddess.

The Decay of Traditional Religion

What had happened in Greece, happened in Rome. The old Greek gods were identified with the old city-states. When these disappeared and the Empire became a reality, the gods faded in significance.[28] Intellectuals criticized the myths and looked elsewhere, in this case eastward, for spirituality. The old Roman religion also began to fade. As one scholar describes first-century Rome: "The spirits of men had fled from the old religion; it still commanded their service but no longer their hearts or their belief."[29] Juvenal documents the lack of piety for the old ways, and himself mocks the structure of the Roman religious myths.[30] In this vacuum of faith, Rome was ripe for the mysticism of the East. Roman faith changed its object and direction. It turned away from official polytheism to the mysteries of the Oriental gods and goddesses.[31]

Hail to the Goddess: Superiority of the Mystery Religions

Roman spirituality was saved by the goddess. As ruler of the dead, of demons and of magic, the one who possessed the key to the door of Hades, and goddess of the underworld,[32] she brought the everyday "techniques" of magical control into the spiritual domain of the mystery religions.[33] As the source of magic and witchcraft, she offered to her initiates the benefits of her cosmic power.[34] This was pagan mysticism with a pragmatic vengeance—the tangible power of the occult joined to a deep sense of personal redemption and union with all things.

Some in Rome were not yet convinced. In spite of the auspicious divine *diktat*, claiming Rome for the goddess, many in the elite class at first viewed the mystery cults with great suspicion. With their bizarre novelties and their obvious foreignness, the mysteries were just not Roman. But religious infiltration was unstoppable. Rome had become the capital and melting pot of the civilized world, "a microcosm of the cosmos,"[35] and the center of a new world religion. Along with the many races and cultures that were congregating in Rome came exotic cults from the East—the Greek mysteries of Eleusis, the cults of Cappadocia, the Phrygian cults of the Great Mother, the Egyptian Isis and Serapis, the *Dea Syria*, the Mithra cult from Persia, the cult of Dionysius, and the "cults of Gnosticism."[36] The goddess offered true and final redemption, which is why so many of the emperors of the first century fell for her charms.

Pro-Choice Spirituality

In spite of initial opposition, these mystery cults proved irresistible, even among the Roman elite. The attractions were many, and one of them was the condition for membership. Race and social position, prerequisites for religious power in the state religion, were of no help in cultivating the spiritual power of the mystery religions. All it took was personal choice and dedication. As the recognized authority, Walter Burkert states: "[the mysteries were] cults which were not prescribed or restricted by family, clan or class, but which could be chosen at will . . . [they were] initiation rituals of a voluntary, personal and secret character that aimed at a change of mind through experience of the sacred."[37]

If you think of all the religious options in Rome as academic courses, the mysteries would be the electives. Electives always appeal to some. Plenty of "students," especially women, found them irresistible. This was pro-choice spirituality at its most alluring. Women, who were struggling for social power in first-century Rome, were given important public offices and recognition in the cults of Isis and Cybele.[38] Thus, certain upper-class women, including wives of Roman senators, became involved in the worship of Isis long before their husbands.[39]

These cults were "personal religions" to which membership was open not by the accidents of birth but by a personal experience of rebirth. They suited the cosmopolitan world of the Greco-Roman Empire.

Roman Gay Pride

Often associated with these foreign cults was a note of transgressive
gender-bending. "In traditional Roman ideology, 'oriental' cults would
inevitably raise questions of gender,"[40] especially those associated with
the goddess. Roman machismo was severely threatened by the effeminate mysticism of the East. And this fear was not without reason, for
certain expressions of paganism have always embraced homosexuality
not as a "civil right," not as an unfortunate aberration of nature, nor as
an incidental non-issue, but as the considered expression of a fundamental theological commitment.[41] This was true long before the birth
of Christ and even as late as the fifth century A.D. After the adoption of
Christianity as the official religion of the Empire in A.D. 312, the cult of
the goddess continued to have success and great visibility. In the latter
part of the fourth century, Augustine in his *City of God* vividly
describes the "games" offered in honor of Tanit, the celestial "virgin"
and mother of the gods.[42] In these games, obscene actors role-played
disgusting acts "in the presence of an immense throng of spectators
and listeners of both sexes."[43] He also describes the public display of the
homosexual priests *(galloi):* "They were seen yesterday, their hair moist,
their faces covered in make-up, their limbs flaccid, their walk effeminate, wandering through the squares and streets of Carthage, demand-
ing from the public the means to subsidize their shameful life."[44]

The mystery cults were thus able to give spiritual significance to
alternate sexual practices.[45]

Personal Redemption

Simon Angus, an authority on the ancient mystery religions, offers this
definition: "a religion of symbolism which through myth and allegory,
iconic representations, blazing lights and dense darkness, liturgies and
sacramental acts, suggestions quickened by the heart, provoked in the
initiate a mystical experience leading to regeneration."[46]

Scholars suggest that this experience of initiation produced a "status dramatization" or ritual change of status.[47] What was once the sole
privilege of the emperor, who stood between the people and the gods,
and at death became a god, was now an experience open to all. The
individual in his initiation experienced himself as the center of the

universe, and, like the emperor, became divinized.[48] This is the experience of *gnosis*.[49] Sallistus (a first-century Latin writer) states: "Every initiation aims at uniting us with the world and the deity."[50] In the liturgy of mystical initiation, ecstasy is so intense that personal identity is lost, and communion with the divine becomes identity with the divine: "I am thou and thou art I." This is the experience of *coniunctione deorum*, the joining of the self with the gods.[51]

The Goddess, Savior from Death

This life-changing experience, provoked by various techniques, from drugs,[52] to induced ecstatic trance via dance and music,[53] to flogging,[54] supposedly allows one to escape the fear of death, and in some sense to escape death itself. One of the few available first-person accounts of an ancient mystery experience describes initiation into the mysteries of the goddess Isis: "I approached the frontier of death, I set foot on the threshold of Persephone [the underworld], I journeyed through all the elements and came back, I saw at midnight the sun, sparkling in white light, I came close to the gods of the upper and the nether world and adored them from near at hand."[55]

This ancient mystic was embraced by the light. Further on, we read this assuring word from Isis: "And when you have completed your lifetime and go down to the underworld, you will find me in the subterranean vault, shining in the darkness of Acheron (a river in Hades), and reigning in the innermost quarters of Styx (eldest of the daughters of Ocean, located at the very bottom of Tartarus/Hell), while you yourself inhabit the Elysian fields (Heaven), and you will adore me frequently, as I am well-disposed towards you."[56]

In the mystical initiation into Isis, the fear of death is destroyed through the experience of *osirization*, that is, a deep association with the resurrected Osiris (lover of Isis), whom the goddess brings back to life. In Egypt, as in Rome with the emperors, this was first limited to the pharaohs, but in the Greco-Roman period, immortality was granted to all who underwent Isian initiation. As Robert Turcan, an expert on Isis, notes: "By resuscitating her husband, Osiris, Isis offered her worshipers . . . the pledge of a victorious omnipotence over evil and death."[57] According to Burkert, in the classic initiation experience, "there is a dynamic paradox of death and life in all the mysteries associated with the opposites of night and day, darkness and light, below and above."[58] In other words, it involves the essential pagan experience of the "joining of the opposites."[59] The only other first-person account of initiation with which I am familiar comes from an ancient text of the magical papyri, which says: "I have been initiated, and I went down into the [underground chamber] of the Dactyls,[60] and I saw the other things down below, virgin, bitch and all the rest."[61]

Here, magic has taken on deep spiritual proportions. Isis, with all her sister personifications, as goddess of the underworld, is able to command an army of spirits to do her bidding to create in her initiates an experience of immense spiritual transformation or rebirth. But this kind of "regeneration" turned out to be the fruit of a pact with the devil; Dr. Faustus gone imperial. The personal cost was enormous. The dedication of a pagan priest into the mysteries consisted of "the offering of his actions, his intelligence and his life" to the Great Mother goddess.[62] This is not play-acting, but radical, total commitment to the powers of the occult.

The Goddess Wins: The Feminization of Roman Religion

The power of occultic gnosis seems to have taken over the elite of Rome. Here lies one of the roots of spiritual, social, and sexual liberation. It is fair to speak of the feminization of Roman spirituality. The early members of the mysteries were women, and the icon of worship was the independent, powerful goddess. Cults to Mars and Mithra, the male gods of war, so popular with the army, now take their humble place behind the all-conquering Isis and her colorful representations.

For in imperial Rome, the macho emperors are now worshiping Isis. The prophecy of the Great Mother regarding Rome had come true. Around the time of Paul, the veneration of the goddess through the mystery cults reaches the elite of imperial power, so that in "the second century of our era these cults were in process of submerging [both] the city,"[63] and the Empire at large.[64] Those devoted to Isis include significant figures in the ancient world of the time. With them, of course, came a host of social climbers, sycophants, and hangers-on of the

Roman court that do not get a mention in the historical record. Some of the goddess's more famous worshipers were, in all probability, Augustus (first emperor of Rome, 32 B.C.), Anthony and Cleopatra (31 B.C., who believed themselves to be the incarnation of Isis and Osiris, another form of Serapis),[65] the emperor Caligula (A.D. 37–41),[66] doubtless the emperor Nero (A.D. 54–68), and certainly the emperors Vespasian (A.D. 69–79), Titus (A.D. 79–81),[67] Domitian (A.D. 81–96),[68] Hadrian (A.D. 117–138),[69] and Julian the Apostate, the emperor who in the fourth century A.D. tried unsuccessfully to turn the "christianized" empire back to paganism.[70]

A Victory Celebration for the Goddess

The apostle Paul was executed in Rome in A.D. 66. Christianity had apparently lost, while the goddess had won.

In A.D. 69, during his campaign in Egypt, the Roman general Vespasian was proclaimed emperor by the army of the East. Believing his success was due to Serapis (Osiris), the consort of Isis, he reputedly restored a blind man's sight and healed a cripple. Clearly these men did not see themselves as mere generals or politicians! In the temple to Serapis "where the priests left him alone with the god,"[71] Vespasian had a deep mystical and occult experience. He immediately left to put down the Jewish revolt; but just as he began preparations for the siege of Jerusalem, he heard of the death of the emperor Nero and hurried back to Rome to claim the Empire. He left the job of destroying the temple and sacking the city to his son, Titus. Interestingly, Titus, who followed his father in the worship of Isis, insisted on entering the Holy of Holies just before it all burned down, perhaps to shake his fist, in the name of Isis—lady goddess of *this* world and of the powers of the underworld[72]—at God the Father, maker of heaven and earth.[73]

Why am I recounting all these details? They are important because we tend to read Roman history as mere politics. However, the events are not neutral history, not just political wars, but spirit wars. The conflict of biblical faith and paganism is an essential part of the drama. There is more here than "wrestling with flesh and blood" (Eph. 6:12 NKJV). Vespasian was a syncretist who promoted the 'worship of various Roman gods, his favorite being the cult of Pax. His other son, Domitian, always in his father's good graces,[74] promoted the worship of Minerva.[75] But Vespasian had a special place for Isis, the goddess of occult magic. Four years after the execution of Paul, on the eve of the celebration of their triumph over Judea and of the destruction of the Jerusalem temple, Vespasian and Titus spent the night in the temple of Isis on the Campus Martius, offering their victory to the *Magna Mater* (the Great Mother). Since initiations took place at night, there is little doubt that father and son were involved in some deep form of occult spiritual experience. They were clearly dedicating their victory over the God of Israel to the pagan goddess Isis. Proof of the importance of this victory of Isis is the fact that the following year, in the name of the Senate, a special coin was struck with the image of the Isian temples in Rome.[76] Why did Rome invest so much to celebrate its victory over a miniscule group of people in an insignificant and distant land? Here is surely a case of Caesar giving unto Isis the things that are of Isis. God, Creator of heaven and earth, is not in the picture.

Isis had won. So powerful was her victory that her presence was felt in at least one early Christian community.[77] According to a modern wiccan priestess of Isis, Caitlin Matthews, it was Isis who functioned in the first century A.D. as the principle of spiritual unity for the whole empire, "a beacon to Christians, Jews, Pagans and Gnostics alike."[78] This triumphal procession to the honor of Isis marked an important event of imperial history. Rome, under the tutelage of Isis, had become "a worthy meeting place of all the gods," as her ladyship had predicted two centuries before.

The Goddess Reigns over All the Religions

Isis was known as the "goddess of a thousand names," and she flourished in the syncretism prevalent at the time. When Isis worshipers confessed her divine ladyship to be "the one who is All,"[79] or the "goddess of a thousand names," they were claiming that she was truly the one worshiped whenever any goddess is worshiped. She was, and is, says Caitlin Matthews, "mistress of the whole globe, the Anima Mundi or World-Soul."[80] This same universalizing confession was made to other gods, simply by the addition of "pantheus"—"all-god," to the name of a specific god. Thus the Egyptian god, Serapis, consort of Isis, was also confessed as *Serapis pantheus*.[81] Indeed, who could be married to the goddess of a thousand names and not make similar syncretistic claims?

What is true of Isis is true of all the pagan gods and religious cults. Ramsey McMullen, professor of history at Yale, and a recognized expert on ancient paganism, describes the variety of spiritual options inherent in paganism this way: "[Paganism] had no single center, spokesman, director or definition of itself; therefore no one point of vulnerability. Everyone was free to choose his own credo . . . worshipers with their own religious ideas . . . circulated everywhere."[82]

I believe McMullen is wrong. One of the most significant outcomes of Alexander's conquests, and thus one of the "major characteristic[s] of the Hellenistic age, was the establishment of *theocracy*, or religious syncretism," that is, the blending of religions.[83] Certainly there was bewildering diversity; but if there was syncretism, it was not because people were especially nice back then. It was because pagan religion does have "a single definition of itself." You can only blend religions if they are blendable. The myriad expressions of paganism do have a common, central core.[84]

A World Religion

Alexander made Roman syncretism possible. Many factors of change were brought about by Alexander:

- the universal spread of the Greek language and culture
- the development of the largest free trade market the world had ever known
- a growing sense of "the unity of the human race"[85]
- a cultural openness to the spirituality of the East

All these combined to produce a deeply *religious* outcome, namely, the emergence "on a stupendous scale"[86] of an all-encompassing religious syncretism,[87] of which Rome was both the beneficiary and the ultimate expression. One historian notes that "syncretism was the religious hallmark of the time."[88] Another speaks of "the ease with which Rome practiced syncretism."[89] This blending and mixings of the numerous "faith traditions" is even described as a *world religion.*[90] These religions and cults, though differing in outward form, came together in a synthesis,[91] unified in the common conviction that behind all the many and varied spiritualities was the same divine spirit. Already, in the philosophy of the Stoics one finds a powerful expression of pantheism. These Greek philosophers of cosmic unity believed that "the divine interpenetrated all in such a way as to admit of no essential difference between God and the World."[92] This was the firmly held pagan belief of the Emperor Marcus Aurelius, Stoic sage and persecutor of Christians.

Interfaith Fellowship

This "world religion" was scrupulously practiced.[93] Religions were not simply placed side by side in a gesture of friendly dialogue. They were theologically intermingled. There are many examples. In a display of interfaith communion, many different gods were housed in the same temple. In Apollo's temple at Didyma, outside Miletus, a visitor in the second century A.D. described the place as a "circle of altars to every god."[94] In other temples, one priest would officiate for half a dozen deities.[95] As Turcan notes:

> For a pagan god, the height of prestige was to dominate the others: . . . Temples gloried in housing gods other than the titular Divinity. A real ecumenism ensured that Atargatis would receive hospitality from Cybele. In a Mithraic crypt, the worshiper could honor Serapis, Attis, Dionysius, Mercury, or even the Gaulish Mercury of travelers, Cisissonius. In Jupiter Dolichenus' temple on the Aventine in Rome, one could worship Mithras, Isis and Serapis. At Brindisi, a single priest carried out his ministry for the followers of Isis, the Great Mother, and the Syrian Goddess.[96]

We know of one pagan priest of the period, Aurelius Antonius, who described himself grandiosely as "priest of all the gods."[97]

Maximus of Tyre expressed a kind of ancient Jewish interfaith, believing that the essence of God cannot be understood but only recalled through symbols: "Why should I examine or legislate about images? Let every kind be divine, let it simply be. If the art of Phidias incites Greeks to recall the god, and honor paid animals does the same for Egyptians, a river for others and fire for others; I will not resent the disagreement; let them simply know, let them simply love; let them remember."[98]

The View from the Top of the Mountain
Is the Same

With a familiar ring of contemporary religious inclusivity, Celsus, a second-century A.D. pagan opponent of Christianity, claimed, "It makes no difference whether we call Zeus the Most High, or Zen, or Adonai, or Sabaoth, or Amoun like the Egyptians, or Papaeus like the Scythians."[99]

In this spiritual utopianism, bringing together the religions was thought to bring about universal peace. Symmachus, a Roman senator, in his report to the Emperor Valentinian in A.D. 384, proposed a policy of religious tolerance, in prose worthy of any present-day spiritual ecologist: "We gaze at the same stars, the sky belongs to all, the same universe surrounds us. What difference does it make by whose wisdom someone seeks the truth? We cannot attain to so great a mystery by one road."[100]

One is reminded of the apostate Christian Gnostics, the Naasenes, who abandoned Christian exclusivity and engaged in interfaith celebrations of the goddess in order to "comprehend the universal mystery," claiming that "everything is spiritual."[101]

We Are the World—Roman Tolerance

From our twenty-first century perspective, it is fascinating to note that *religious tolerance* is not the exclusive property of our religiously enlightened and socially evolved sophistication. Religious tolerance was a fact of life in the Greco-Roman world. In Rome, in Athens, and in Corinth—indeed everywhere in the ancient empire—the altars and cults flourished side by side, with much interchangeability.[102] Scholars speak of "the almost complete absence of intolerance."[103]

Did this mean the arrival of utopia?

There was tolerance not because the ancients were more enlightened or peace-loving—the record would indicate the contrary—not because of some long-lost golden age of societal bliss, but because the religions shared essential notions about the nature of spirituality and the unseen world. Ancient universal tolerance only proves the successful imposition of imperial power over an immense geographical area, and the dominance of pagan religious ideas throughout that vast empire.

Tolerance was nevertheless imposed.

The Pax Romana Included Religion

This "world religion" was no mere theory. The rubber met the Roman roads at two levels—politics and spirituality. Roman state religion and the spiritual pagan practices that blended with it functioned as a symbol of imperial unity for a population of endlessly diverse people.[104] Ancient geopolitics, expressed in military might and economic advantage, ultimately found in religious syncretism its quasi-irresistible power. Civic loyalty, obligatory patriotism, and political necessity, as well as deep commitment to pagan religion, stood behind the confession demanded of every loyal Roman citizen, including Christians: "Caesar is Lord." Christians who refused were condemned as both atheists and anarchists, disturbers of the Roman peace.[105]

In some form or other, political power, polytheistic religion, occult spirituality, and various expressions of alternate sexuality (seen particularly in certain Eastern mystery religions) merged in the Roman culture to make this pagan colossus seem impregnable to the Christian message. Totalitarian political power joined with a syncretistic, all-tolerant world religion to insist on religious peace.[106] The mystery religions, especially the cult of Isis, fit easily into the domain of the Roman Prostitute, giving her direction and added vigor. The Roman "peace" was tolerance only if one conformed to the religious/political powers that ruled. Those powers were ready to shut the mouths of dissidents, leaving them nowhere to run—as rebellious slaves and early Christians discovered. In spite of its supposed tolerance, ancient paganism crucified believers for their religious convictions. The political forces in power were just as "exclusive," intolerant, and narrow-minded as the much-maligned fundamentalisms, ancient or modern.

Rome welcomed the goddess Isis, but not the God of Paul. Of all the imported religions, only Christianity was judged intolerable for purely religious reasons.[107] Syncretism and tolerance only went so far.

The tolerant religionists, including Marcus Aurelius, felt obliged to stamp out the one religion that refused the pagan paradigm for personal liberation and peaceful coexistence. For political and religious reasons, the Beast and the Prostitute conspired together.

Conclusion—The Beast and the Harlot Go Global

Rome is a photograph of human complexity. She is both all that one would want and much that one must despise. Who can fault Rome's entertaining and comfortable life, since it offered a sense of spiritual significance? However, the utopia turned into a nightmare. Rome mercilessly exploited slaves, entertained itself by watching live crimes against humanity, bloated itself on material excess, and brought a stench to the world with its moral degradation. Weakened and corrupt, it was finally incapable of defending even the city of Rome against the barbarian invaders from the north.

Classic is the story of "the fall of Rome." Rome causes us to wonder whether human society, fed by the lie, will always mix shame and glory in this disappointing way. Why do we still hope in human progress? History suggests that things might even get worse. In the famous words of Lord Acton: "All power corrupts but absolute power corrupts absolutely."

The apostle John's vision of the Beast and the Harlot, described in the Book of Revelation, suggests a world system even more expansive than Rome. Though John was thinking first about the Rome of his own time, the prophet's image also predicts a more powerful world system to come. John, through the Spirit, looks at Rome and quadruples it. The ancient photo is blown up to planetary proportions. Here is the biblical way of looking at the future—ancient Rome as a picture in miniature of the coming, all-encompassing, global village, and it is not a pretty picture. It is certainly not utopia.

We stand on the threshold of the global village. Many with immense power and wealth, empowered by a brand-new spirituality, believe that an earthly, planetary utopia is just around the corner.

Chapter 3

World Peace or
Global Beast?

> We stand at a critical moment in Earth's history, a time
> when humanity must choose its future. . . . [W]e are one
> human family and one Earth community with a common
> destiny. We must join together to bring forth a sustainable
> global society founded on respect for nature, universal
> human rights, economic justice, and a culture of peace.
>
> PREAMBLE, THE UNITED NATIONS' *EARTH CHARTER*[1]

Welcome to the Global Village

When I was a young schoolboy attending Quarry Bank High School for
Boys in Liverpool, England, with my boyhood pal, John Lennon, we did
not know it, but the sun was setting on the British Empire. In school
assemblies on important national holidays, we would sing Sir Edward
Elgar's anthem to the glory of Britain, which, to the tune "Pomp and
Circumstance," went something like this:

Land of Hope and Glory, Mother of the Free,

How shall we extol thee, Who are born of thee?

Wider and still wider Shall thy bounds be set;

God who made thee mighty, Make thee mightier yet!

Singing that song, the patriotic hairs on the back of my little neck
would stand up. How times have changed. John Lennon became a planetary icon and was assassinated by a deranged fan. The National Union

of Teachers has demanded that Elgar's jingoistic sentiments be replaced
by a more global-friendly version. The new words go something like
this:

> Music and our voices Unite us all as one,
> Let our sound be mighty, Sung by everyone.
> Deeper still and deeper Shall our bounds be set,
> Bring our world together, Make us closer yet.[2]

In now mostly coed British schools, a much bigger empire—the
empire of the planet—is raising the hairs on little schoolboys' (and little
schoolgirls') necks. This is equally true in America where the National
Education Association shares the same utopian worldview as its educational cousins across the pond. A symbolic and disturbing preview of
the future stands at the entrance of a Milwaukee local school. It is a sign
that reads: "All people are essentially good." After the metal detectors,
there is a second sign that reads: "Welcome to the Global village."[3]

A Common Destiny

As in ancient Rome, we now stand before an all-encompassing empire,
this time, truly global. If there was any doubt that globalism is the
major agenda for a group of very powerful people in our day, the
United Nations' statement, quoted above, would remove it. UN visionaries believe the earth to be at *a critical moment,* and the earth community to possess a *common destiny.* The challenge that faces us,
according to this statement, is to realize a *global society.* By global they
mean "all scientific, cultural, religious and economic human activity . . .
integrated into one worldwide network."[4] You could think of it as . . . a
World Wide Web!

We no longer need the futurologists to speculate about globalism.
It is already here. But they speculate anyway. Widely recognized futurologists, Alvin and Heidi Toffler, declare: "We are witnessing the sudden eruption of a new civilization on the planet. . . ."[5] William Greider
speaks of "a new ideology struggling to be born—a new global consciousness."[6] With equal urgency, ex-Soviet leader and now world
statesman Mikhail Gorbachev declares: "Globalization cannot be
stopped."[7]

There is much in our present world that justifies this vision.

Facts: A Common Global Culture

What would have taken centuries to put in place may, with modern technology, take only a few generations. Like the Greek city-states, nationally sovereign countries are ceding their power to global political, legal, and economic structures.[8] Nelson Rockefeller predicted such a movement in 1962 in a lecture at Harvard: "And so the nation-state, standing alone, threatens in many ways to seem as anachronistic as the Greek city-states eventually became in ancient times."[9]

Like the spread of Greek and Latin languages and culture in antiquity, a uniform "Anglo" culture, sometimes described abroad as "cultural imperialism," is slowly unifying the globe through movies and sport, technology and the English language.

- *Star Wars* was a megahit because it was a global success. Kids the world over want to "be like Mike." Tiger Woods is so popular in Thailand that Thai civil servants may no longer play golf: the government was losing too much time on the links.
- In ancient Rome, an unprecedented network of dependable roads aided communication throughout the Empire. Today, air travel and the Internet have produced global communication that surpasses the wildest dreams of our ancestors. Organizations such as *Unifem* connect women across the globe in a "chat room" about common issues and dreams. Terrorists send coded messages from caves, while cancer patients compare notes, putting research ahead by years.
- The common language of "chat rooms" is English. When German and Japanese executives meet in Paris, they speak English. More people may speak Chinese than English, but international meetings are not conducted in Mandarin. Just as the ancient empire liberated commerce, we trade through multi-national companies and international structures like the World Trade Organization. Globalism is big business. America On-Line/Time Warner Inc. chairman Steve Case, speaking at a technology conference, outlined his vision to globalize his 219 billion-dollar media conglomerate. From being a "U.S. company with some foreign outposts," he wants to become a global player through "aggressive" acquisitions and investments. He

states: "In the next five to ten years you will see that we are really serious about becoming a truly global company."[10] Such global companies represent enormous power. Fifty-one of the one hundred largest world economies in the world are trans national corporations.[11]

Hardly a day goes by without some reference to global concerns.[12] A search for "global" on my search engine produced 26,000,005 sites! Satellite technology *(Earthshots)* allows pinpoint photography of any square yard of the planet, including you in your jacuzzi! As of June 2002, 139 countries had signed a treaty creating the world's first permanent international war crimes tribunal (The International Criminal Court) to bring to justice people accused of crimes against humanity. Such an institution may have beneficial effects, but, as in ancient Rome, there will soon be no place to run.

The Desertification Treaty, developed by the UN and ratified by the U.S. Senate,[13] claims jurisdiction over seventy percent of the earth's land area; but it is concerned about all land use. To combat desertification, the treaty seeks to prevent land use that its enforcers think may *lead* to desertification. A companion treaty is now being developed by the UN Commission on Water for the twenty-first century. According to an expert observer, the United Nations is, in fact, "creating the structure in international law and, through its extensive bureaucracies," will "control the use of all natural resources on earth."[14]

You may argue that globalism should not be a fearful but an enriching development. As they were in Rome, the economic advantages of an empire are enormous. Just as the ancient empire liberated trade, we now face the everyday reality of global trade through multinational companies—there are presently 55,000 corporations doing business all over the world, and $1.5 trillion in foreign currency changes hands everyday.[15] We see international structures like the World Trade Organization, the World Bank, the International Monetary Fund, the annual World Economic Forum in Davos, Switzerland,[16] and the coordination of the world's stock exchanges. Says a UN official, "A new 'world order' will be achieved through the globalization of industries like banking and finance." And everyone seems to be better off.

Such coordination of countries, industries, and governments binds our modern world together in a way that leaves no point on the globe independent of the coming planetary imperialism—a reality AT&T exploits with its ad campaign: "One World . . . One Card." In a variety of ways, globalism affects the way we think about the future.

Theory: The End of America as We Know It

That was my doing. I had insisted they come in by themselves, just the leaders of the world around a single big table . . . to look past their nation agendas . . . to see what really was at stake here, in the summer of 1992, at the Earth Summit in Rio . . . just the leaders of the world, the UN secretary general . . . and me.

Maurice Strong, organizer of the UN Earth Summit.[17]

Many have dreamed of a planetary empire, a one-world community to realize earthly utopia. Some "geo-politicians" in the highest echelons of government envisage the end of nation-states in order that a peaceful, world community should be born. Deputy Secretary of State Strobe Talbott, who defined, shaped and executed the Clinton administration's foreign policy from 1992 to 2000, believed: "In the next century, America will not exist in its current form. All states will recognize a single global authority."[18]

Maurice Strong, a key globalist figure, senior adviser to the UN general secretary and to the president of the World Bank, believes the following about sovereign nations: "The concept of national sovereignty has been immutable, indeed a sacred principle of international relations. It is a principle which will yield only slowly and reluctantly to the new imperatives of global environmental cooperation. What is needed is recognition of the reality that . . . it is simply not feasible for sovereignty to be exercised unilaterally by individual nation-states, however powerful."[19]

Such a planetary vision is also shared by the bi-partisan and highly influential Council on Foreign Relations.[20] As one would expect, General Secretary of the UN Kofi Annan has as his goal "global society for all."[21]

A globalist theory that stands any real chance of succeeding is necessarily uniformist and collectivist. One theorist makes the point with disarmingly honesty: "This global culture will rest on a shared view of the universe, a common story of human origins, and a shared set of values and goals, and a basic set of behavioral patterns to be practiced in common."[22]

Or, as the Club of Rome says: "A world consciousness . . . must become part of every individual so that the basic unit of human cooperation and hence of survival is moving from the national to the global level."[23]

As a culture, we seem to be ready for it.[24] Moreover, there are powerful people in the globalist movement, deeply committed to making this happen. Barbara Marx Hubbard is one. Author of *The Book of Co-Creation*, and once a Democratic vice-presidential candidate, Hubbard claims in her *curriculum vitae* to be "establishing Evolutionary Circles throughout the world to support small groups in their emergence as universal humans, founders of a global civilization." These "universal humans" adhere to the following creed: "I take personal responsibility for generating evolutionary conspiracies as a part of my work. I will select and create conspiratorial mechanisms . . . that will create and perform evolutionary breakthrough actions on behalf of people and planet. One people, one planet."[25]

Such a statement is hardly the classic definition of democracy, namely "one man, one vote."

Some observers contest the inevitability of a global culture of this nature and point out a certain number of opposing facts.
- Most of the world speaks Chinese, not English.
- The present world seems to be breaking up into seven or eight civilizations, rather than gelling into one.
- Civilizations seem to wish to remain separate, even as they use a common language and Western technology.[26]

Such objections, while doubtless true for the present, fail to take into account a number of other key factors in the global equation:
- the breakdown of the moral fiber of Western culture and its powerful influence on the rest of the world;

- the determination of dedicated ideologues, since elites have always been the agents of revolutionary change;
- the capacity of such ideologues to employ threats, real or imagined, to seize the power of central control.

Strategy of Control

Bread and circuses kept the Romans content with their lot for a long time. How similar is our successful Western capitalism, centered in the USA. Just as Rome set the standard for the rest of the Empire, so America seems to represent and articulate many of the contours of the planetary community.

Global Bread

Natasha, a visiting Russian friend, stood in the aisle of our local supermarket, transfixed before an unimaginable number of choices. Her dreary daily chore in her own country had been to stand in line for hours, hoping to buy the one variety of meat that lay on the butcher's shelves. She would stand in line to look at the item, write her order on a ticket, go pay for it, then stand in line again to pick it up. As tedious as waiting was, it was less difficult than the choices she had before her as she stood in an ordinary grocery store in California. She seemed overwhelmed. "How do you ever decide?" she asked, visibly shaken by the vast array of goods she saw.

A decade ago, it would have been easier. Grocery stores carried about nine thousand items; they now stock about twenty-four thousand. Revlon makes 158 shades of lipstick; Crest toothpaste comes in thirty-six sizes, shapes, and flavors. With Natasha in our grocery store that day, I counted thirty-two choices of chocolate flavor for drinks. As a measure of our opulence, which gets very close to decadence, we are offered choice where there really is none. AT&T offers "the right choice" among so many comparable phone companies; Wendy's slogan, "there is no better choice," is strictly true, but there is probably no worse choice either; though Pepsi claims to be "the choice of a new generation," Coke counters as "the real choice" while the customer drinks essentially the same fizzy water; "Taster's Choice is the choice for taste" amongst a score of same-tasting instant coffees. The extra glut, though keeping the price down, is sheer waste.

No culture in history has ever come close to realizing the generalized material plenty of the present American economic dream. Most of the fifty-one transnational corporations that make up the hundred largest world economies are in fact American.[27] California has the fifth largest economy in the world. Most of the billionaires are American, and the poorest American is fabulously rich relative to most of the world's population.

The World Circus

With all its technological and industrial power, America, like ancient Rome, has become a vast playground of unlimited entertainment, the envy of the rest of the world. A social critic perceptively observes: "Television is *the* primary force in our lives. . . . Television happened overnight. At some mysterious point in the 1950s, television ceased to be just an odd-looking gizmo—a radio running a picture track—and entered the bloodstream. It became part of our nervous system. It is who we are. It is what we do. And more important, it is how we feel."[28]

Commercial television has joined bread and circuses in a medium in which entertainment and advertisement melt into a seamless "advertainment," for everyone's watching pleasure.[29]

Do you love movies? Cable gives you hundreds of stations and endless choices, which always can be supplemented by visits to the local video store. Within two miles of my home, there are eight video stores, some of them hawking products that regularly break up marriages and provoke sexual crimes. The violent content of contemporary films caused *Chariots of Fire* producer David Putman to compare the feel of our movie culture to the depravity of the Roman Coliseum.[30]

Do you love football? For you there is high school football on Friday night, college football all day Saturday, pro football all day Sunday, and, to get ready for the next weekend, Monday Night Football. Do you love golf? The Golf Channel allows you to watch the sport of gentlemen 24/7. With sports obsession comes gambling (as it did in Rome); casinos and state lotteries have appeared everywhere. Americans wager more than $600 billion a year; in 1974 it was a mere

$17 billion. Every week, millions of "disposable" dollars are wasted for the kick that gaming delivers. Every month casinos are built to keep up with the demand.

Do you love pornography? The Playboy Channel provides round-the-clock porn.[31] Internet pornography, with its 70,000 sites, is one of the few on-line sectors making money. Americans spend four billion dollars yearly to rent 700 million porn movies, more than they spend on major league baseball. While 400 "regular" movies are made each year, the porn industry makes 11,000.[32] *Esquire* rejoices in "the pornographication of the American girl." A generation ago, Malcolm Muggeridge could already say: "Never . . . has a country been as sex-ridden as America is today."[33] Now, he would have to add his beloved Britain.[34] We are an "erotomanic" culture, so obsessed with lustful entertainment that our modern decadence looks unnervingly similar to that of ancient Rome.

A civilization addicted to spectacle in which the citizen is the anonymous viewer begins to think of itself as a part of the spectacle. Like the Romans, we are on show, more concerned with our public image than our private commitments. Like the Romans, we are bathed, perfumed, manicured, and toned to an obsession. The video culture gives ultimate expression to "democratic" entertainment. We watch videos of ourselves being "videoed." Hence the success of "reality television," which gives us public voyeurism in the privacy of our living rooms, beginning with *The Jerry Springer Show,* which has morphed into *Survivor, The Mole,* and the *Truman Show.* "Reality television" was never more real than in the horrendous shooting of people in a Texas church in 1999, when at least two people involved had the strange reflex of making a movie of the event as its grizzly details unfolded. Tragically, one version was taken by one of the gunman's eventual victims, pushing the envelope of *Cinéma Vérité* as far as it can go. Neal Gabler's thesis develops just such a theme in his book *Life: The Movie*[35] (which is not about the Roman culture but about ours), and Neil Postman underscores the same truths in his *Entertaining Ourselves to Death.*

While the masses complacently entertain themselves to death, educational standards plummet and the elite prepare our planetary future (political, economic, and religious) with a blueprint right out of the

1960s. We are living in a moment of the greatest sustained period of prosperity in the history of the world and, through television, the most extensive availability of constant entertainment. Yet during this period we have experienced a revolution that has led to the disintegration of America's time-honored intermediary social institutions and that has shredded its ethical boundaries.

Erosion of Intermediary Social and Moral Structures

On its bread and circuses regime, Rome witnessed the erosion of social structures, often leaving the individual face-to-face with the state. Our own bread-and-circuses approach may well do the same. The most radical American revolution took place not in 1776 but in the last generation of the twentieth century. In those forty or so years, during a period of international success for Western culture abroad, we have witnessed unprecedented cultural deconstruction at home. Presented in the emotional language of democratic rights and fair play, a radical vision has taken control of the Western mind. For example, pro-"gay marriage" forces state their case in patriotic revolutionary terms: "Just as our forefathers rejected King George's oppressive laws in 1776, we should reject today's unfair laws regulating marriage."[36]

Is there any comparable relationship between unfair taxes and the redefinition of marriage? By presenting radical social change as simple justice, the Left claims that there has been no "culture war," just the normal progress of American democracy. We must be aware of the revolutionary character of our immediate past in order to see its implication for the future.

Eighteenth-century America changed some political and economic arrangements and, via an armed uprising, broke politically with the Motherland. Late twentieth-century America broke not with political arrangements, but with a worldview. It has vilified the covenantal marriage and family, which have served as essential building blocks of civilization, and has put another, socially destructive model in the place of the family. That model hallows autonomy, admires uninhibited personal freedom, advocates a variety of sexual choices, and leaves the individual defenseless before the "Nanny State."

Roger Kimball argues that in the 1960s, America suffered an upheaval of dramatic proportions. A "momentous social and moral assault" has been unleashed on "our educational and cultural institutions." We have lost our moral consensus and our ability to engage in rational discourse, all replaced by "powerful feelings."[37] In the words of Gertrude Himmelfarb, a respected American historian, "There has been a culture war and the Left won it."[38]

There certainly have been some major changes in American culture in the last generation, in particular in the destruction of authority, sexual boundaries, and traditional spirituality, which can only be described as major victories for the optimistic New Left revolution. Here is a partial list of victors:

- The sexually liberated over the sexually inhibited
- Women as breadwinners over women as mothers and home-makers
- The feminists over the patriarchs
- Children's rights over parental authority
- Humankind over mankind
- Ms. over Miss and Mrs.
- Divorce over life-long monogamy
- Cohabitation over marriage
- Recreational sex over procreational sex
- A woman's right to abort her child over the unborn child's right to life, liberty, and the pursuit of happiness
- A collapsing birth rate over the baby boom
- Gays over straights
- Gay marriage as a moral ideal over sodomy as a moral outrage
- "Omni-gender" over male/female
- Moral chaos over moral consensus
- Freedom over commitment
- Rights and entitlements over responsibilities and service
- The Me generation over the We generation
- Immediate pleasure over deferred gratification
- Guilt-free, shameless self-consciousness over a sensitive conscience
- Lust over modesty

- "New History" over Patriotic History
- Columbus as villain over Columbus as hero
- Indigenous People's Day over Columbus Day
- Multiculturalists over the American melting pot
- Government by courts over government by consent of the people
- Living constitution over written constitution
- Postmodern over modern
- Global over national
- Computer screen over the book
- Power plays over pursuit of truth in the academy
- Politically correct speech over free speech
- Partisan commentary over dispassionate news reporting
- Information over understanding
- The irrational over the rational
- Earth-based spirituality over materialism
- Pet "care-takers" over pet owners
- Animals over human beings
- The goddess over God
- Spirituality over doctrine
- Post-Christian culture over Christendom
- The many ways over the one way
- All "holy books" over the Bible
- The Gnostic Gospel of Thomas over the biblical Gospels of Matthew, Mark, Luke, and John
- The "Death of God" over God as the Creator and source of all life
- B.C.E./C.E. over B.C./A.D.
- Winter break over Christmas
- Earth Day and spring break over Easter
- The Age of Aquarius (pagan spirituality) over the Age of Pisces (the Fish of Christianity)
- Multifaith pagan America over Christian America

This fast-moving revolution has occurred in one generation, as the second millennium gave way to the third.

The Feminization of Society

Compared to ancient Roman feminism, the present expression is an avalanche that sweeps all before it. Feminism is the most powerful movement of change in Western society during this recent revolutionary period. Feminism is not all bad. It brought some excellent changes to our society—an added respect for women and their giftedness, a clear identification of male chauvinism, a new sensitivity to various forms of abuse, and a need to define very carefully what we mean by patriarchy.[39] However, movements, like swords, always have two edges.

A color photo of a nude woman with outstretched arms in the traditional place of Jesus Christ at the Last Supper is part of an art show, "Committed to the Image: Contemporary Black Photographers," featured by the Brooklyn Museum. It is symbolic of the place women are claiming in our radically reconfigured world—Jesus as a naked woman.[40] Is anybody confused? Many are—about their own gender identity. Social commentators document the "feminization" of the culture, evident in the military,[41] sport,[42] law,[43] and the church,[44] to name a few representative areas. The feminist approach has led to what some have called the feminization of American foreign policy. Richard Tarnas, in his best-selling *The Passion of the Western Mind,* sees this development as profoundly therapeutic: "The crisis of modern man is an essentially masculine crisis, and I believe that its resolution is now occurring in the tremendous emergence of the feminine in our culture."[45] Masculinity is considered nearly pathological.[46] Feminization will save us.[47] There is no place here for "one-flesh" heterosexual marriage as the context where the masculine and the feminine meet and are reconciled and sanctified according to God's design, where males are civilized and females granted real power. Rather, the new feminizing psychologists propose to heal our innate male and female egotism by various forms of androgyny: men must become more female.[48] Such an approach creates all kinds of identity problems.[49] Women must become more male by assuming autonomous power, and men must tone down their urge to forge ahead. So hampering the natural, God-given differences between men and women is socially corrosive to the essential structures of a balanced society, namely, marriage and the family.

Feminist Theory

The women's liberation movement has tried to resolve the natural tension between two values—the importance of the individual and that of the larger community—by using its own deeply ideological analysis of sex and gender. For feminism, radical sameness is the solution for injustice. The following statement makes this clear. In the ideal, egalitarian world: "When we no longer ask 'boy or girl' in order to start gendering an infant, when the information is as irrelevant as the color of a child's eyes . . . only then will men and women be socially interchangeable and really equal. And when that happens there will no longer be any need for gender at all."[50]

Such an attitude is not just theory. It has quickly been transformed into a kind of coed obsession.[51] Male/female interchangeability rejects the notion of separate male and female spheres and translates immediately into campus coed bathrooms, coed high school wrestling, women reporters in the male locker rooms, and women on the front lines of combat. Journalist Anna Quindlen, with gender-neutral consistency, finds it unfair and insulting to women that they are not drafted. She agrees with Carol Forell of the University of Oregon School of Law, who states: "Failing to require this of women makes us lesser citizens."[52] Such feminist liberation has also given rise to the precipitous decline, since 1960, in the social prestige accorded to motherhood, the vertiginous collapse of the birthrate, and the unspeakable slaughter of the innocents, which increased dramatically when abortion was made legal in 1973.

According to a number of social commentators, like Mary Ann Glendon,[53] Jean Bethke Elshtain,[54] Gertrude Himmelfarb,[55] Wendy Shalit[56] and Elizabeth Fox-Genovese,[57] feminism has caused the community to suffer for the sake of the individual and has produced massive breakdowns in the social fabric of marriage and the family.[58]

The Divorce Culture

As in ancient Rome, the so-called "liberation of the woman" undoes society's fabric of intermediary structures and produces autonomous individuals, answerable ultimately only to themselves and the state. However, feminism has not seen the dangers of the independence it has fostered. They see dangers not in their unprotected state of independence, but in what they consider to be the constraints of marriage. For certain feminists, marriage is dangerous to women's health. In the *Divorce Culture,* Barbara Dafoe Whitehead documents how sexuality in the 1960s was "liberated" from its traditional conjugal confines, producing the inevitable explosion of divorce—now at over 50 percent.[59] With divorce comes the undermining of normative marriage and the two-parent family. Professor Lawrence Stone of Princeton observes: "The scale of marital breakdowns in the West since 1960 has *no historical precedent* that I know of. There has been nothing like it for the last 2000 years and probably longer."[60]

COHABITATION—LIVING IN SIN IS NOW THE NORM

Presently, one-third of all babies are born out of wedlock. According to a "Report to Congress on Out-of-Wedlock Childbearing" by the National Center for Health Statistics, 68.7 percent of black babies are now born illegitimate, which means that less than a third of black American babies are born to married couples.

In 1969 a Gallup poll found that only 21 percent of the population supported premarital sex; in May 2001, 60 percent were in favor (67 percent of young adults).[61] Cohabitation in 1965 concerned only 10 percent of households; in 1994 it involved more than 50 percent.[62] We now have a whole generation of liberated sluts and cads, freed from the chains of marriage, responsible to no one—democracy gone nuts! Said a college student: "The sexual revolution is over and everyone lost."[63] There is certainly an initial exhilarating sense of freedom; but that liberty is exercised with the permission of an all-powerful state, which is the only party to accrue true power in this situation.

HOMOSEXUALITY

Rome was home for alternate sexuality. But Rome had never been anything but pagan in its religious convictions. What is surprising is how alternate sexuality has invaded the once-Christian society of the West. The feminist dismissal of the significance of male and female difference clearly invites the normalization of homosexuality, literally, the sexuality of sameness. This is the final stage of making males into females, or, in the case of lesbians, making females into males. In recent years, the normativity of heterosexuality has been destroyed by the rise of state-protected and -promoted homosexuality and bisexuality. By way of illustration, fourteen mainstream mental health establishments in tandem with the Interfaith Alliance declared homosexuality "normal" behavior, and sent a booklet, *Just the Facts*, to 14,500 school board presidents. Not surprisingly, pressing homosexuality as "normal," our schools have become sexually moral neutral zones, where our youth are no longer given ethical and social norms by which to behave. In California, the Department of Education's Tax Force proposed a number of pro-homosexual recommended mandates for public schools to follow. These include:

- Integrating pro-homosexual viewpoints throughout all public school curriculum;
- Requiring the personal questioning of children regarding homosexuality and transsexuality;
- Using taxpayer dollars to establish "gay/straight alliances" on campuses;
- Establishing a response system whose purpose will be to "provide rehabilitation to perpetrators" of discrimination against homosexuals and transsexuals;
- Training every public school teacher and staff member on how to implement these regulations.[64]

State-sponsored, legalized homosexual marriage will surely put the final touches on the social destruction of biblical, creational marriage. The general council of the United Church of Canada recently declared that homosexuality is not a sin, and that, by implication, gay marriages are perfectly allowable.[65]

Moral Collapse

The current collapse of morals and marriage is unprecedented in the history of the West. Gertrude Himmelfarb, professor at Brooklyn College and the Graduate School of City University of New York, where she was named distinguished professor of history, speaks of the change from virtues to values as "the true moral revolution of our time."[66] By virtue she means "a fixed moral standard." "Value is a subjective, relativistic term; any individual, group, or society may choose to value whatever they like."[67] The change has been stunning. After the horrendous crime against the World Trade Center towers on September 11, 2001, a young Yale student had this observation: "Absent was a general outcry of indignation . . . my generation is uncomfortable assessing, or even asking, whether a moral wrong has taken place."[68] This is true across the board. Only a generation ago, the intermediary social structures of marriage and family were held in high esteem, along with the supporting moral structures of norms, shame, and modesty. Not any more.

No Norms

"Normal" for many people now means freedom from norms. Those who have norms are described as undemocratic extremists, imposing their personal values on others. In the year 2000 a judge ruled that a fifteen-year-old boy from Massachusetts should not be barred from class while wearing female dress such as high heels, wigs, and padded bras. His therapist suggested that forcing the teenager to wear boys' clothing could endanger his mental health. At a court hearing, Judge Linda Giles, a self-identified lesbian, said the school's stance amounted to "the stifling of a person's selfhood, merely because it causes some members of the community discomfort."[69] Here it is clear that the appointment of homosexual and lesbian judges is not a morally neutral act, because a homosexual judge will promote homosexual "values" that hold individual freedom as the highest good. For judges like these, "normal and lawful" in areas of sexuality means no norms at all.

What is "normal"? Recent research carried out by Brook, the youth sex advisory service, found that young people seventeen to twenty-five years old (64 percent of young men and 54 percent of young women) agreed that it was "normal" for a person to sleep with more than ten partners before getting married.[70]

No Shame

There is an old German proverb that says: "So long as there is shame, there is hope for virtue." As we have noted, virtue has given way to personal values. "Around 1960, something happened. Shame antibodies went the way of the top hat and spats," says James Twitchell, author of the book *For Shame*.[71] Twitchell gives the example of how shame no longer accompanies unwed pregnancies,[72] nor does it dominate contemporary religion, psychology, politics, or education. The baby-boom generation of "liberation" tends to see shame as an obstacle to self-esteem and self-fulfillment.[73] "Shame is the canary in the mine shaft of culture, that gives us 'boundary protections.'"[74]

No Modesty

Wendy Shalit, a Jewish college student at an Ivy League school, was so distraught with what she saw on her campus and in the culture at large that she wrote *A Return to Modesty*.[75] She shows how we all, but especially women, who suffer the most from it, have become a people without modesty. A culture with neither shame nor modesty is a culture of lust. Many of our ads and shows lack any sense of modesty. The TV show *Temptation Island* is all about lust. Miller Genuine Draft joins lust with theft to sell its beer. The young gardener is being seduced by the beautiful, bikini-clad mistress of the house, struggling to open her last ice-cold Miller. After sizing her up, he snaps open the cap and leaves with the beer. Modesty also must be thrown aside as one more crimp on our program of liberation through personal choice and animal desire.

D. H. Lawrence once said: "Liberty is all very well, but men cannot live without masters. . . . Liberty in America has meant the breaking away from all dominion."[76] In the opinion of the sociologist Wilfred M. McClay, America has become *The Masterless*.[77]

Breakdown as Achievement

One-world visionaries are rejoicing as they see the debacle of disintegrating morals. The world is not really falling apart, but *reconstituting* itself. The breakdown of structures is the major achievement of the 1960s, for it paves the way for utopia. Only by tearing down the old can humanity rebuild. The *ancien régime* must be guillotined to make way for the new day of revolutionary *liberté, égalité,* and *fraternité*. According to Joseph Campbell (the mind behind George Lucas's *Star Wars* trilogy): "We are at this moment participating in . . . the greatest ever . . . leap of the human spirit."[78] Jean Houston, guru to ex-First Lady Hillary Clinton, agrees with Campbell's optimism: "Other times in history thought they were it. They were wrong. This is it."[79] Houston believes we are in a state of "breakdown and breakthrough . . . what I call a whole system transition."[80]

I was invited to speak to the Christian student group at UC Davis the same weekend as the celebrations of Earth Day. The sound of tom-tom drums and the smell of pot from the campus green just beyond the amphitheater door accompanied my lectures on Christian theism. UC Davis in 1996 seemed stuck in a sixties time warp. Radicals celebrated the ongoing breakdown of culture with the theme "Kiss Chaos." How telling! In a *uni*-versity, supposedly committed to a common, structured, coherent *uni*-verse of discourse—literally, one truth—chaos and the breakdown of society are embraced as the true road to liberation. Here was the pagan, monistic circle in full deployment on a post-academic college quadrangle!

The time warp is prophecy. Berkeley and Davis wave the 1960s program of social, sexual, and spiritual liberation as the blueprint of the coming planetary community. The coherent character of the cultural revolution provides the agenda for tomorrow's planetary "love-in." Oddly enough, the 1960s liberation package is now being applied globally. It is a social map applied on a larger scale. Aging hippies, male and female, now in business suits, plan the future of the globe with the old flower-power paradigm they have been developing since college days.[81]

Creeping Planetary Control: A New Day for the UN

Police control was a fact of life in Rome. Planetary control seems light years away for us. But imagine Lake Superior invaded by minute algae that double their number each day. For years, this small plant life would grow unnoticed in such a vast expanse of water. However, the day would come when the lake would be a quarter covered. The next day it would be half-covered, and the next completely choked.

Behind the theories and the present realities of globalism there already exists a worldwide political mechanism to bring it about—the United Nations. Most Americans pay little attention to the United

Nations and assume that nothing serious ever happens there. Alas, they are wrong.[82] Many are calling for a renewed role for the UN.[83] Globalist theologian Lloyd Geering does not call on the church or God the Savior. Rather he declares: "The UN's time has finally come. It is only within the framework of that global organization that the common problems of mankind can be collectively addressed."[84]

Reorganization of the UN for Peace and Global Governance

The emerging global Nanny State is happy to oblige. Mikhail Gorbachev insisted to an international forum of many of the world's leaders that "new structures were needed to govern globalization."[85] These structures have been developed within the UN. In the 1990s, General Secretary Kofi Annan appointed Gorbachev's good friend Maurice Strong (an immensely important personality of the globalist movement) to reorganize the United Nations.[86] On July 14, 1998, Strong published his initial plan, a ninety-five-page document, entitled *Renewing the United Nations: A Programme for Reform*. This is not a cost-cutting analysis. It is a step-by-step program to implement many of the recommendations advanced by the UN-funded Commission on Global Governance in its 1995 report entitled *Our Global Neighborhood*.[87]

In every nation where there is a UN presence, all UN activity will be consolidated under the authority of a "Special Representative of the Secretary-General." All UN activity will be headquartered in a single, special facility to be known as "UN House." All services will be delivered under a single flag—the UN flag. And the program will be backed up by a standing UN army. The UN was originally created and has thus far functioned to serve its membership of sovereign nations. But the UN is now gearing up to provide sovereign "security for the people" within those nations. As the UN is seen to protect individuals from the state authorities that presently govern them, these structures will break down and we will end up with only two entities: the global government (and its official representatives) and the individual.

Other UN changes include the creation of a World Court, an "Assembly of the People," and a Petitions Council. The Assembly of the

People is to consist of three hundred to six hundred selected representatives of Non Governmental Organizations (NGOs) accredited by the United Nations. The function of the Assembly of the People is to provide direct input to the General Assembly from these nonelected "representatives" of "civil society."[88] Needless to say, the agenda of those deemed "uncivil," those who have not been recognized by the UN as NGOs, will not be considered. The UN algae already can be seen over large sectors of the global lake. As an astute observer stated a few years back: "Global governance is not an event; it is a process. It is a process that has been underway for years. By the year 2000, enough of the policies will be in place, and sufficient restructuring of the UN will have been accomplished, to claim that global governance is the new reality. A reality from which there is no escape."[89]

Though independent government bodies have not yet ratified such decisions, this thinking shows us what those in power desire. Such globalism is actively promoted through the UN Convention on Climate Change, the Convention on Biological Diversity, the Convention on the Rights of the Child, the Convention on the Law of the Sea, the Convention on Chemical Weapons, the Convention on the International Criminal Court, the Convention on the Elimination of All forms of Discrimination against Women, the Convention on World Heritage Sites, the UN Worldwide Biosphere Reserve Network, the Convention on Wetlands, the Convention on International Trade in Endangered Species, the Ecosystem Management Policy, the American Heritage Rivers Initiative, the Sustainable Communities Initiative—and a host of other UN policies that now dominate domestic policy in the United States and other Western powers. These policies—initiated, implemented, and enforced by the United Nations—are *de facto* global governance.[90] And willing one-world politicians take up the refrain. In a press conference in South America, then-President Bill Clinton said: "What I am trying to do is promote a process of reorganization of the world so that human beings are organized in a way that takes advantage of the new opportunities of this era, and permits them to beat back the problems."[91]

This ambiguous, spin-doctored phrase is political "Clintonese" *newspeak* for globalism.

Other major UN power grabs include plans for the disarmament of all sovereign states,[92] a UN police force and standing army,[93] a common world currency and economic system,[94] "world education,"[95] a global taxation system,[96] a global commons,[97] and extensive collectivization via the Earth Charter and Agenda 21, which Jaspers calls "a massive blueprint for regimenting all life on Planet Earth in the 21st century."[98] I wonder how many of my readers know such a document exists. A UN-sponsored description of the effects of Agenda 21 states: "Effective execution of Agenda 21 will require a profound reorientation of all human society, unlike anything the world has ever experienced."[99] All this is done in the name of planetary peace, what one bumper sticker calls "whirled peas"!

Writing in the 1970s, Francis Schaeffer said, "The future is open to manipulation. Who will do the manipulating? . . . Whoever achieves political or cultural power in the future will have at his disposal techniques of manipulation that no totalitarian ruler in the past ever had."[100]

Without absolutes, said Schaeffer, the modern scientist will lose objectivity and science will become mere technology. He warned of "chemical and electrical manipulation"—the all-seeing eye of computer technology as well as mind-altering drugs.[101]

The electronics are in place for a global control that not even Schaeffer could have imagined a generation ago—satellites to monitor every inch of the planet; computers that move huge amounts of data across the planet in seconds; sophisticated bar-coding and microscopic chips that allow genetic identification of everyone on the planet (alive or dead). Genetic engineering and cloning will have countless uses for human behavior manipulation.

Such achievements can be used for good or evil. "Spirit entities," channeling through human vessels, have indicated the Internet's usefulness for their global schemes: "The Internet is a paradigm for future communities of the world because it balances naturally without control and as a result this is the perfect place to create this space of ultimate empowerment."[102] The Internet, like other human achievements, could be a powerful tool of global control.

The Kings of the Earth Conspire Together

As I followed the news articles on a number of Internet news sites, several scheduled "globalist" events in New York caught my attention. In August and September of 2000, international meetings brought together a mix of religious and political world leaders broader than any ever gathered. Here was the schedule of these historic events:

- World Peace Summit of Religious and Spiritual Leaders
  On August 28–31, 2000, the "World Peace Summit of Religious and Spiritual Leaders," bankrolled by Ted Turner, brought some 1,200 leaders to the UN to discuss religion and world peace.[103] As in Rome, pacification is essential. In his plenary address, in a summit on religious peace, Turner tore into evangelical Christianity, to the whooping cheers of the assembled dignitaries. He maintained that Christianity "was intolerant because it taught we were the only ones going to heaven."[104] Turner was introduced by his friend, the omnipresent spiritual pagan, Maurice Strong.[105] At the end of the summit, a permanent International Advisory Council of Religious and Spiritual Leaders to the UN secretary-general was named.[106]

- UN Department of Public Information/NGO Forum
  At the same time took place the UN Department of Public Information/NGO Forum: "Global Solidarity: The Way to Peace and International Cooperation." This gathering brought together over a thousand representatives of NGOs to focus on how these powerful lobby groups can participate in the decision-making process of the UN. NGOs are not democratically elected, but claim to represent the peoples of the world. In UN global-speak, they are referred to as "civil society." In the main, they are radical pressure groups on which the UN leadership chooses to bestow official NGO status—thus we have nonelected UN elite granting official status to nonelected pressure groups, such as the Lucis Trust (a theosophical, occult organization), many radical feminist organizations, Planned Parenthood, and homosexual groups.[107] To the NGOs that organized the disruptive riots in Seattle and Davos in 2000, Kofi Annan declared a week later in Montreal at the World Civil Society Conference

(NGOs): "the NGO revolution is the best thing that happened to the UN in a long time."[108] The NGOs tend to define what is "customary international law," rulings that always attempt to trump national laws.[109]

- State of the World Forum
  A few days later, during September 4–10, 2000, Mikhail Gorbachev's State of the World Forum took place at the New York Hilton. Maurice Strong was an honored guest here too. Annually, since 1995, Mikhail Gorbachev has hosted his forum, bringing together annually hundreds of globally powerful guests, including 141 heads of state and 59 former heads of state. In 2000 this powerful group discussed how to structure the new global order, as sustainable human system management.[110]

- The Millennium Summit
  During September 5–8, 2000, the Millennium Summit was held, uniting all the heads of state throughout the world to discuss a complete reorganization of the UN. Maurice Strong was there too because he had been charged by Kofi Annan to produce the working draft. At this summit, many world leaders endorsed the new UN along globalist lines. President Clinton was there, identifying the UN as the peacekeeper of tomorrow's world and calling for a UN standing army that would take precedence over national sovereignty.

This planned event, though few noticed it, brought together, essentially at the UN, a who's who of one-world elitist visionaries. It constituted an assemblage of power never yet seen in the history of the planet. It took place on the threshold of the new millennium, a symbolic moment with glaringly obvious future intentions.

But you may object that these UN goings-on are far from the real centers of power, and that freedom-loving people the world over would never be enticed by the collectivist, regimented society proposed by the one-worlders of the UN. Supporters of democracy would *never* fall for this. Globalist Lincoln P. Bloomfield of the Massachusetts Institute of Technology recognizes this difficulty and comes up with the answer: "[A global takeover] would be possible if our national leaders utilized a grave crisis or war to bring about a sudden transformation in national attitudes. . . ."[111]

The Liberating Effects of Global Crises

The doomsday clock is ticking towards a day of reckoning...

MAURICE STRONG[112]

I sat bewildered. I expected a developed, theological appeal for religious unity from the world's spiritual leaders. But the first two plenary sessions of the Parliament of the World's Religions were devoted to the need of a one-world government that would solve the ecological crisis. Unity will come from crisis; and for this reason, crises are positive, whether they are environmental pollution, grinding Third World poverty, terrorism, overpopulation, economic or political instability, war, or biological and nuclear threats. Multiple UN agencies are working day and night to identify and publicize all kinds of crises. Dr. Rashmi Mayur, a popular one-world speaker at UN gatherings, is typical. "The world is not working, and each day we are getting closer to an unprecedented catastrophe, possibly bringing an end to human civilization. . . ."[113] In his autobiography, Maurice Strong presents a fictional scenario for the end of the year 2031, which postulates a world that has degenerated into chaos, conflict, and societal breakdown on a colossal scale. "It may be fiction," he says, "but it is not far-fetched. I am convinced that it is the kind of world that we will have in, or around, the year 2030 if we continue on our present course."[114] In the opinion of another UN official, "Within ten years time, you're going to see the beginnings of an embryonic world order."[115]

Mikhail Gorbachev has often sounded the same alarm. The destruction of the World Trade Center towers, bringing much of the world together in horrified outrage, allowed Gorbachev to seize the occasion to say: "It is now the responsibility of the world community to transform the coalition against terrorism into a coalition for a peaceful world order. Let us not, as we did in the 1990s, miss the chance to build such an order."[116] However, it will probably take a massive nuclear threat from a rogue nation or terrorist organization to produce the kind of crisis about which Drs. Mayur and Bloomfield speak. The likelihood is strong.[117] If such a catalyzing event occurred and some manner of UN dreams were put in place, what kind of a society would be on offer?

An Agenda with Teeth

Women's issues and the "liberation of sexuality" became official US foreign policy during the 1990s.[118] It is an agenda with teeth. The World Bank was reorganized by James D. Wolfensohn, who became its president on the appointment of President Clinton in 1995. Wolfensohn is a protégé of Maurice Strong,[119] an apostate Christian and serious practitioner of "New Age" spirituality, who is one of the most powerful, nonelected world politicians of the modern age. Strong says of the "revolutionary"[120] work of Wolfensohn that it is has made the bank "a development leader rather than merely a lender."[121] In other words, the World Bank will only lend money to countries that accept its definition of "development."[122] One observer describes its present policy as "the imposition of a Westernized feminist ideal that is controversial even in North America."[123]

A new form of "cosmopolitanism" is upon us, destined, by a small group of very powerful people, to "civilize" and unite the globe. The new empire of the planet will be founded upon the great achievements of Western technology, capitalism, and democracy, its *pax mundi* (world peace) ensured by the state-of-the-art invincible weaponry from the Western sector. But a new view of the human being will bring personal liberation to all. Article 12 (a) of the Earth Charter reads: "Eliminate discrimination in all its forms such as that based on race, color, sex, sexual orientation, religion, language and national or social origin."[124] The buzzwords, "eliminate discrimination" actually mean the promotion of a new multisexual, polyreligious autonomous humanity, liberated from the oppressive structures of normative heterosexuality, the patriarchal family, and biblical religion. This is, as the Beijing feminists declared, "*a crucial social agenda which affects all humanity*." Such an agenda will create a brave new "democratic" world based on the elimination of the old. With appropriate optimism, the proponents of social destruction and reconstruction claim that their experiments eventually will bring about a better world, even if no one knows for sure where things are leading.[125]

To assure its success, such a vision needs a religion. The liberated "Western woman"—the symbol of the new ideology—needs the power of the goddess to realize global revolution. At the Beijing Conference, the goddess was everywhere on display.[126]

With infectious optimism, some believe that the USA has become the dispenser of an "emerging *American* wisdom tradition," which joins Western technology to Eastern spirituality to save the planet.[127] Like ancient Rome, America, the sole superpower on the present world stage, has become worthy of the goddess. "Nothing," says contemporary Isis priestess Caitlín Matthews, "is going to delay the Goddess's second coming."[128]

Chapter 4

Religious Utopia
or Spiritual Deception?

The Goddess Has Come to America

Said Katherine K. Hanley in her words of address at the official opening of a new Hindu temple in her constituency: "This date marks the inauguration of the first Durga [a Hindu goddess] shrine in the United States of America; Fairfax County is pleased to join in increased public awareness and community involvement in celebration of the Durga Temple."[1]

The goddess has arrived in Washington. At an auspicious moment in ancient history, she arrived at the cultural and political center, Rome. Now she comes, in her vaxrious manifestations,[2] at the dawn of the third millennium, the "Age of Aquarius,"[3] to America, leader of the free world and powerhouse of the global village. But the way had been prepared. As radical theologians in the 1960s were declaring the death of the God of the Bible, others announced the rebirth of the gods and goddesses of ancient Greece and Rome.[4]

From the birth of Christendom, the goddess has lurked in obscure corners of the world; but she has made a stealthy comeback.[5] Had you been listening hard enough, you would have heard her whispering in meetings of the world's religious and spiritual leaders at the United Nations: "*America* is [now] worthy to become the meeting-place of all the gods."[6] She is an outsider to America's Christian traditions, just as she was an outsider to the traditional religion of Rome. But her future here looks bright.[7] The title of a book by Richard Grigg, *When God*

Becomes Goddess: The Transformation of American Religion, shows that America's cultural elite is rushing to lay out the welcome mat for her divine ladyship.[8] Grigg, a Roman Catholic theologian, declares that religion in America is not in decline, but in the "process of transformation": "significant elements of traditional religious belief and practice are passing away, but a new kind of religiosity is poised to take its place."[9] Does he mean the religiosity reflected in the bumper sticker, "Ankh if you love Isis"?[10] To what religiosity is he referring?

Ex-Roman Catholic theologian Mary Daly welcomes this "second coming" of the goddess: "The antichrist and the Second Coming are synonymous. This Second Coming is not the return of Christ but a new arrival of female presence. . . . The Second Coming, then, means that the prophetic dimension in the symbol of the great Goddess . . . is the key to salvation from servitude."[11]

This goddess savior now speaks fluent American English and will liberate our planet. Daly's thinking is utopian myth-making with a vengeance. We are living in a significant moment in history: As the goddess encountered stunning success in Rome, so she experiences acclaim in American corridors of power and throughout the globe.

Harry Potter for Adults

Jean Houston (friend and counselor of ex-First Lady Hillary Clinton) believes we are in "a whole system transition, . . . requir[ing] a new alignment that *only myth can bring* [emphasis mine]."[12] Creating a "Harry Potter for adults," Houston proposes the myth of Isis and Osiris, so popular among the power brokers of first-century Rome. At the highest levels of power in Washington, Isis, the goddess of magic and the underworld, is promoted as the saving myth of tomorrow's social, cultural, and spiritual "alignment."[13] "Never," says Houston, "has this mythic knowing been more needed than today."[14]

The goddess has entered the mainstream and main street. *Hot Topics,* an in-your-face clothing store for teens, includes a rack of books on witchcraft. Jennifer Hunter's *21ˢᵗ Century Wicca: A Young Witch's Guide to the Magical Life,* turning the imaginative into the real, is a bestseller. Fantasy becomes political as witchcraft is popularized and is tied to feminism and women's new identity. In 1993 Cynthia Eller, in *Living in the Lap of the Goddess: The Feminist Spirituality Movement in America*, complained how few women below thirty were engaged in feminist spirituality (witchcraft).[15] Since then, we have seen on screen: *The Blair Witch Project; The Craft* (teen witches), *The Crucible; Sabrina: The Teenage Witch*, and *Charmed*, among others. To children we offer the imaginary; to adults we move to reality, which includes wiccan services on army bases and prisons, as well as witch-clergy performing marriages with the blessing of the New York City Council.[16]

Jean Houston recognizes her debt to Joseph Campbell,[17] guru of George Lucas, producer of *Star Wars*. According to Campbell, who was raised as a Roman Catholic,[18] "myths are the clues to the spiritual potentialities of human life ... [to be found by] turn[ing] within." They are "what human beings have in common."[19] This includes the myth of the Goddess. The United Church of Christ publishing arm, the Pilgrim Press, commends to the faithful the work of theologian Wendy Hunter Roberts, a pagan priestess, and says of her book, *Celebrating Her:* "Deep within the womb of the earth lies a memory of a sacredness nearly buried under the weight of patriarchy. . . . More and more women— especially those with Christian backgrounds—are being drawn to this empowering, goddess-centered worship."[20]

Beware! The goddess does not lead us into the heart of Christianity, but right out of it, as Sue Monk Kidd's book, *The Dance of the Dissident Daughter: A Woman's Journey from Christian Tradition to the Sacred Feminine*,[21] joyfully affirms. The movement seems unstoppable in mainline churches, which have accepted a connection between Christianity and a highly visible and passionate movement in contemporary society—feminism.

As they did in ancient Rome, social and religious forces have joined. Whatever good feminism has offered (such as equal pay for equal work and an awareness of abuse) should not blind us from seeing the deeper agenda of goddess spirituality. Here, the "dance" becomes an inevitable "slide." The driving force is anti-Christian. Feminist Deena Metzger, perhaps without realizing it, catches the biblical image for apostate religion when she solemnly declares: "We must allow ourselves whatever time it takes to re-establish the consciousness of the Sacred Prostitute."[22] With the rebirth of pagan goddess worship, we see the outlines of the coming worldwide apostasy, the "planetary Prostitute."

For the moment this liberating consciousness represents a sense of empowerment for many who have lost their spiritual way. It is shocking but true that once "Christian" America now looks more and more like the ancient pagan empire of Paul's day, which was "a goblet seething with myths."[23]

Preparing a Chamber for the Goddess

I came to the US for the first time the same year as the Beatles, in 1964. While in my home country of England there were pubs on every corner, in America there were churches. America was the great Christian citadel of the modern period, the fortress of the faith in a world of atheistic humanistic unbelief. But times have changed. To be sure, the impression persists that the nation is still rooted in its Christian past. The polls could not be more encouraging. Ninety-seven percent of Americans believe in God, and 90 percent believe God loves them. Mega churches are bulging at the seams, and presidents still go to church hugging a Bible. Nine out of ten homes possess a Bible,[24] and one out of three Americans claims to be "born again."[25] Yet something is radically amiss. As a cultural religion, Christianity is coming unglued. "Born again" sociological believers no longer believe the classic teachings of Christianity.

A "Christian Nation" No Longer

Vast numbers of red-blooded Americans, including many prominent leaders who claim a "born again" Christian experience, also accept Deepak Chopra, goddess spirituality, abortion, homosexuality, and religious syncretism (all religions lead to God). The following example shows the shift. This testimony comes from a famous basketball star, speaking in the 1960s: "The choice is simple . . . between the eternal and the passing . . . between Jesus Christ and the world, *I've made my choice.* I love Jesus Christ . . . How about you?"

Thus spoke Bill Bradley in a tract distributed throughout the nation's universities by Athletes in Action, documenting his life-changing encounter with the Christ of the Christian gospel. By the

1990s, Bradley, ex-senator and presidential candidate, seems to have had a second conversion experience: "Christianity offers one way to achieve inner peace and oneness with . . . the world. Buddhism, Judaism, Islam, Confucianism and Hinduism offer others. Increasingly I resist the exclusivity of true believers."[26]

Bradley has become a syncretist, and his experience is not unusual. According to sociologist W. C. Roof, nearly half of America's most conservative born-again Christians said all religions were "equally true."[27] Harvard historian Eugene Taylor, in *Shadow Culture*, speaks of the "Third Awakening" of American spirituality, this time a pagan one.[28] He argues that native esoteric spirituality, which was once marginal, is now considered normal. Just as the Roman elite turned to the pagan mystery religions of occult power, so cutting-edge leaders of modern society are discovering the power of the new spirituality. This subtle anti-Christian shift in modern society is now accepted as sociological "fact." Said sociologist Alan Wolfe, "We've gone from a predominantly Christian country to one of religious tolerance, and that's never been reported as a news story."[29] Of course, such tolerance, while appearing respectful of other opinions, actually masks a crisis of faith—the refusal to believe that there are any real differences in religious truths—as Bill Bradley's tolerance illustrates. The drying up of personal convictions leaves a moral hole into which rush the deep waters of syncretism, in which paganism thrives. Francis Schaeffer predicted this in the early 1970s, when he saw the invasion of Eastern spirituality: "Pantheism will be pressed as the only answer to ecological problems and will be one more influence in the West's becoming increasingly Eastern in its thinking."[30]

A New Religious America

In 1888 the German church historian Philip Schaff made this prediction: "America, favored by the most extensive emigration from all other countries, will become more and more the receptacle of all the elements of the world's good and evil, which will there wildly ferment together, and from the most fertile soil bring forth fruit for weal or woe for generations to come."[31]

What Schaff sensed with the faintest of intuitions, Harvard professor and committed syncretist, Diana Eck, documented in a four hundred-page book, *A New Religious America*. She states: "The United States has become the most religiously diverse nation on earth. . . . This is an astonishing new reality. We have never been here before."[32] The mosques, Hindu and Buddhist temples, and the Sikh *gurdwaras* rising out of the ground all over the fruited plains are obvious "architectural signs of a new religious America."[33]

In my sleepy little town, called Escondido ("hidden"), the local paper carried a seemingly innocuous ad in the religion section: "Spiritual but not religious? Believe in God but haven't found a church that fits? Then the Church of Today is for you. We emphasize spirituality more than religion; we believe there are many paths to God."

All this plus "spiritual education for children, a large, fun playground and a contemporary, professional music team," shows how much American religion has changed. In one generation the melting pot of races has become the melting pot of religions, and America has irreversibly (at least for the foreseeable future) embarked upon the normalization of pagan religious syncretism.

Wellesley College's "Multi-Faith Chaplaincy" has been called "a spiritual revolution on campus," and the campus revolution is happening nationally.[34] This change is not inevitable evolutionary progress. It is contemporary regress. The "many paths to God" of the Church of Today, like the Chapman University's All Faith's Chapel,[35] is only a twenty-first-century version of pagan Greco-Roman temples. The charming senior minister preaches the same spirituality of syncretism as the pagan priest Aurelius Antonius, who described himself as "priest of all the gods."[36]

Just how far has this new religious plurality gone? A few examples must suffice.

Hard-Core Paganism

The *Times* of London made the connection in its article entitled "Oldest Religion in Britain Was Reinvented in the 1960s."[37] The giant publishing house, Harper, in its religion section, on the same page with C. S. Lewis, features a book *Paganism Today: Wiccans, Druids and the Ancient Goddess Traditions for the Twenty-first Century*. Says the introduction: "The number of practicing pagans is increasing dramatically, yet paganism remains shrouded in misunderstanding."[38]

HarperSanFrancisco will help to fix that! So accepted is pagan witch-craft that Wiccan soldiers have won the right to have "Wicca" engraved on their dog tags, and wear on their uniform the witches' pentagram.[39]

The Interfaith Movement

The same goal of syncretistic unity is ultimately achieved in a much subtler way via good works and goodwill. One of the major ground rules of the omnipresent interfaith groups is the agreement not to pros-elytize. Tolerance of every belief system becomes the highest good. Rabbi Martin Lawson, president of the Inter-religious Council of San Diego, states that since the group's purpose is "mutual understanding and respect," its members must leave "things of a proselytizing nature" at the door. "No effort to convert guests to any religious belief is per-mitted."[40] This sounds fair, but the principle favors the absolute prin-ciple of the relativity of truth. Behind the tolerance lurks an ideology unwilling to allow Christian belief. "It's all the same source, whether you call it God or the big bang." The message here is "different but ulti-mately the same."[41]

Evangelical Mystics

My final example of subtle syncretism in American churches highlights a spirituality known as "centered prayer." Using much Christian termi-nology, this approach borrows from Eastern, pagan meditation, and encourages the constant repetition of mantras (specific words or sounds), the suspension of rational thought, and the rejection of dual-istic categories (true/false, right/wrong) in order to produce a unitive experience of God. Though its practice may be well-intentioned, the results can be devastating to Christian orthodoxy. One of the leaders of this movement, Brennan Manning,[42] called "a modern-day saint" by the evangelical magazine *Aspire*,[43] nevertheless states: "[Do you see] why no Christian can ever say one form of prayer is not as good as another or one religion is not as good as another?"[44]

Such pagan syncretism is influencing not only mainline Christian denominations but devout evangelicals as well. The church must renew its vigilance.[45]

Mainline Protestants

Such religious relativism leaves confusion and ignorance in the ranks. Only 21 percent of America's Lutherans, 20 percent of Episcopalians, 18 percent of Methodists, and 22 percent of Presbyterians affirm the basic Protestant tenet: salvation by grace, not by good works. It is a theological principle the Vatican, too, has accepted in its 1999 accord with the Lutheran World Federation, but only 9 percent of the Catholics in the United States agree with it. Paul Hinlicky, a leading Lutheran theologian, points to "an absolute collapse of mainline Protestantism in this country."[46] At the 2000 Peacemaking Conference of the PCUSA, a keynote speaker, Dirk Ficca, asked the question: "What's the big deal about Jesus?" He argued that Jesus is okay for Christians but that there are other paths to God.[47] The same phenomenon of collapse is happening in worldwide Judaism, where the biblical beliefs of most Jews have eroded.[48] We can thus speak in general of a collapsing Judeo-Christian worldview.

Superstitious America

Americans are daily bamboozled by astrologers, psychics, palmists, mediums, and clairvoyants similar to the augurers, magicians, and soothsayers of ancient Rome. "Can you cast a spell to snag me a man or two?" a caller asks psychic Serena Sabak. Answer: "Seventy-two hours before the next full moon, mix the following ingredients in a glass bowl: one quart of distilled water, the petals of six red roses, a teaspoon of vanilla, a quarter teaspoon of cinnamon. When the moon is at its fullest, set the potion where it can absorb the magical light. Sprinkle a little on your skin. You will see the results almost immediately."[49]

Serena will rush you her magic tarot cards.[50] If these don't work, you might try a "Three Wishes Miracle Doll, with Magic Wand," which, according to Haitian and African magical traditions, grants you three wishes: "guaranteed result," for the low, low sum of $14.95 + $4.25 S&H.[51] The common use of horoscopes, the Psychic Hot Line, fortune-tellers, and seers (who offer help in criminal investigations) suggests that our culture is returning to the ways of superstitious Rome.

Syncretism and Superstition Need Spiritual Power

As I sat in O'Hare Airport, waiting for another delayed flight, I got into conversation with a young businessman. Raised a Southern Baptist, he now believed everybody—Buddhists, Hindus, people from all religions—would be in heaven, as long as they had faith. Faith, he said, was everything. I asked him how he would like to be in a room with Osama bin Laden and his henchmen, all of whom had more *faith* than he. He thought for a moment, and then said, "You have a point there."

Many ancient Romans turned away from official syncretistic polytheism and popular superstition to the mysteries of the Oriental gods and goddesses.[52] Today the situation is comparable, attracting people who

- equate discernment with intolerance;
- were raised believing it outrageous that any religion could claim to be the only true religion;
- are confused by the multiplicity of religions but who desire social harmony;
- believe civility to be a higher good than truth;
- desire a religious synthesis that also gives spiritual power.

Enter the goddess.

"It may be," says present-day Isis priestess Caitlín Matthews, "that Sophia is about to be discerned in much the same way as she was in 1st century Alexandria: as a beacon to Christians, Jews, Gnostics and Pagans alike."[53] The old Isis of "many names" will once again bring a world syncretism, this time on a planetary scale, driven by initiates imbued with her spiritual power.[54] If America could offer such a synthesis, says Diana Eck, this would be "the greatest form of lasting leadership we [could] offer the world."[55] Here, fleshed out in deeply religious terms, we see the "emerging American wisdom tradition"—America's new vocation—that will save the planet.[56]

The Meaning of Goddess Spirituality

In the deconstructed postmodern world of fractured beliefs and autonomous, unconnected people, the goddess brings good news. She offers an integrated worldview that addresses the great concerns and hopes of our day: ecological wisdom, economic justice, human rights, women's liberation, equality and harmony between the sexes, personal significance, global peace, utopian dreams, and deep spirituality.

The goddess is the most powerful symbol for pagan religion because she expresses its essence. She represents the maturing fruit of consistent pagan thinking about the nature of the universe that *one divine principle* joins everything together. We call it "monism," that is, the theory of "oneness."

A leading intellectual and apostate Christian, Lloyd Geering, emeritus professor of religious studies at Victoria University, whose books are promoted by the Jesus Seminar, approvingly agrees: "Unlike the dualistic character of the Christian world, *the new global world is monistic* [italics mine]. That means that the universe is conceived as essentially one. . . ."[57] Think of a circle. Everything is in that circle—the divine, the human, animals, rocks, trees, etc. Everything in the circle shares the same nature. The circle is it, divine and self-generating. This oneness is captured in the emotive image of the inclusive soft-core womb of the goddess, from which everything emerges and returns. Such monism characterized both the religious paganism of the past and that of the 1960s revolution. It also defines the vision of global harmony for the future. It has sometimes been referred to as the "perennial philosophy."[58] The old lady keeps coming back, hoary with age, but decked out in a brand new party dress and lots of makeup.

Humanity Is All-Powerful

The goddess assures us that everything, including our inner self, is divine. The well-known witch Starhawk gives this definition of her: "She is the great forces of birth, growth, death, and regeneration that move through the universe. Her many aspects are the faces we put on these forces so we can interact with them. She is immanent within us as well as in nature."[59]

The two thousand mainline "Christian" women at the Re-Imagining Conference of 1993 were reminded, "The Goddess [Sophia] is the place in you where the entire universe resides."[60] Joseph Campbell is enamored of the goddess story because in it "the world is the body of the goddess, divine in itself, and divinity is not something ruling over and above a fallen nature."[61] This goddess pantheism can be found in all the non-Christian religions, even where her name is absent.

The divinity of all things is expressed in all the non-Christian religions—witchcraft, Hinduism, American Indian shamanism, and supremely in peace-loving Buddhism.[62] Its ancient teaching proposes the same view of God: "You're not going to find truth outside yourself. You become a Buddha by actualizing your own original innate nature. This nature is primordially pure. This is your true nature, your natural mind. . . . it is always perfect, from the beginningless beginning. We only have to awaken to it."[63]

You are God or, as Harold Bloom discovered when reading the ancient Gnostic texts: "I am uncreated, as old as God!"[64] Liberated from his Jewish upbringing, Bloom became a pagan monist, or a Gnostic, as he calls himself.

For the religion of tomorrow, according to Geering, "'God' . . . will no longer refer to an objective spiritual being." Rather, the term *God* "sums up, symbolizes and unifies all that we value. That is why we speak of the God within us."[65] This divine/human being will not be encumbered by the confines of heterosexuality, or any structures imposed by an external Creator. On the issue of sexuality, as well as the specific identity of God, the Parliament of the World's Religions' *Global Ethic* was notably silent. The two pillars of the liberal religious revolution for a unified paganism—the diffuse nature of God and the liberation of sexual practice—stand strong and tall.[66]

Global Utopia

What is true about *human* nature is also true about nature. Guilt-ridden exploiters of the environment find redemptive satisfaction in thinking that the earth is divine. This fabulous, functioning ecosystem can be explained as development from within,[67] another way of speaking about evolution. Says Geering: "The universe cannot be explained from sources outside itself for the universe has no outside."[68] If the universe itself is "divine," then it is worthy of our worship. "To worship God in the global era would mean, among other things, that we stand in awe of this self-evolving universe."[69] In this adoration, the goddess is the essential symbol. Geering explains: "The new global religion will draw not only from the more ideological faiths of [monotheism] but from the preceding nature religions . . . who stood in such awe of the forces of nature. . . . Mother Earth would be a consciously chosen symbol referring to everything about the earth's eco-system. . . . In the religion of the coming global society, the forces of nature, the process of evolution and the existence of life itself will be the objects of . . . veneration."[70]

Worldwide Religious Harmony

Paganism in the form of global spiritual unity is now proposed as the future of the church and of global religion. Many religious organizations (the World Council of Churches, the United Religions, the Parliament of the World's Religions, the Interfaith Movement, and other mechanisms) are seriously dedicated to the sole task of bringing about a one-world religious reality. The present work of the "spirit" is producing an "invisible geometry to shape the religions of the world into a single truth." The new Pentecost is also the second coming. Christ is now undergoing "a mass incarnation among human beings all over the world, and manifesting himself in all the religions."[71]

A mainline academic press proposes a six-volume set of books in the *Global Spirit Library*, readings from Buddhism, Hinduism, Judaism, Christianity, Islam, and Confucianism, showing how these major world religions contribute to the spiritual bringing together of the planet.[72] This vision is promoted by virtually all the major religious publishing houses, and it is one of the common unifying themes of the professional guild of the teachers of religion in American colleges and universities, the American Academy of Religion. Syncretism appears as the revolutionary message of the Jesus Seminar, though appropriately dressed in other vocabulary.[73]

Syncretism in a so-called "Christian" world is only part of the picture. The new spirituality for the masses, whether they know it or not, presented in all its Hollywood glitz and dazzle, turns out to be pagan-Buddhist. We all thought we were being royally entertained, but we were being royally had. For, in an age which, on the surface, abominates "prosyletizing," George Lucas states that he made the Star Wars trilogy, in his own words, "to bring Buddhism to America."[74] How are the Buddhists doing?

The preparation has been long and laborious. Madame Blavatsky, "the most famous occultist of the 19th century,"[75] expressed hope to bring the East and the West together through occult spirituality. At the end of the nineteenth century, Blavatsky claimed that her *Secret Doctrine* was the revelation of "the universally diffused religion of the ancient and prehistoric world, . . . the source of all religions,"[76] which in the twentieth century would be more and more accepted.[77] The essence, she maintained, of this "universal religion" (note the globalist implications) was Buddhism.[78]

At the first Western Buddhist Teacher's Conference in the 1970s, a group of Buddhist meditation teachers met in Dharamsala, India, to discuss the transmission of Dharma in the modern world—for according to the globalist vision of Mahayana Buddhists and Bodhisattvas, "there can be no real enlightenment until all are enlightened."[79] The judgment they made in the 1990s of their progress is upbeat: "Strong bridges have been built from East to West, and the Dharma has arrived in the New World." How interesting that its arrival took place about the same time the goddess got into town! The Dalai Lama, so to speak, embraces her ladyship when he says: "I believe deeply that we must find, all of us together, a new spirituality."[80]

The Power of Goddess Spirituality

Today women are rediscovering Isis, . . . each of us can
personally experience the healing presence of the Goddess within us.
All women are Isis and Isis is all women.

KATHLEEN ALEXANDER-BERGHORN, RADICAL FEMINIST[81]

The healing presence of Isis? As I recounted in another book,[82] I attended the official "seminar" put on by the Fellowship of the Healing of Isis, as part of the Parliament of the World's Religions in Chicago in 1993, and saw, firsthand, what this is all about. In a typical hotel seminar room, a fragile little priestess, all dressed in white robes, suddenly became possessed of an unusual spiritual power and proceeded to wail in fear-inspiring moans. Others in the audience followed suit, and they were just getting going, because we were invited, as in the ancient Isian temples, to "enter the second chamber." That is when I decided to leave, but not before realizing that the "healing of Isis" had to do with a trance-like experience of spirit possession.

In Touch with the Goddess

Whatever Jean Houston was doing to help First Lady Hillary Clinton get in touch with the dead Eleanor Roosevelt, the following is how Houston describes her role in helping a certain Normandi Ellis, a lover of the "Egyptian mysteries," to get in touch with the ancient Isis/Osiris myth. Houston served, she says, as "Ellis's *evocateur*, her Thoth [according to Egyptian religion the divine revealer of secret knowledge], helping her to enter states of consciousness in which she found herself living in the myth."[83] According to the myth, Isis, Egyptian goddess of magic and of the underworld, the Shamanness and Necromancer *extraordinaire*, every year conjures up her deceased husband, Osiris, in the realm of the dead, and restores him to life. Harold Bloom fills in the details: "Central to shamanism are its supposed mysteries: flight, levitation, gender-transformation, bilocation, and animal and bird incarnations. All these phenomena, however startling, are merely means to the single end of shamanism: restoring the undying self of the dead."[84]

"The power and effectiveness of shamans—witches, sibyls, druids—emerges from their ability to communicate with the *non-human*: extra-terrestrial and subterranean forces, and the spirit-world of the dead."[85] The practice was known at the time of Paul. The ancient writer Lucian (around A.D. 100) says of necromancers: "I heard it said that by incantations and initiations they [the necromancers/shamans] could open the gates of Hades [the underworld of death], take whomever they pleased there and bring them back again safe and sound."[86]

The Isis myth suggests that we have divine, occultic power over death within ourselves to save ourselves and our planet. So when Houston says: "Never has this mythic knowing been more needed than today,"[87] she is proposing as the solution to the world's problems a thoroughgoing pagan occultism that became so popular in the halls of power of ancient Rome. Repeated observance of the Osiris and Isis rituals, says Houston, "maintains our continuing attention to the powers of the divine . . . [to] the union of spirit and matter, and the assurance of survival after death."[88]

Guilt-Free Mysticism

The goal of pagan spirituality, this mystical experience of oneness with the divinity, is clear, and is stated clearly—*to stifle guilt*. This is why the occultic "Jesus" who channeled messages to Helen Shucman, author of the best-selling New Age text, *A Course in Miracles*, says to the reader: "Do not make the pathetic error of clinging to the old rugged cross. . . . Your only calling here is to devote yourself with active willingness to the denial of guilt in all its forms."[89] But there is more to a spiritual high than trance-like ecstasy. There is an experience of *dominion*, as Marx Hubbard describes it. Going beyond the limitations of the mind also goes beyond rational definitions of right and wrong. Bruce Davis of the Manson family, now a born-again Christian, says about LSD that it "enlarged my sense of what was permissible . . . the unthinkable became the thinkable and the thinkable became the doable."[90] By embracing evil, pagan spirituality produces a temporary, counterfeit euphoria of *virtual redemption* and relief from guilt.

Anything that reminds one of guilt must be eliminated from the throbbing heart of the nation, the public square. If this is now true of the public square of this once "Christian" nation, it will certainly be true of the planet's.

Occultic Power

The Nechung Monastery in Dharamsala, India, is the locus of the official oracle, the place where "Tibetan Buddhist contact with the spirit world reaches official heights."[91] The current medium, or *kuden*, is the thirteenth to serve the Tibetan State Oracle. The event begins

> with twenty Nechung monks seated in a circle. Some blow blasts on long cylindrical horns, while others strike brass gongs and lacquered drums. The *kuden*, riding the sound of the music, goes into a trance and invokes the spirits. As possession occurs, a quiver runs through his body. His breathing becomes labored and his eyes take on a wild, startled

look. This is replaced by a distant stare as he begins to visu-
alize himself as a . . . deity at the center of a celestial man-
sion. His own consciousness cast aside, he has become Dorje
Draken, the chief spirit minister and bearer of counsel for
the State Oracle of Tibet.[92]

In spite of the impression that Buddhism is a nonthreatening
movement of religious ideas, particularly those of love and self-
sacrifice, it is here, at this occult shrine, that the Dalai Lama, one of
the most respected religious leaders of our day, comes for spiritual
counsel and empowerment.

Going within, your self sits at the center and reigns supreme. Here
is a classic example from Barbara Marx Hubbard: "All my life I have
heard an inner voice . . . my dearly Beloved . . . the guidance from my DB
is 'I am you.' . . . Over a period of six weeks I started to invite what I call
my universal self to take dominion within the household of selves that
I am. . . . I have been experiencing an identity shift such that I can now
say to you, 'I am the beloved that I seek . . . the universal human.' "[93]

Paganism always offers spiritual power.

Humanity Is God: Mystical Ecumenism

This kind of experience will bring the religions together. Says Episcopal
pagan priest, Matthew Fox: "Mysticism . . . has never been tried on an
ecumenical level."[94] The Roman Catholic scholar, Paul Knitter, is seeking to put that right. He states that there is "a growing awareness among
contemporary Christian theologians that a new method for a 'global' or
'world theology' is needed."[95] He calls for a "new kind of theologian
with a new type of consciousness—a multidimensional, cross-cultural
consciousness . . . [who will] 'pass over' to the experience . . . that nur-
tures the creeds and codes and cults of other religions."[96] Diana Eck,
describing the deep fellowship of Buddhist and Trappist monks at
Thomas Merton's monastery, Gethsemani, in Kentucky, says: "Religious
communities, even monastic communities, may have many differences,
but in the depth of spiritual life, there simply are no borders."[97] Some
believe that as more individuals find their divine identity in this pagan,
mystical oneness, the planet will shift into a unified, altered state of
consciousness, making this-worldly utopia possible.[98]

Utopian Dreams

There is a new American dream that pushes our frontier to the East and out to encircle the entire planet, out to the fuzzy edges of the cosmos to catch a ride with Heaven's Gate and Timothy Leary's ashes. Respected journalist Tony Schwartz,[99] with a sort of cockeyed optimism, defines a "new, emerging American wisdom tradition," a pagan version of the health and wealth gospel that joins material ease with spiritual meaning, Western capitalism with Hindu meditation. This hybrid cocktail, made and mixed in the USA, will save the planet.

Specifically, people will have to change. "Only by *reinventing ourselves at a profound level* will we release the Earth Community from its present impasse,"[100] believes Sally McFargue, professor at Vanderbilt Divinity School.[101] How profound? Willis Harman, a favorite spiritual counselor to Mikhail Gorbachev, informs us about how profound this self-reinvention must be. Harman describes a group of intuitive, globally sensitized people who make up "an expanding fraction of the populace," capable of perceiving "a shifting underlying picture of reality." They see "the connectedness of everything to everything" and place "emphasis on intuition and *the assumption of inner divinity* [emphasis mine]."[102]

Because globalism is a unique, untried event in human history, it functions to justify this kind of optimistic expectation of human transformation. Globalism provides the pretext, evolution the mechanism. According to Geering, the global reality is causing us to create "one unified species [through] a global consciousness/super-consciousness. . . . Possibly the human species could become so united in love and goodwill that there would be some kind of spiritual center. . . ."[103] Indeed, this possibility becomes a requirement. Hedging his bets, Geering warns that if it does not happen, someone will have to make it happen! "If the global society emerges, it will *require* [emphasis mine] humanity to develop a new consciousness and a new form of spirituality."[104]

Now, though, is the time for optimistic enthusiasm. The planet, fired by this high-octane spiritual energy, will soon take its final evolutionary jump into utopia. Here is the vision, in ultimate, lyrical prose: "Functioning in a context of love, trust and safety, small teams of people around the world join with one another for the betterment of all. Eventually, a sufficient, unified field is built, which 'jumps' the entire system to a new level of consciousness. All humanity, all life on this planet and throughout the universe shifts to an exalted level of love and awareness."[105]

The Goddess Reigns Supreme

In this coming utopia, the goddess will reign supreme when all her enemies have been subdued. This global religion consists, positively, of a deeply held conviction of the truth of paganism, and negatively, of a very careful and painstaking demolition or elimination of opposing beliefs.

Absolute Knowledge

At its core, this new religion is no more tolerant than those it constantly accuses of intolerance. What the general public often hears are the emotive appeals to broadmindedness and nonjudgmental tolerance. Wendy Hunter Roberts, a pagan priestess, declares with a disarming lack of prejudice: "We have no one, true, and only way."[106] In similar terms, the Buddhist Dalai Lama, wrapping his arms around all the religions, expansively declares: "The concept of only one religion and only one truth is bad . . . love and compassion for mankind is necessary to be happy, while complicated philosophy and doctrine are not."[107] Religious truth, say others,[108] is so great that each religion can only contribute a part. Those who claim to "have the total truth have missed the real point."[109]

Even though pluralism publicly claims openness and tolerance while accusing Christians of exclusivist bigotry, there can be found statements of deep, personal conviction, and exclusivity regarding *the truth* of the pagan system. Apparently there is a limit to openness! For instance, Stephen Hoeller, bishop of the Ecclesia Gnostica of Los Angeles, claims that Gnostic "Christians" believe that "direct, personal and absolute knowledge of the authentic truths of existence is accessible to human beings."[110] Richard Alpert, on LSD, heard "a voice inside that spoke truth."[111] Hameed Ali, a Sufi (Islamic mysticism), believes that Sufism has "the clearest and most precise understanding. . . . direct knowing is just there, available with clarity and precision."[112] Such deep conviction as to the truth of paganism gives rise to intolerance for its opposite, theism.

The Pagan Antithesis

When one digs deeper into religious tolerance, one finds commitment to an immutable pagan worldview, a conviction that paganism is right and Christianity is wrong. There is tolerance only for other *pagan* approaches, and deep intolerance for biblical truth.[113]

The following chart is part of a list proposed by *MasterPath: The Divine Teachings of Light and Sound*,[114] a spiritual path to find the god within. The left column is the "esoteric" (what is within), spiritual paganism. The right column is the "exoteric" (what is outside), or biblical Christianity. According to Masterpath, the column on the left is truth; the column on the right is illusion.

PAGANISM	CHRISTIANITY
Truth	Illusion
Esoteric (Inner)	Exoteric (Outer)
Entering Heaven While Living	Entering Heaven After Death
Saving Oneself	Being Saved
Worship of Spirit Within the Individual	Worship of Outer Personality
Resolving of Karma	Forgiving of Sin
Many Lifetimes Lived in Soul	Only One Life to Live
Attaining Self and God Realization	Second Coming—a Futuristic Event in Time and Space
Everyone [Christ]	Only One Saint for Yourself
Living Master	Dead Master
Disciple's Lower Nature Crucified	Savior Crucified
Disciple's Energies Collecting in Third Eye	Savior Resurrected
Disciple Leaving Body Consciousness	Savior Ascended

Here we see clearly the exclusionary character of contemporary paganism. The ad is written for New Age, pagan yuppies, and it makes no attempt to charm the public with notions of tolerance and broadmindedness. It is a lucid expression, from the pagan perspective, of the classic religious antithesis in which monism and theism are recognized as mutually exclusive.[115]

BACK TO THE FUTURE

In other terms, the new, global religion seeks to undermine Christianity by presenting itself as cutting edge spirituality that will save the planet, and Christianity as hopelessly and intolerably out of touch. According to this approach, Christianity's worldview has "been slowly dissolving from Western consciousness." The "remnants" of Christianity—heaven and hell, God on his heavenly throne, the last judgment, Christ as Savior—now merely "exist like islands of the past in the fast-flowing tide of secularization which is giving rise to the new, [evolving] global world."[116] We are outgrowing the need for a God like the one we find in the Bible.

But note this! Oddly enough, in some ways, the evolutionary tide is going backwards, turning back on its tail! The outgrowing is becoming ingrowing. Geering admits that "the new story of the earth, in reminding us of the earthly matrix from which we have evolved, is reviving in us some aspects of very primitive human thought, namely the worship of nature as the Great Mother."[117] He actually proposes to go back to the pre-Israelite paganism of ancient Canaan![118] In this, as in many other areas, we are going back to the paganism of the Roman Empire. But if one is obliged to go backwards to find the "new," then it is not the "age" or "newness" of any particular belief that is the real issue. That is a smokescreen. The fact is we are in the presence of mutually irreconcilable, equally ancient notions. Biblical faith is being bustled out, not because it is old, but because it does not fit; not because it makes no sense, but because it sings a different tune, discordant with harmonic religious convergence. As United Religions board member Paul Chafee clearly stated: "We cannot afford fundamentalists in a world this small."[119] So much for all-inclusive united religious tolerance.

THE TIME FOR GLORIFYING GOD IS OVER

This is the new message of the church, according to Episcopalian bishop John Spong. He affirms that the church will never again speak to the postmodern world[120] unless she abandons her "theistic definition of God,"[121] that is, God as separate from his creation. Such is the program specifically adopted by Robert Funk, founder of the Jesus Seminar, in his "Twenty-One Theses," and put into explicit wording by Lloyd Geering: "The time for glorifying the Almighty (male) God who supposedly rules *is now over* [my emphasis]."[122] At the very least, one might ask where the spirit of inclusiveness, openness, and tolerance can be found in such a statement.

The pagan juggernaut is moving, in and outside the churches. Nothing, especially biblical orthodoxy, must be allowed to get in its way. Christianity will be allowed to survive only if it converts to paganism, if "God becomes goddess." We are reassured that "all religious traditions will contribute," but with the caution: "Those that can respond most flexibly . . . to the current challenges are likely to offer the most."[123]

The "new" absolutism and the imperious necessity of a certain kind of unity suggest the emergence one day of an intolerant, unbroken monistic circle, which will, with the help of the state, cover the earth as the waters cover the sea.

The Harlot and the Beast Embrace: The Goddess Mounts Her Throne

Consider the following scenario.

As the band plays "Hail to the Chief," the exciting new First Couple emerges from the presidential helicopter to wildly ecstatic applause. The year is 2040, your grandchildren are getting married, and you will make the ceremony. The president of the United States of the Americas, one of the world's five administrative regions, is giving a policy speech on human rights, public civility, and the importance of whole-hearted support for the fledgling experiment in global governance. The normally all-business, no-nonsense "policy wonk" today is decked out in seasonal soft pink. Her lesbian lover at her side, the president makes an emotional appeal to "fair-minded" citizens of the community of nations for tolerance of all sexual practices and religious options, in the old tradition of American democracy and of global human liberation. Officially married, the First Pair is also very religious, though their spirituality is not exactly classically American. They are often photographed emerging from one of the high-class witches' covens that now proliferate in Washington, D.C.[124] Personifying contemporary broadmindedness, they have no intention of imposing their religious commitments on anyone. Indeed they magnanimously see all religions as extremely important, essentially the same, and a necessary component of government policy. The president's speech climaxes with an impassioned invocation of the powers of Isis, Egyptian goddess of magic and unifier of the cosmos, and an emotional call for increased government funding for all participating faiths and "life-choices." It concludes with a solemn commitment to end, once and for all, every form of intolerance and exclusivistic "hate-speech," for the imperious necessity of world peace. The crowd of gays and "straights" alike gives the president a long and enthusiastic standing ovation and a rousing rendition of "God Bless the Americas."

Fiction? What will impede the joining of pagan religion and political power, with so many key world leaders intent on making it happen? The following are a few who are working hard to accomplish a similar dream.

Religious Commitments of Globalist Politicians

Mikhail Gorbachev, the last leader of the atheistic Soviet Union, now calls for "a new synthesis of democratic, Christian and Buddhist values" if the planet is to survive into the next generation.[125] Upon analysis, this is nothing less than the prostitute borne on the back of the beast, that is, apostate religion joined with political power. Notice the choice of words. The language is coded but the meaning is clear:

- *Synthesis:* Gorbachev makes no bones about deploying both the spiritual and the political in one concerted effort;
- *Democratic:* This does not mean "one man, one vote," as in classical democratic theory, but some form of global collectivism which will ensure "sustainable growth," that is, what the elite

determine to be the desirable living conditions for the people (*demos*) of the global village;
• *Christianity and Buddhism:* This is a hybrid mix of two unmixable religious categories that can only produce apostate religion.

The Global Harlot

Gorbachev's religious proposition, the blending of Christianity and Buddhism, is not an idle remark.[126] It reveals the heart of his vision. This mix is proposed by the members of the small but significant Theosophical movement, which has great influence in the corridors of power that were occupied by figures like Gorbachev. Using slightly different terminology, they describe "the new world religion" as the collaboration of the "two Brothers, the Buddha and the Christ."[127] To celebrate the unity, they propose "Three Spiritual Festivals, 2002." They call upon people of goodwill to celebrate the Christian festival of Easter, the Buddhist/Hindu festival of Wesak, and their own "Festival of Goodwill" during which they promote their "Great Invocation" prayer to their Ascended Masters, the "hierarchy."[128] Such prayers are considered "the most potent tool available to us for planetary transformation."[129]

The growing cooperation between various religions helps "prepare the way for new revelations of spiritual truth" and the coming of a "great spiritual Teacher." Says Diana Eck, "The most energetic and significant spiritual dialogue in recent years has surely been the Christian-Buddhist dialogue. . . . It would be impossible to count the number . . . involved in the past three decades."[130] This can be noted in the hundreds of books from all the major publishers, proposing this theme, as well as in numerous academic conferences. To cite just one, Pacific Lutheran University housed the Sixth International Conference of the Society of Buddhist-Christian Studies in August 2000. One hundred and seventy scholars discussed for a week the subject "Buddhism, Christianity and Global Healing." Such a joining removes from Christianity what is essential to it—God's self-revelation as Creator and Redeemer, separate from the creation, and leaves Buddhism's spiritual atheism perfectly intact.

The Global Beast

The major focus of discussion at Pacific Lutheran was the UN's Earth
Charter, drawn up, you remember, by Maurice Strong and Mikhail
Gorbachev. During the exchange it was recognized by all that "the
Charter . . . reflects central Buddhist beliefs."[131] Thus, a leading
Buddhist scholar, Daisaku Ikeda, has declared: "We can use the Charter
as a tool for transformation. . . ."[132] Professor John Cobb, the well-
known process theologian, proposed "earthism"—which is the char-
ter's subject matter—as humanity's common bond. Theologian Paul
Knitter spoke of "the need to bring both prophetic and mystical quali-
ties to the task of moving the Earth Charter from vision to reality."[133]
Religion will serve a political agenda—and vice versa.

At the Earth Charter's launching ceremony in the Hague in June
2000—with both Queen Beatrix of the Netherlands and Ruud Lubbers,
former prime minister of the Netherlands, present—the authors,
Gorbachev and Strong, made impassioned appeals for its implementa-
tion under UN authority.[134]

RELIGION AND POLITICS AT THE UN

The United Nations is clearly a global, political structure; but from its
inception, some have sought to press its spiritual significance as well.
Alice Bailey, leader of the occultic Theosophical Society[135] and founder
of the Lucifer Publishing Company in 1922 (renamed the Lucis Trust,
and now a recognized NGO of the UN), said before she died in the
1950s: "[Thanks to] the efforts of the UN . . . a new church of God,
gathered out of all the religions and spiritual groups, will unitedly
bring to an end the great heresy of separation."[136] She went so far as to
state that "within the United Nations is the germ and seed of a great
international and meditating, reflective group . . . [whose] point of
meditative focus is the intuitional or buddhic plane—the plane upon
which all hierarchical [occult] activity is today to be found."[137] Here
global politics and Buddhist religion are clearly joined.

The devil is often in the details. The Lucis Trust has been in charge
of the Meditation Room at the UN since it was established in the 1950s
by the secretary-general, Dag Hammarskjöld, a Lutheran who became

a Buddhist. But the devil is not only in the details. On May 17, 2001, I received a mailing from the Lucis Trust, from their posh address, 120 Wall St. 24th Floor,[138] which states:

> Today is a climaxing time of change. Humanity is passing through an extremely difficult transition period in which the old forms are dying out and new ones are coming to life. . . . Always in such times of necessity, and to inaugurate the new age, a Teacher comes forth. . . . But we should not look for this teacher to come forth as a traditional religious figure. Instead, he will come for all humanity . . . the facilities of the entire world of contact and communication will be at his disposal. . . . He comes to give a message, which will heal . . . which will give to humanity an expression of some hitherto unrealized aspect of divinity.[139]

Doubtless such a "Teacher" would be both a world politician and a pagan religious leader who would integrate religion and politics in a new synthesis. It is not outlandish to think that such a "Teacher" could even be a lesbian witch, a priestess of the goddess. For world politician Maurice Strong,[140] his preferred "Teacher" certainly must be an *apostate* Christian.[141] Once an elder of a Christian church before he turned to occult paganism, Strong's world savior will be a truly "Planetary Prostitute," a genuine article Antichrist![142]

In the meantime, the United Religions Initiative (URI) proposes to become for the world's religions what the UN is for the world's nations. Set up on July 14, 2000, and now an official NGO, this mechanism is one more example of the determination on the part of some to bring global politics and the world's religions together for the betterment of humanity.[143]

Why It Must Happen

This unholy alliance of the planetary prostitute with the planetary beast is doubtless inevitable because many powerful people,[144] with well-meaning motives, are driven by an all-consuming passion for a united world,[145] beguiled by the perennial temptation—utopia.[146] But with no possible transcendent hope, paganism's dreams for utopia must focus on this world.[147] If the earth is the goddess, and if utopia is to happen, it must happen here. She must reign over her domain. Besides, our human reputation is at stake. Humanity's pretensions to be able to build a global Babel must be realized to save us from ourselves. Why will this project work any better than that of ancient Rome? Have we changed that much to become a superior race? For some, the present time is the last hope for such utopic dreams to become a reality. This time it *must* happen, or it will never happen. Globalism is the pretext, pagan empowerment the means. And by definition, it can only happen by human effort, so every aspect of life, including the religious and the political, must be utilized. The circle must be unbroken or the spell will be. There can be no place for dissent. If necessary, "goodwill" will be enforced by state power, for the sake and good of humanity. But "humanity" is an odd commodity, as the social commentator Stephen Lasch perceptively remarked: "The capacity for loyalty is stretched too thin when it tries to attach itself to the hypothetical solidarity of the whole human race. . . . We love particular men and women, not humanity in general. The dream of universal brotherhood, because it rests on the sentimental fiction that men and women are all the same, cannot survive the discovery that they are different."[148]

This is true of people in general, and of males and females in particular. It is also true of religion. The fiction of sameness will be exposed. In the meantime, to maintain the fiction (or "the lie," as the Bible describes it), Christians could be faced with a state-enforced ultimatum: "Deny the Christ of the Bible and worship the goddess of global Babel—to save the planet."[149] Have we not heard this before? "Confess Caesar as Lord and save the Empire."

Conclusions

There are many reasons to think that the future planetary community will not look anything like the democratic, "Christian" America, as defined in its founding documents, but much more like ancient, totalitarian, pagan Rome, where the simple admission, *sum christianus* ("I am a Christian"), was a capital offense. Since the goddess has claimed America, and America now leads the planet, her real designs are for imperial, global control. Francis Schaeffer, not long before he died, with remarkable prescience, described the world's future, in similar terms, as "proud humanism . . . joined to the acme of the occult."[150]

I raise the specter of a global colossus, a future pagan Babel, not to scare or sensationalize, but to promote clear thinking. If there is none, God's people "will be destroyed for lack of knowledge." I hope my read of history is wrong, and I do not claim a prophetic gift; but from the evidence presented here, a global pagan kingdom cannot be far off the mark. If the Roman Empire described in chapters 1 and 2 provides a historical parallel, it shows, despite the promise of liberation, the totalitarian nature of pagan culture. In the difficult times to come, what should Christians do and say? Christianity will not be the official imperial religion in the new world system. It will be the odd-man out, a metaphysical party-pooper, unable to participate in the global celebration of political and religious peace. So how will Christians survive?

First they must listen, and there is much to hear. We know that this is not the first time Christianity has been under similar attack. As we noted in the first chapters, the gospel was preached in the ancient world under comparable circumstances; and so we should *listen to history.* Specifically, we must *listen to Paul,* the apostle sent with the gospel to the original Roman pagans. In the syncretistic, conformist pagan empire of his day, Paul did not hold back. In spite of constant opposition and overwhelming odds, when paganism seemed to have won total victory, he showed the Christian way forward. His preaching of the Christian utopia provoked inevitable religious conflict between Christianity and false utopian myths of imperial paganism. But the gospel finally turned the pagan Empire upside down. If we are going to understand our times, we must turn our attention to the rabbi. Paul, and the master he represents, must be heard in the context of global Babel. Paul must be read in the light of his historical context within the ancient Roman Empire, but he also must be read in relation to the coming pagan empire in which we and our children are called to witness.

It is time to listen to Paul.

Part Two

The age of the "Christian West" is coming to an end. As in first-century Rome, the state can no longer support the social and moral agenda of the church. We live in a post-Christian, postmodern, post-Constantinian[1] world, where a new, "democratic" ideology of religious and sexual freedom sweeps all before it. Christians are confronted by a new reality, forced to look again at the Bible with different questions and expectations. The revival of paganism in our time is "apocalyptic," in the original sense of that term as "unveiling." Triumphant neo-paganism clarifies the contrast between its worldview and that of the Bible and promotes its political/religious agenda as the only one.

Capturing the pagan mind by looking at the message of Paul is not, in the first place, to find a pragmatic method of evangelism for pagan questions, though this must be done. In order to capture the pagan mind, from Paul's perspective, one must understand its radical difference from the "mind of Christ." The reason is simple.

The pagan and Christian visions of utopia cannot be reconciled. For paganism, the coming utopia is a human achievement; for the Bible it is the work of God. As Paul programmatically says: "[Pagans] worship and serve the creation rather than the Creator" (Rom. 1:25). Nature worship is the "lie." Worship of the Creator is the "truth." There is deep logic here. In paganism, Nature is divine, self-generating, and worthy of worship. There is no Creator. There is no transcendence. Nature itself, including humanity, brings the universe to perfection. This cosmos is all there is. C. S. Lewis warned against this view when he said: "Aim for heaven and you will get the earth too. Aim for the earth and you will get neither."

For Christianity, the starting point is the Creator/creature distinction. God exists independently of the creation he made. He is both the

89

Creator of life and of its utopian transformation. Thus, the biblical notion of utopia begins with God's act of creation and concludes with his act of recreation. This is the essence of Paul's "theocentric" teaching.

Capturing the pagan mind is also essential for understanding Paul, whose message was the Christian response to the pagan worldview. Understanding what Paul calls "the lie" clarifies the truth. If it was the Christian message for ancient Rome, it must surely be the Christian message for planetary "Rome." At this deep level, nothing changes.

It is appropriate to hear Paul address us as we stand on the threshold of the global village. Of all the original apostles, it was Paul who was born in a pagan city, took the gospel to the pagan world, and understood the pagan religious option. Of the biblical writers, Paul is the only one specifically commissioned by God to speak to and of the pagan condition. He is called as "the apostle to the pagans";[2] his goal is the "sanctification of the pagans";[3] and everything he writes is influenced by the inclusion of the pagans in the people of God.

Paul speaks from a social context that our culture is fast resembling. The pagan past is our planetary future. Historic biblical Christianity finds itself in direct confrontation with the religious claims of a political empire intent on delivering a this-worldly utopian answer to human needs, based on the misleading myths of pagan spirituality. It is helpful to realize that we are not the first to face such a situation. In spite of modern evolutionary mythology, nothing really changes. The options are the same, and there are only two. In his teaching of option number one—the Bible's worldview—Paul makes no compromise with option number two—paganism. Unlike many teachers in the church today, Paul warns his ex-pagan converts to have nothing to do with the pagan myths and lifestyle from which they had been delivered.[4] Rather, he sounds the note of profound antithesis and mutual exclusivity—for the sake of clarity, in order that people might know the truth and be saved. In these confusing times, if anyone can make sense of things, it is surely Paul.

In the days of my youth, I remember bonneted Salvation Army ladies who, with great verve and flourish, played little box-shaped wind instruments called concertinas. With both arms extending it outwards and then compressing it inward they could produce a mighty, rushing wind and powerful, animated sound. Paul's thought may be represented as a kind of intellectual outward and inward movement, following the exhaling of God's creative Spirit.

The first move outwards, farther than the human mind can see, is the miraculous breathing forth of the vastness of the original creation, what I call "the birth of creation." This is the backdrop against which to see everything else Paul says.

The second movement is like the contraction of the concertina into its original, lifeless shape—all the wind sucked out of it, silent and inert. This movement of compression represents the death of creation, as creation life is slowly but surely, through the fall, sucked out of the cosmos. The movement of contraction ultimately necessitates the crushing of God the Son, as his life is snuffed out at the cross.

The third and final movement extends the concertina even further than its first move. On this move, God breathes out again from his divine life, in a glorious celebration of the rebirth of God the Son at the resurrection and the glorious rebirth of the whole creation as a necessary consequence.

This movement of life, death, and back to life is dimly reflected in the natural order, where summer is followed by winter and then returns with the spring. This wonderful, cyclical symphony of nature is celebrated by paganism at the winter and summer solstices as expressing the entirety of existence. For all its hype, paganism is a very limited and stunted view of things. It only ever gives you more of the same. Alas, by enclosing everything, including God, in the circle of life, it fails to account for the full picture. Beyond the dependable, natural cycles stands the absolute beginning of the universe as well as its final, radical transformation. Behind both of these stands the powerful mystery of the transcendent God. About these the Bible and Paul are concerned. There is no question more radical than this, nor can the question of the meaning of life be treated in a more comprehensive manner.

But before we study Paul's gospel, we need to know who Paul is.

Chapter 5

Paul—Not Your Average Rabbi

A Prophet Like Moses

Why listen to Paul? He was a squint-eyed rabbi who gave up a prestigious teaching possibility to wander around Greece and Turkey, making enemies of his Jewish compatriots and causing minor riots wherever he went. What possible relevance do his brief letters and treatises have for the twenty-first century?

Appearances can be deceptive. I once was asked to address a study group that had read my book *The Gnostic Empire Strikes Back.*[1] As my host began to introduce me, a towering gentleman hovered over my five-foot-seven-inch frame. "You're Peter Jones?" he exclaimed in surprise. "I thought you were six-foot-four!" Reality doesn't always match expectations.

Paul was physically and socially unimpressive, but he wrote spectacular copy. He was possibly the greatest ancient Greek author,[2] not for his style so much as for his power. Paul risked his life to bring the gospel to the heart of the "Gentile" Roman Empire, but many in the Gentile church would gladly eliminate the messenger.

My wife recently spent a writing week in Los Angeles. Without wheels, a stranger to the neighborhood, she went out to find a church for Sunday worship. She met the interfaith chaplains (husband and wife team) of a nearby university, who declared their love of Jesus, but found Paul to be a poor benighted soul with deep psychological problems. "Poor Paul is quite touching," said the woman pastor with a benevolent sigh. Such an attitude about Paul is common. An organizer of a gay parade declared that Jesus would have been at the front of the parade, but that Paul would not have been welcomed. Give me Jesus. You can keep Paul.

Paul faced marginalization in his own time as both Jews and pagans, and even Christian converts in the churches he founded, questioned his apostolic authority. The apostle Peter had to come to his defense,[3] while Paul defended himself against charges that he "peddled" and "distorted" the word of God.[4] He was called "an aborted fetus" by some in Corinth,[5] and others there denied his right to be an apostle.[6] In answer to the original Corinthians who began to have difficulty submitting to Paul's teaching, Paul wrote two letters. In the first he asks, "Am I not an apostle? . . . Even though I may not be an apostle to others, surely I am to you! For you are the seal of my apostleship in the Lord" (1 Cor. 9:1–2). In the second letter he indicates that the opposition to his authority had intensified: "Do we need . . . letters of recommendation to you? . . . You yourselves are our letter, written on our hearts. . . . Make room for us in your hearts" (2 Cor. 3:1; 7:2). This impassioned plea communicates the painful rejection Paul faced.

Throughout history, Paul's reviews have been mixed. He probably would have had a three on *Amazon.com*—as many fives as ones. Many of his critics would have given him "ones." For them, he was the *haereticorum apostolus*—"apostle of the heretics";[7] a "dishonest, hypocritical evil-doer, cheat and con-artist";[8] "a dirty little Jew";[9] "a cheat, a hateful imposter, a genius of hate, the true Satanic anti-Christ . . . the 'glad tidings' [of Jesus] were followed by the *worst* tidings—those of St. Paul";[10] "a monstrous imposition on Jesus."[11] At the end of the nineteenth century, many Germans saw Paul as a psychopath leading the Christian faith back into Judaism. The Nazis painted Paul as the great corrupter of the European spirit, because he re-Judaized the gospel.[12] A blue-eyed, blond-haired Aryan Jesus was the monstrously racist result.

However, Paul had fans as well. Those who would have given him a "five" rating were many great thinkers in the history of the church. Some hailed him as a "prodigious genius";[13] "the second founder of the church, after Christ and alongside Peter . . . the first after the Unique . . . a theological superman . . . the model of the Christian

throughout history . . . unequaled Christian theologian and philosopher";[14] "the founder of Christian theology";[15] "the founder of
Christianity."[16] One line of opinion throughout the ages has seen Paul
as the most powerful human personality in the history of the church—
a figure upon whom later Christian theology was built.

The huge discrepancy and the violent intensity of these opinions
tells us that Paul is a crucial figure. But if we are to understand him, we
need to take a look at his place within the original Christian movement.
We cannot content ourselves with the opinions of secondary sources.

Hit by a Metaphysical Mack Truck

The traffic has slowed to a crawl. The rubber-neckers cannot resist. On
the main road into Damascus, an accident victim lies helpless and
blinded. He is not any old commuter, but Saul, the infamous public
prosecutor, carrying arrest warrants from the high priest to imprison
Christians and wipe out their heretical faith. This arrogant protégé of
the Jewish leadership lies in the gutter, holding up traffic.

This bizarre incident did more than hold up traffic. What kind of
event was it that brought this brilliant career to a screeching halt? What
took the top of the class to the bottom of the pile?

Something Earthshaking Happened

That something earthshaking happened no one can deny. Scholars have
debated for centuries about what really happened on the Damascus
road,[17] but no one contests the dramatic change. Saul became Paul; the
Jew became a Christian; the representative of the high priest became an
apostle of Jesus Christ, and the proud careerist became a humble servant. In losing everything associated with his past, Paul loses all sense
of being an up-and-coming star. His self-understanding is radically
changed, so he will say that his goal is no longer to promote himself but
to know and promote Christ.[18] There is no more self-righteousness, an
attitude reflected in his use of the third-person pronoun as he recounts
his own experience of change.[19] From a brilliant young man who was
eager to climb the social ladder, Paul gave up thinking of himself as
the "first" and accepted a position at the end of the parade as the
"last."[20] From a life of boasting, implicitly and explicitly, about his

achievements, Paul now boasts in his weakness.[21] He calls himself the "worst of sinners" (1 Tim. 1:16) and the "least of the apostles" (1 Cor. 15:9). Following this event, Paul becomes a stunning early example of the saying of Jesus: "The first will be last, and many who are last be first" (Matt. 19:30).

In one particular passage, Paul gives us a window into his soul as he describes his former life as a successful but very proud man, convinced he was right, and having all he needed for success (see Phil. 3:3–6). But his career, his ambitions, and his successes came to a screeching halt. At Damascus, the proud Paul is brought low. A sense of his human unworthiness in the presence of God's great holiness replaces a sense of human achievement. This, of course, is the experience of the Old Testament prophet, classically in the case of Isaiah, who declares, upon seeing the Lord, high and lifted up on his throne: "Woe is me for I am ruined. For I am a man of unclean lips, and I live among a people of unclean lips, and my eyes have seen the King, the Lord Almighty" (Isa. 6:5).

A Meeting with God

A naturalist, who believes that there is nothing outside nature or beyond the natural order, can believe neither Isaiah nor Paul, and is obliged to interpret Paul's words to correspond with some recognized *natural* phenomenon—inner mystical transport, moral crisis, or psychological collapse. This is not what Paul says. His account is much more like Isaiah's—"my eyes have seen the King, the Lord of glory." He speaks of a totally unexpected, objective rendezvous with the God of Abraham, Isaac, and Jacob, initiated by God, not by Paul. Paul is the object, and Christ the subject. Something assailed Paul from the outside, as he says in his own words—"Christ Jesus took hold of me" (Phil. 3:12).[22] Paul's experience, described in these terms, recalls that of the prophet Jeremiah, who declares to the sovereign Lord: "You overpowered me and prevailed" (Jer. 20:7),[23] or of Jacob: "I saw God face to face, and yet my life was spared" (Gen. 32:30).

The objective character of this experience enters the narrative in a variety of ways: the risen Christ appeared to him;[24] he and his fellow travelers saw a blinding light at midday, and Jesus spoke to him;[25] God, at a specific moment, revealed his Son to him;[26] he saw the Lord.[27] That the resurrection occupies such a crucial place in Paul's theology (see below) indicates just how significant was this initial meeting with the resurrected Christ.

Paul was a theist, like the writers of the Old Testament he had studied from his childhood. He believed in the God who has an existence independent of the creation he made. He believed that the Creator God, at very specific times and for particular reasons, had intervened in human history—just as he intervened in the case of Moses at the burning bush, or in the case of Isaiah in the temple at Jerusalem[28]—to further the cause of redemption. Just as the experience of Moses never became the way of enlightenment for every Israelite, so Paul never once proposes his experience on the Damascus road as the paradigm for general Christian conversion or spirituality. Rather, like the "burning bush" for Moses, this event singles him out as a unique spokesman for Christ,[29] a member of a unique group upon whose witness the church for the ages to come was to be founded.[30]

The changes were so radical in Paul's life that his entire worldview and thinking process was turned inside out. Though the bald statement of fact that Paul offers us about his experience already tugs at us for a response, the radical changes in his life speak even more loudly. The worldview revolution is so great that only an event of the nature he describes—the objective reality of a meeting with the risen Lord—can explain them.

HIS WORLDVIEW IS REVOLUTIONIZED

Paul met the risen Lord—and this experience brought about a complete transformation of the way Paul understood reality. Only this could have dislodged the stubbornly-held conviction that Christians were condemned apostate Jews. As one scholar has perceptibly noted, on the Damascus road Paul's thought patterns changed forever:

> The appearance of Jesus proved to Paul that the Christian proclamation was correct; that Jesus had been raised from the dead; that he must therefore be the Messiah . . . and Son of God; . . . the exalted Jesus identified himself with the

Christians . . . [which] established that the church, which Paul had been persecuting, was indeed the people of the Messiah. But if a people, who did not observe the Law as the Pharisees defined it, were the people of the Messiah, then salvation could not be by the Law; it must be the gift of the Messiah . . . to all men [including] the Gentiles.[31]

A MISSION TURNED UPSIDE DOWN

Saul's ardent desire to be number one in the purest form of Judaism is transformed into an awareness of having been seized by the risen Jesus to represent him to the far off and the far out. Saul's hatred is turned to love, and he is willing to go into the filthy bowels of the earth to win unlovely, sin-stained pagans. The proud racist becomes a lover of all kinds of people, in every condition.

Some Rabbi!

People who think they are Jesus Christ or Napoleon are found in psychiatric hospitals with other inmates who believe them. Those who order other people around with "commands from the Lord" are undesirables in the labor market. How did Paul, who believed himself to be fulfilling the role of a second Moses with the authority to give divine commands, avoid an early and long career in a rest home for religious fanatics?

Paul is no ordinary rabbi or teacher to be consulted for his wise but pedantic opinions. We cannot tear Paul out of the heart of New Testament revelation and leave him on the side as a take-it-or-leave-it oddity. To dismiss Paul as an unnecessary extra in New Testament revelation would be a historical, theological, and methodological error of monumental proportions.

Paul is no ordinary rabbi because he is one of the *essential* founders of the Christian faith. He occupied an indispensable and vital place in the process that gave the church a completed revelation of the fullness of God's redemptive plan. I would like to show this in a carefully constructed argument, so fasten your seat belts and hang on. I hope you will agree that the trip is worth it.

The Foundation: Jesus, Not Quite Finished

Unlike the Koran, the Bible did not fall from the sky ready-made. Not only did Old Testament revelation take hundreds of years to unfold, but New Testament revelation took time as well. This is very important when thinking about the place of Paul in the original Christian movement and his authority over the church in every age. According to the New Testament, Paul is not just an optional extra, a self-imposed dictator who took over the church's view of Jesus for his own ends. Paul occupies a crucial and essential place in the original formulation of the Christian message.

Though Jesus on the cross cried out, "It is finished" (John 19:30), he knew that the *history* of redemption was far from over. After the cry of dereliction from the cross, other redemptive events still had to take place. God dealt definitively with sin at the death of his Son; God resurrected Jesus from the dead; Jesus appeared to his disciples after the resurrection; he ascended to heaven; he sent the Holy Spirit to the church on the day of Pentecost. So, while Jesus is the big event, he never wrote down a word and died before many of the key redemptive events took place. His task was to accomplish redemption, to *do* it, to *be* it. He appointed others to be witnesses of these events, both in spoken and in written form.

During his earthly ministry, Jesus informed his disciples of their role as public witnesses in the future: "There is nothing covered that will not be revealed, and hidden that will not be known. What I tell you in the dark, speak in the light; and what you hear in the ear, preach on the housetops" (Matt. 10:26–27 NKJV). That apostolic witness he defines as the foundation of the future church. When Peter, representing the other apostles, declares that Jesus is the "Christ, the Son of the living God" (Matt. 16:16), Jesus' response is most illuminating. He states that this divine revelation about himself, coming from the mouth of the apostle, would be the rock or foundation on which he would build the church.

This is what the apostles in their witnessing, preaching, teaching, and writing do. They lay the foundation about Christ in the church. This is what Paul says. There is no other *foundation* laid than Jesus

Christ.[32] But God takes his time to reveal his mind. Thus an enormous segment of the Christian foundation is laid in the revelation embodied in the Old Testament, long before the coming of Christ. Jesus, the other apostles, and Paul constantly affirm this. The Old Testament is cited verbatim hundreds of times, and scholars have estimated the number of allusions to be in the thousands. No New Testament author ignored the Old Testament. They all agreed with and based their own thinking on what Jesus had said: "I have not come to abolish [the Law and the Prophets], but to fulfill them" (Matt. 5:17).

Paul, for example, writing to the Roman church, states that the gospel he preaches was "promised beforehand through the prophets in the Holy Scriptures" (Rom. 1:2). Paul is affirming that *everything* contained in the New Testament gospel was already revealed in promised and prophetic form in the Old. The New Testament is an inspired exposition of the Old. As Saint Augustine said in the fifth century: "The New is latent [hidden] in the Old; the Old becomes patent [revealed] in the New."[33]

In other words, the apostolic interpretation of the Old Testament Scriptures in the light of their fulfillment in Christ is a fundamental element in the church's foundation. The revelation of Christ's coming is the foundation of the church; for in his gift of Christ to us, God gave us everything. There is nothing God could have added.

The function of Christ's apostles, who are directly named by him, is to bear witness to the unique, historical event of Christ's coming, and particularly to the powerful, unique event of the resurrection.[34] Just as the work of Christ took place in history, accomplished by the unique man Jesus, so also the apostles' witness was unique, not to be repeated for every generation. The apostles belong not to the time of the church but to the time of the incarnation.[35] On this event stands the historical character of the Christian faith, namely God's act of redemption in space and time. When the church of the third and fourth centuries clarified the issue of the New Testament canon, they made the same statement.[36] They recognized the significant difference between the time of Christ and the apostles and the time of the church.[37]

Paul's Claims

Paul claimed to be part of that "apostolic foundation" in several ways.

HE CLAIMS TO BE A TRUE APOSTLE

Paul is an apostle/spokesman of Christ, not by personal design or desire but by a special intervention of God:[38] "not from men nor by man, but by Jesus Christ and God the Father, who raised him from the dead" (Gal. 1:1). Notice that the raising up of an apostle is set in the same context as the raising of Jesus from the dead, that is, as a unique divine act that is part of God's redemptive plan.

Paul's gospel comes from an objective, revealed, outside source and differs from anything else that might masquerade as gospel. The theistic character of this claim is remarkable. "Flesh and blood,"[39] he says, did not enter into the paradigm. The term "flesh and blood" stands for created, human existence as opposed to the reality of God the Creator. Paul is claiming that his message comes through *no human intervention.* It came "out of the blue." Paul's only explanation is: "It pleased God to reveal his Son to me."[40]

HE CLAIMS TO BE PART OF THE ORIGINAL FOUNDATION

Paul argues that what he preaches is in full agreement with a widely recognized, ancient formulation of the gospel that he had received from the original Jerusalem apostles,[41] and which he introduces with the following words: "For what I received I passed on to you as of first importance" (1 Cor. 15:3). To this creedal formulation, of utmost importance, Paul does something most unusual. He writes himself into it! "Last of all," he writes, "he appeared to me" (v. 8), thus bringing the creed to a conclusion. There is only one satisfying explanation. He clearly considered his call and ministry a significant fact in the history of redemption, to be cited alongside the others. His call and ministry are part of the original apostolic foundation and thus part of the gospel in which the Corinthians "stand and by which they are saved."[42]

HE CLAIMS TO BE A FOUNDATION LAYER

"According to the grace of God which was given to me [as an apostle], as a wise master builder I have laid a foundation" (1 Cor. 3:10 NKJV). In the Old Testament, those building the Mosaic temple were called "master-builders."[43] Precisely because he is part of the foundation,[44] Paul can claim to be a foundation layer/master builder of the *new* temple,[45] namely, the church. Others build on this foundation, which is Christ.[46] Apostles lay the foundation by being Christ's appointed spokesmen. Paul is claiming to do what Jesus said he himself would do, namely, build the church on the apostolic foundation.

Paul addresses the subject of the new temple in his letter to the Ephesians. He encourages the Ephesian Christians to be built up into Christ.[47] He exhorts them to understand his "skillful insight"[48] into the nature of this new temple, given to him by revelation. The term *insight* is found both in the building of the Mosaic sanctuary, and then in the Davidic/Solomonic temple. God says to Moses: "Moreover, I have appointed Oholiab son of Ahisamach, of the tribe of Dan, to help him. Also I have given skill [or insight] to all the craftsmen to make everything I have commanded you" (Exod. 31:6).[49] It is apparent that with the notions of "wise master builder" and "skillful insight," Paul is presenting himself in this unique apostolic role of foundation layer for Christ's church. That is why he can say that there is only one Jesus, the one Paul preaches;[50] that there is only one gospel, the one he received.[51]

What is more, Paul was accepted as such by the other apostles. They gave "him the right hand of fellowship" (Gal. 2:9) and endorsed his labors. In other words, the original foundation layers, appointed directly by Jesus during his lifetime, recognized the essential contribution Paul was called by Christ to make. These "pillars" recognize three things about Paul: (1) the similarity and complimentarity of Peter's and Paul's missions; (2) the practical evidence of the truth of his preaching from overwhelming numbers of Gentile conversions; and (3) the divine origin of Paul's apostolic call.[52] Paul is thus accepted as an authentic spokesman of the Christian faith by those uniquely placed to do so. Paul's preaching was the same as theirs, and he can openly affirm this—"Whether, then, it was I or they, this is what we preach, and this is what you believed" (1 Cor. 15:11). At the same time, what Paul had to offer was different and absolutely crucial for the future of the church. His contribution was both unique and essential and completed the original work of apostolic foundation.

Paul: Apostle of Jesus Christ for the Pagans

Since the early leaders of the church were Jews, the significance of Christ is explained first and mainly from this Jewish-Christian point of view. But the founding apostles recognized that Paul was uniquely commissioned with the gospel concerning the pagans.

So much does Paul's preaching and teaching ministry integrate the "mystery of the Gentiles" into the original gospel of early Jewish Christianity, that he speaks of "my gospel."[53] This is not a different gospel such as the followers of the early heretic Marcion believed. It is rather the *full version* of the one and only true gospel. A much respected New Testament scholar rightly observes: "Paul's Gospel given him by revelation was not a gospel differing in kerygmatic content from that of the early church." Rather it was a message which included "a new understanding of the pattern of redemptive history in these final days."[54]

This "new understanding" comes from the revelation granted to Paul concerning the present inclusion of the Gentiles and the significance of this event in redemptive history. Paul's gospel is given to him directly by Christ and reveals clearly and definitively a new mystery, namely, that Gentiles are now to be included in the people of God. Everything Paul writes and teaches develops this theme. Paul knows himself to be a spokesman of God's wisdom in a final phase of history that is inaugurated by the resurrection of Christ, and his message is for the whole pagan empire then and now. His task is to reveal and to articulate the inclusion of Gentiles, which was predicted in the Old Testament[55] and announced by Jesus.[56]

Paul is not just a missionary who out of a deep conversion experience became an unusually effective witness. He is *the* apostle to the Gentiles, handpicked by God for the purpose, chosen and endowed like the great prophets of old. Paul's "Gentile" version of the gospel "completes the word of God,"[57] for the inclusion of the Gentiles is the last redemptive event before the second coming.[58]

Why should we listen to Paul? Because without him *the Word of God is incomplete*. Just as the *events* of redemptive history are incomplete without the event of the Gentile inclusion, so the *revelation* of redemption, the New Testament, is incomplete without the Pauline gospel. To Paul is given the divinely inspired word of *explanation* of the last redemptive event before the Second Coming.[59] Paul is not an optional extra. His gospel is the last essential component of God's Word for our time. The key role that the Gentiles will play in the early history of the church and Paul's place in the establishment of the Christian faith emerge not as peripheral extras but as essential and constitutive elements. The survival of the church depended upon it becoming an essentially Gentile phenomenon.

One can already say that Paul constitutes an organic and indispensable part of the apostolic witness concerning God's saving acts in the person of Jesus.

Paul: Last Apostle

All of these considerations—that Christ intended a foundation; that foundations can be laid and finished; that Paul's part in the foundation is his revelation that the pagans are to be included in the body of Christ— suggest the appropriateness of seeing Paul as the *last apostle*.[60] There was a reason Paul was a latecomer, and Paul takes the time to explain it. This is what he says: "Last of all, he [Christ] appeared to me" (1 Cor. 15:8). Implicit in this statement, I believe, is the claim to be the last apostle who brings to a conclusion the original founding Christian message.

Someone might ask at this point, "Could Paul, who was not there at the beginning of the church, be the *first* in a new line of 'apostles of Christ,' disconnected from the earthly Jesus but adapted to the new situation of the church in history?" However, Paul himself counters this objection, claiming not to be the first of a new line, but the last of the old. He claims to be "last of all." He is last on a list of original historical witnesses of the resurrection appearances.[61] He even acknowledges his exceptional case by referring to himself as one "abnormally born," as if anticipating readers' objections.

Two pertinent questions arise: (1) How did Paul know he was the last apostle? and (2) What are his grounds for making such a claim?

How Did Paul Know He Was the Last Apostle?

It is possible to think that Paul was merely making an educated guess about his relationship to the other apostles, simply observing, as he looked around, that up to this point he was the last.[62] There are, however, compelling reasons to believe that he was claiming to be the definitive last apostle of Jesus Christ.

He uses very specific language. He appears to know that the apostolic group is complete, for he says that "[Christ] appeared to *all* the apostles."[63] And further, he describes himself very specifically in relation to that group, with the definite article, as "*the* one [apostle] abnormally born."[64] This specificity goes along with the statement in the very next verse, where Paul confesses to being "*the* least of the apostles."[65] Again, we have to do with an identifiable, distinct group in which the individual apostle Paul occupies a unique position.

His language is foundational, not off-handed. Paul is reminding the Corinthians, as he begins chapter 15, what is of "first importance." He is rehearsing the gospel he preached to them by which they are saved, except if they believe in vain.[66] Remember, he already presented himself to them in chapter 3 as a "foundation layer."[67] The foundation he laid was Jesus Christ, and Christ was revealed to him by direct revelation from God.[68] Paul is reminding them that he, as an apostle by divine appointment, is a direct source of this saving gospel. He is a reliable source of gospel truth. The issues raised are most serious. Correct belief is a matter of spiritual survival.

His language is also creedal. Most commentators agree that we probably have here an early statement of the common gospel from the earliest times of the church. Notice the confessional cadence of the text, and the obvious repetitions, so typical of confessions: "that Christ died for our sins according to the Scriptures, that he was buried, that he was raised on the third day according to the Scriptures, and that he appeared to Peter, and then to the Twelve" (1 Cor. 15:3–5).

There is something quite remarkable about this creed. Paul wrote his first letter to the Corinthian church around A.D. 50. He cites a creed containing elements that indicate a Palestinian/Jerusalem origin.[69] The creed thus dates from the late 30s or early 40s. It is a creed universally accepted in the early church, as far as Greece, less than twenty years after Christ's crucifixion. Such "hard" evidence is remarkable in that it seriously undermines the present liberal attempt to identify orthodoxy as a late imposition upon an early "Gnostic" Christian movement.[70]

What is perhaps even more remarkable is that Paul writes himself into this creed. All this indicates that his statement about his place in relation to the other apostles is not an off-handed remark, but a solemn declaration of great theological, even creedal, importance.

What gives him the *chutzpah* to do this?

WHAT ARE HIS GROUNDS FOR MAKING SUCH A CLAIM?

Paul bases his claim to the status of "last apostle" because of the Scriptures. He grounds his claim in the Old Testament, and specifically in a passage having to do with the Servant of the Lord. While Christ is confessed in the New Testament as the Servant of the Lord,[71] Paul, as an apostle of Jesus Christ, seems to take on many of the elements of that servant role.[72] As an alternative to his title as "apostle of Jesus Christ," he will use the term "servant of Jesus Christ."[73] Specifically, the title is appropriate because the Servant's mission seems to describe so clearly the mission of the original apostles. Comparing his ministry with that of the other apostles in these verses,[74] and trying to show both his sense of unity with them and also the particularity of his apostolate to the Gentiles, Paul uses two expressions, "not in vain" and "labor."[75] The terms are not innocent. They recall the ministry of the servant in Isaiah who "labors in vain."[76] I believe Paul is making this allusion to explain why it pleased God to call him as the last apostle.

The servant's mission is twofold. First, he is sent to "bring Jacob back . . . and gather Israel" (Isa. 49:5). But he goes without success. "I have labored to no purpose; I have spent my strength in vain and for nothing" (v. 4). Then the Lord commissions him for a second task: "I will also make you a light for the Gentiles" (v. 6). Paul reads this as a prophecy of the apostolic mission. The original apostles were sent by Christ to the house of Israel, but met with relatively little success. Paul describes this hard grind of the Jewish apostles when he deals with this subject in another letter. Again, he cites a text from Isaiah: "All day long I have held out my hands to an obstinate people"[77] (Rom. 10:21). Compared with the Gentile mission, where God's grace was "not in vain," Peter and the other Jewish apostles finally met with great resistance. But Paul reads this as being the fulfillment of God's plan. Here is the proof. He cites Isaiah as he turns away from unbelieving Jews to the pagans. He says to the Jews: "We *had* to speak the word of God to you *first* [because Isaiah predicted it]. Since you reject it . . . we now turn to the Gentiles. For this is what the Lord has commanded us: 'I have made you a light for the Gentiles, that you may bring salvation to the ends of the earth'" (Acts 13:46–47).

Paul knows from Scripture that the Gentile mission is *last* because the Jewish mission is *first*. Thus he goes to the Jew first, and then to the Gentile, according to the necessity laid down by Scripture and the command of the Lord.[78] Peter, James, and John give Paul "the right hand of fellowship," thereby recognizing Paul's special calling[79] that his gospel for the Gentiles was the same as theirs. These men were the major players in the earliest expression of the Christian faith. All three share Paul's view of Christ the divine Son.

Since the Gentiles are *last*,[80] and Paul is "the apostle to the Gentiles"[81] sent to the "ends," literally "last" of the earth,[82] it only stands to reason that the mission he received by revelation would be the *last* saving effort before the end,[83] and that he would thus be "the last apostle," whose role was to inaugurate, reveal, and explain it.

Paul does claim to be *least*. His unending sense of shame for having persecuted the church forever reminds him of his human unworthiness.[84] He nevertheless understands the enormity of his place in the plan of God. His apostolic *lastness* is crucial for the world. "There is no doubt," says Scandinavian Johannes Munck, a highly-recognized Pauline scholar of the mid-twentieth century, "that Paul is speaking of himself as a figure in New Testament redemptive history."[85]

Paul: Second Moses

There must be an appropriate biblical category for one called to such a unique and faithful rereading and reinterpretation of the original gospel message, in perfect accord with the Old Testament Scriptures, inspired by the Spirit of God. There are good biblical reasons to think that Paul and the other apostles operated in the New Covenant as Moses did in the Old. Another highly recognized Scandinavian scholar and New Testament professor at Harvard, Krister Stendahl, agrees with this assessment: "[Paul's] self-understanding reaches one of its high points when . . . the comparison given [by Paul] is not one between Moses and Christ, but between Moses and *Paul*."[86]

From Paul we get a number of significant indications that this is the case.[87] His claim, as noted above, to have received, by revelation, "architectural" *insight* for laying the foundation of God's final temple recalls the great temple builder, Moses, to whom the Lord says: "Make this tabernacle and all its furnishings exactly like the pattern I will show you" (Exod. 25:9). Both Moses and Paul receive divine revelation for God's dwelling place on earth. As a wise master builder, with the authority of a second Moses, Paul lays the foundations of the New Covenant the way Moses laid the foundations of the old. These implicit parallels become explicit in his second letter to the Corinthians where Paul directly compares his *end-time* apostolic ministry with the ministry of Moses.[88] He says: "We are very bold. . . . not like Moses" (2 Cor. 3:12–13).

Paul is no ordinary rabbi. Rabbis were not noted for their "boldness" but for their scrupulous care in retaining and protecting as inviolable every word their master spoke. But this rabbi is different. Paul so understands the forward and future elements implicit in his teacher, the great prophet Moses' writings, that he takes his teacher's place. In claiming *great boldness* (or "freedom," or "clear speech"), "not like Moses,"[89] Paul the rabbi is teaching the way Jesus the rabbi taught— "with authority."[90]

Actually, Paul does to Moses what Jesus did to Moses. In the Sermon on the Mount, Jesus says: "You have heard that it was said 'Do not commit adultery'" (Matt. 5:27). Jesus is here citing the seventh of the famous Ten Commandments.[91] But then he goes on: "But I tell you that anyone who looks at a woman lustfully has already committed adultery with her in his heart" (v. 28). Jesus is bringing out the deep intention of the ethical implications of the Mosaic law, but he does it from a position of unusual authority—"But *I* tell you . . . ." Many Bible scholars see Jesus functioning here in the role of the second Moses.

Paul does the same thing. As an apostle of Christ—that is, a spokesman of Christ, and as witness of the resurrection—Paul does the same thing to Moses' words with regard to the creation. He uses "boldness" or "freedom of speech," not in the sense of being a loose cannon, but of being in a position to see with much more clarity what Moses intended. He is a prophet granted the same kind of authority as Moses, but standing where he does, as apostle of Christ, his revelation supersedes that of Moses. This is very clear in one particular text, where Paul writes: "So it is written: 'the first man Adam became a living being'; the last Adam, a life-giving spirit'" (1 Cor. 15:45). It would appear that, as he cites and comments on an Old Testament Scripture from the hand of Moses, Paul is himself *consciously writing Scripture* and rewriting Moses.

MESSING WITH GENESIS

Paul's argument is clearly made up of two striking affirmations about two Adams. The first phrase—"the first man Adam became a living being"—is clearly a citation from Genesis, the classic account of the creation of man.[92] But the observant reader will note that this Old Testament citation has been altered. There are fingerprints all over this quotation of Holy Scripture. With surprising audacity Paul has "tampered" with the inspired Mosaic text. Even though Moses had formally warned that no one should add or subtract from what he was writing according to the command of the Lord,[93] we catch Paul inserting two additions. He inserts between "the" and "man" the word *first* and then adds the man's name, "Adam." These are clearly Paul's additions. They are not in the Old Testament verse. They are intended to set up with clarity what Paul will say by comparison in the second part of the verse—in the following way. The addition—"first"—prepares for Paul's teaching about the "last man." The second addition—"Adam"—sets up Paul's teaching about *the person* of Christ in comparison with *the person* of Adam. In other words, Paul is not quoting carelessly or making free with a stylish embellishment. The Genesis text has been deliberately remolded for the sake of a finely-tuned, logical argument about the future of the cosmos.[94]

In view of the liberty Paul takes with the sacred text, one must ask about the relationship between the solemn formula, "it is written," used here and throughout the New Testament to cite holy, inviolable Scripture, and Paul's conception of his *own* apostolic authority. If Paul intends us to take his *additions* to the Moses text as "Scripture," it also appears that he wishes us to do the same with his following *commentary* on Moses' words.

If Paul has so blatantly added his own interpretations to the text of Genesis, is not the whole second phrase—"the last Adam [became] a life-giving spirit"—a comparable Pauline addition to and interpretation of the sacred text?[95] In other words, would not the phrase "it is written," as a description of inspired Scripture apply not only to what Moses wrote, including Paul's additions, but also to what Paul added as a second, complementary phrase?

Certainly the second phrase is nowhere to be found in the Old Testament, nor is it a quotation from other pre-Pauline or Pauline literature. So there are only two possibilities: either it is of "undetermined origin," or it is a Pauline comment seeking to lay bare the fuller meaning of Genesis in the light of the Christ event. The latter is surely the most satisfying explanation, for it expresses so powerfully the Pauline view of the end of history and the significance of Christ in a way only Paul could have written.

Recognized scholars[96] argue that Paul's major addition (the second phrase—"the last Adam [became] a life-giving spirit") properly belongs *within* the quotation from Scripture. This does seem to be the case, for two reasons:

1. Both phrases are perfectly presented in a parallel structure, indicating that they constitute a logical and organic whole. One stands in admiration at the economy of words coupled with the unsurpassed density of theological import, all presented in a structural parallelism that reaches the level of poetic and literary beauty.

2. The ultimate proof that both phrases have been deliberately structured by Paul to be taken together is that they share the same verb—"become." The verb is expressed in the first phrase—"the first man Adam *became* a living being"—since it belongs to the Genesis quotation. There is no verb in the second

phrase, even though it needs one. As is often the case in good literature, the verb is not repeated. Literally the second phrase reads: "the last Adam, a life-giving spirit." But the verb is *unquestionably* assumed.[97] In other words, the Genesis citation and the Pauline addition are so closely wedded together that the verb of one is presupposed in the other, such that the second phrase cannot stand on its own, and must have the "inspired" verb of the citation in order to make sense.

If the second phrase is Pauline, then this verse tells us in no uncertain terms how Paul conceived of his own writing ministry, and the manner in which he interpreted all the Old Testament texts cited in his epistles.

At the very least Paul is proposing that his additions *within the citation* of Genesis should be received as Scripture, believing himself empowered to alter the text of Moses, not with a view to disfiguring it, but with a view to bringing out what he believed were its implicit implications for creation's future. It is not difficult to believe that he also intends his larger, theologically potent addition (which makes even clearer those implications) to be received as Scripture. The conclusion seems warranted that *Paul, as he cites and comments on Scripture, is consciously writing Scripture.* In this verse we can look over Paul's shoulder and watch him acting as a "second Moses" interpreting Moses.

It is by this boldness that he can add to Old Testament Scripture in order to make its full meaning plain. Is not this the essence of New Testament revelation—the forward-pointing character of the Old Testament is made plain by Christ and his apostles[98] in the fullness of time? The phrase of Augustine—"the New is latent in the Old, and the Old becomes patent in the New"—as the classic statement of the nature of Scripture throughout the history of the church is also a helpful way of understanding what Paul is teaching about the resurrection here. When Paul says to the Corinthians that he uses much boldness, "not like Moses," who had to put a veil on his face,[99] he means that the glorious revelation of the New Covenant granted to him as an apostle enables him to lift the veil from the Old.[100] What was latent now becomes patent. What Moses could only see dimly as a future event,[101] Paul has seen taking place. So we have the following procedure worked out: the resurrection (the new) is implicit in the creation (the old), and the creation (the old) becomes explicit in the resurrection (the new).[102]

Paul has seen the first expression of an event that will bring an end to the world as we know it. He sees in creation an implicit promise of resurrection. Paul reads the implications for new creation in Moses' account of the old creation just the way Jesus reads in the law of Moses its implications for the new law of the kingdom. In both cases there is end-time clarification and intensification. Hate is murder; mortal flesh anticipates immortal flesh. In this case, the apostle of Christ is acting in the same way as Christ, the final prophet. Both thus function in the prophetic role of the second Moses, laying the divinely-revealed foundation of God's reconstruction of the cosmos.

I beg my twenty-first-century readers of Paul to bear with me as we delve into a few specifics. I do not wish to overwhelm you with the details of the Greek text. However, it is crucial to note that we are confronted not with an illumined guru who emits insight from the depths of mystical ecstasy, but with a credentialed prophet who has witnessed the space-time, history-ending event of the resurrection. Paul's apostolic ministry is the God of theism intervening in a particular saving way in the flow of history. He miraculously acts on the creation to change it, but also gives the divine explanation of this act through the prophets he raises up for this purpose. This was the way Paul saw it.[103] His call was an act of God with no natural explanations. The church received him as "a messenger of God," indeed "as Jesus Christ."[104] No modern-day radical scholar or New Age guru can convincingly make this claim, even though they seek to turn Paul's claims to mush. Paul you must take or leave. If he was mistaken about the resurrection, then nothing he says can be taken seriously. To reject what he says here is ultimately to reject everything he says.

A Biblical Worldview for Converted Pagans

Paul was marginalized in his own time, and many in our own day wish to exclude him from Christianity. The "Give me Jesus, you can keep Paul!" approach fails to do justice to the organic nature of New Testament Christianity and to the history of redemption in which

Paul's contribution was essential. Though Christ is indeed the final word of God,[105] that word is richer than the earthly ministry of Jesus. The word of Christ includes everything Jesus did, including the words he spoke through his fully-authorized spokesmen, the apostles.

As Paul addressed the Corinthians and their problems, he did so not simply because he had founded the church and was their "father in the gospel." He spoke not simply as a successful missionary. He also spoke in the name of Christ, as an apostle of Christ, bringing the revelation concerning the meaning of the mystery of the Gentile/pagan inclusion into the people of God. What he gave to the church of all time, and to converted pagans in particular, was not simply another interesting account of "how to get saved," important though that is. He provided for once-pagan Christians, tempted to return to paganism in one form or another, a biblical *worldview.*

The Sanctification of the Pagans

Paul was not content to convert pagans: he wanted them to persist in the faith, to become mature, to become holy, and to be witnesses in the pagan world of their day.[106] Deriving this goal from Old Testament prophecy, Paul wanted to see the God of the Bible praised and glorified in the pagan nations.[107] In order to do this, the pagans needed to hear the gospel, know the God of the Bible as Creator, Redeemer, and Consummator, and understand their special place in the world—a total program, a full-scale worldview. Paul travels the Graeco-Roman world in fulfillment of Scripture, so that "those who were not told about him will see, and those who have not heard will understand" (Rom. 15:21, citing Isa. 52:15). He does this specifically "so that the Gentiles might become an offering acceptable to God, sanctified by the Holy Spirit" (Rom. 15:16). Here "sanctification" is not just a moral category. At its heart, sanctification means knowing one's particular place in God's created order. In a word, it means understanding and putting into practice the Bible's worldview.

Paul, in his apostolic calling, has the concerns of both an evangelist and a pastor/teacher.[108]

- As an evangelist, he seeks pagan conversions, namely, a change of heart and mind at the initial hearing of the gospel—"speaking to the Gentiles so that they may be saved" (1 Thess. 2:16).
- As a pastor/teacher, he seeks their sanctification, a change of thinking and acting in the long-term living out of the faith—"leading the Gentiles to obey God by what I have said and done" (Rom. 15:18).

Bringing pagans to biblical faith, to biblical thinking, and to holy living is no mean task. As a T-shirt in a recent gay parade loudly and proudly proclaimed: "I can't even think straight." So, says Paul, the pagan lifestyle is "influenced and led astray to mute idols,"[109] and known for the "futility of [its] thinking."[110] Such thinking is futile because it is based upon a false starting point, "the lie" rather than "the truth."[111] "The depraved mind,"[112] which is the thinking of "foolish hearts,"[113] inevitably judges the truth of the gospel as "foolishness,"[114] and leads to degraded living.[115] To such people, without God and without hope,[116] Paul's gospel brings hope and sanity and the life-giving God of the Bible.

Changing the way pagans thought and behaved required the mind of a genius as well as the divine inspiration of the Holy Spirit. In Paul's letters we have them both. His writings contain the program God gave to Paul adapted for ancient pagans in the first century—a powerful declaration of the Bible's worldview and its utopian perspective. What was valid then is equally valid now. We need to capture the pagan mind by considering Paul's life-changing proclamation of the Bible's total message of good news about time and eternity for a pagan planet.

It is time to dig in.

Chapter 6

The Birth of Creation

The gruesome opening scene depicts the murder of the hero's wife. But squeamish viewers need to keep their eyes open, for without that scene, *The Fugitive* is incomprehensible. The tortured life of the lone hero makes sense only in the light of that scene.

The first five minutes of the story are important to Paul. To proclaim the gospel (about Christ, redemption, salvation, and resurrection, and the future of the cosmos), Paul starts with the beginning—creation. The starting point of his theology is not that "Jesus died for our sins" but that we "worship God as Creator." The lie is not first our rejection of the cross but our worship of creation.[1]

The new creation flows directly from the original creation.[2] God the Redeemer, who saves us from our mess, is the Creator who made things good in the first place. The person and work of the last Adam can be understood only in relation to the first Adam. Authors give only a nod to Paul's doctrine of creation, failing to discuss its integral place in Pauline theology.[3]

Just as the opening scene of the Old Testament begins with the overarching statement—"In the beginning God created the heavens and the earth"—Paul always begins his letters with a reference to "God." The Old Testament never ceases to laud God as Creator and defines the origin of all things in the God of utter transcendence. Paul never loses that perspective as he elaborates the gospel for the pagan world, which personified the forces of nature and praised imperial state-craft but offered no accounts of origins. Paul, drawing attention to that silence, points to the knowledge of the Creator in everyone.[4]

The verse we have discussed above, 1 Corinthians 15:45, evokes the importance of creation. Paul writes, "So it is written: 'The first man Adam became a living being.'" After World War I, Lloyd George, the British foreign minister, said of defeated Germany: "We must squeeze the German lemon 'til the pips squeak." If we squeeze this verse until it squeaks, we see the kernel of Paul's message for the spirit wars of contemporary global culture.

Paul's phrase "the first man *became* a living being" is not a nod to evolution, for it is in a larger Old Testament text that reads: "The LORD God formed man from the dust of the ground and breathed into his nostrils the breath of life, and man became a living being" (Gen. 2:7). This text affirms God as Creator of all things. Meet the God of Paul.

According to Paul, Who Is God?

For Paul, the title "God" is a reference to the transcendent, personal source of all things. The Hebrew title, "Jahweh," the "I Am," is more specifically related to the source of life. As a Jewish boy, Paul would recite Israel's historic confession, the Shema, twice a day: "Hear, O Israel: The LORD [I Am] our God, the LORD [I Am] is one" (Deut. 6:4). Not surprisingly, he cites this same Old Testament and Jewish creed in his letters.[5] For Israel, the oneness/uniqueness of Jahweh, the only source of life, means that he *must* be the Creator. "For all the gods of the nations are idols, but the [one, unique] LORD [I Am] made the heavens" (Ps. 96:5).

To this God, Paul often gives the name "Father." Knowing the Father represents the very depth of Christian spirituality, as Jesus himself had already revealed.[6] At *the* crucial moment in the history of redemption, when everything was on the line, Jesus uttered this prayer of deep filial devotion: "Abba, Father, . . . everything is possible for you. Take this cup from me. Yet not what I will, but what you will" (Mark 14:36).

Paul articulates this truth in two of his letters. To the Christians at Rome, he says: "For you did not receive a spirit that makes you a slave again to fear, but you received the Spirit of sonship. And by him we cry, 'Abba, Father'" (Rom. 8:15). The Spirit, through the work of Christ, brings people into intimate relationship with God. To Gentile converts in the Galatian church, Paul says: "Because you are sons, God sent the

Spirit of his Son into our hearts, the Spirit who calls out, 'Abba, Father'" (Gal. 4:6). This idea is not unique to the New Testament. Intimacy with God as Father is the goal of God's saving project in the Old Testament: "I will be a Father to you, and you will be my sons and daughters, says the Lord Almighty" (2 Cor. 6:18). Paul sees this goal already realized in the church in pagan Corinth.

Father as Creator

God as Father is not God as Santa Claus. Intimacy with "the Father" expresses the immeasurable condescension of God the transcendent Lord, for "Father" means "generator" or Creator. Note the following example: since Paul was the means for the Corinthian believers' coming to faith, he calls himself their father. "Even though you have ten thousand guardians in Christ, you do not have many fathers, for in Christ Jesus I became your father through the gospel" (1 Cor. 4:15).

Jesus himself associates the Father directly with creation,[7] and a number of texts in Paul that exhort Christians to give thanks to God the Father[8] should doubtless be read in the light of his statement that all creatures should give thanks to God the Creator.[9] God the Father has all dominion, authority, and power,[10] for he is, says Paul, the "one God, the Father, from whom all things came and for whom we live" (1 Cor. 8:6). Notice that "Father" and source of "all things" are associated. As did Moses, Paul makes the connection between: (1) God's oneness, (2) God's unique character as compared to idols, and (3) God's identity as Creator.[11] Paul taught these truths to the Corinthians as well as to skeptical Greeks in Athens: "The God who made the world and everything in it is the [Creator in whom] we live and move and have our being" (Acts 17:24, 28). In associating "Father" with "Creator," Paul is reiterating Old Testament notions. Moses declares to Israel: "Is he not your Father, your Creator, who made you and formed you?" (Deut. 32:26). The prophet Malachi repeats Moses: "Have we not all one Father? Did not one God create us?" (Mal. 2:10).[12]

Paul's doctrine of God the Creator is not an incidental leftover from his Jewish past, but an integral part of his gospel proclamation. The creation-redemption connection is essential not only because Christian spirituality depends on it, but because it is grounded in the mystery of God's very *nature*. Christ and the apostles reveal that God the Creator is the "triune" God: Father, Son, and Holy Spirit. It becomes gloriously clear through the life, death, and resurrection of Jesus that the Creator and the Redeemer are one and the same. Specifically, the Christ of the gospel, the eternal Son in human form, is also active in the work of Creation, as the Gospel of John and the Book of Hebrews affirm. According to John, the Son (also the Word), is God "through whom all things were made."[13] Hebrews makes the same astonishing claim. Of the Son, the radiance of God's glory, the Scripture says: "In the beginning, O Lord, you laid the foundations of the earth, and the heavens are the work of your hands" (Heb. 1:10).[14] Having declared that "there is but one God, the Father, from whom are all things and for whom we live," thus insisting on the oneness of God the Creator, Paul adds: "and one Lord, Jesus Christ, through whom are all things and through whom we live" (1 Cor. 8:6). In creation, Christ is the agent through whom things come into existence.

This phrase is developed more fully in Colossians, where Christ is "the image of the invisible God, the first born of all creation" because "he is before all things" (Col. 1:15, 17). "First born" does not mean that Christ is the first creature, but that he reigns supreme as the Creator over the whole creation he made,[15] as Paul's next phrase makes clear: "All things were created by him and for him" (v.16). As in First Corinthians, Christ is at the center of the gospel message and the divine agent of creation.

All acts of God are trinitarian, involving the three persons of God working together. Thus, the Spirit is also active in creation, as a number of Old Testament texts affirm.[16] Specifically, in the Genesis account, the Spirit, like a bird incubating its eggs, "hovers" over the original unformed mass to bring it to form.[17] The Spirit is known in Paul as "the power of God," and is involved in the recreative act of resurrection.[18] It is in this colorful language of incubation that the idea of a transmission of energy from God to the original creation seems to be implied.[19]

Those who take the name of Christ ("Christ-ians") cannot avoid understanding themselves in relationship to God the Creator. Christ, their divine Redeemer, is the very source of all created life. The original creation is the great work of their Savior, and the whole of creation owes its existence to the preexistent Christ.[20] This surely means that redemption is the redemption *of creation*. Christians, of all people, must affirm and celebrate the Savior's original handiwork.

Paul speaks about the "mystery, which for ages past was kept hidden in God, who created all things" (Eph. 3:9). Elsewhere he makes the same affirmation: "God [the Creator], who said, 'Let light shine out of darkness,' made his light [the light of the Redeemer] shine in our hearts to give us the light of the knowledge of the glory of God in the face of Christ" (2 Cor. 4:6).[21] In other words, the Christian gospel of redemption (what Paul calls the mystery) flows directly and organically from the very heart of God the Creator, the "God who created all things and who caused light to shine."[22] He also says that God as Creator is the Savior/Benefactor of all, but especially Savior/Redeemer of those who believe.[23] Sunlight and gospel light are closer than you might think, for creation and redemption are not mutually exclusive realities. They stand together the way the persons of the divine trinity are related—distinct yet united in a deep community of being and purpose.

It has been the sign of Christian intellectual "chic" for a generation or more to read the New Testament gospel through the eyes of contemporary, democratic notions of liberation. Such an approach no longer works. "Liberation" is destroying our communities, our families, our marriages, our personal sense of sexual identity, and, what is disturbing in terms of the future of society, the rising generation's sense of clear moral obligation. A compromised church finds itself parked in a back alley of cultural irrelevance. Meanwhile, other Christian groups have finally risen up to "defend the family" or to "fight for traditional values" and stand as unconscious accusers of the church, which has sometimes equated the gospel with "Jesus died for our sins." The Christian gospel has been truncated and diluted in two ways. It has become either a take-it-or-leave-it Christian version of contemporary ideology, or it remains a mere program for personal salvation—a high-speed gospel train to heaven. As society implodes into lawlessness in the name of choice and freedom, Christian believers may no longer read the gospel through the "insights" of modern culture, nor may they dispense it as a "gos-pill" for aching souls. We must understand the scope and intentions of the gospel, not through the buzz words of *diversity* and *choice*, nor as a quick, one-way ticket "outta here," but as the New Testament authors did, *through a fully-worked-out biblical doctrine of creation.*

How Does God Create?

GOD CREATES FROM NOTHING

"The first man Adam *became* a living being" (1 Cor. 15:45). According to Paul, Adam became the first human being at a particular moment in space and time. Here is what *became* means. Moses' mother was commanded by the Pharaoh's daughter to accept a paid position as nurse to her own infant son. The Hebrew woman was to bring the baby to the palace when he was weaned. This was Moses' first down payment on the despoiling of the Egyptians! The narrative of Moses' birth and early childhood continues: "And the child grew, and she brought him unto Pharaoh's daughter, and he *became* her son" (Exod. 2:10 NKJV). At a given moment, the mother had to hand over her son to the Egyptian princess, at which time the boy Moses *became* the adopted son of Pharaoh's daughter.

Moses used this verb, in the same tense, in Genesis 2:7, when under divine inspiration he wrote: "The first man *became* a living being." Neither the verb nor its tense describes a slow process of evolution, but clearly indicates an instantaneous change of state, of a moment of becoming, a point in time when one enters a new form of existence. In Adam's case he went from nonbeing to being, just like the entire physical cosmos, which, as modern scientists are now saying, had a beginning. God created everything *ex nihilo,* from nothing—a miracle. Adam is not an eternal spirit, romping for eternity past in the heavenly playing fields of the Lord and falling into matter through foolishness or desire as religious paganism often affirms. Adam, as a created human person, body and spirit, has a true and unmistakable beginning.

According to Paul, the circuit-blowing, paradigm-transforming event that gives resurrection life to Christ's dead body has a parallel in past human experience, in God's original creative act of *making* the world in the first place. People have a hard time believing in resurrection; but the original creation was just as miraculous, and the results of this are there for all to see. The "just so" naturalistic explanations given by scientific evolution have dulled our senses to the wonder of physical life.[24] How did animate life come from inanimate rocks? "Quite simple, really," says the evolutionist, with a straight face. "A prebiotic soup, by sheer chance, formed in the hollow of a rock, and the rest is history—natural history!" But no one has solved the very "unnatural" problem of origins. Paul, like the biblical authors in general and the church throughout history, locates the origin of the cosmos in a miraculous act of God, *the God*, says Paul, "who gives life to the dead and calls things that are not as though they were" (Rom. 4:17). Through Christ, God speaks the word of power, and creation comes into being.

Part of the divine speaking is giving names.

GOD CREATES BY NAMING

All parents want their babies to speak. My wife and I have seven children, and I remember longing for the day when each child would be old enough to speak to me. The best part was when they said my name—*Dadda*. God, too, loves to hear his name on the lips of his children.

Paul makes use of the name *Father* in an intriguing prayer addressed to God. Like the Lord's Prayer, which begins: "Our Father," Paul begins his prayer: "For this reason I kneel [an attitude of prayer] before the Father,[25] from whom his whole family [or fatherhood] in heaven and on earth derives its name" (Eph. 3:14–15).[26] "The Father" gives his name to father-defined families, and is a clear reference to the Creator.[27] In this same letter, Paul, with the same verb, "every name that is named," refers to the totality of the created cosmos over which Christ reigns.[28]

In the Genesis account of the creation, there is much emphasis placed on the specific identity of each created form. Each type of vegetation, every species of animal, is brought forth "according to its kind,"[29] and thus has a particular character and identity. That is why everything must be named in order to be clearly distinguished. God *called* the light "day." He *called* the darkness "night."[30] This is what Paul surely means in speaking of the Father naming all the families/*patrias*. Isaiah the prophet exhorts Israel to think about creation this way: "Lift your eyes and look to the heavens: Who created all these? He who brings out the starry host one by one, and *calls them each by name*. Because of his great power and mighty strength, not one of them is missing" (Isa. 40:26).

The New Testament deepens the biblical doctrine of creation by revealing in explicit terms that creation was the work of the divine Trinity. As we noted, Paul declares that creation, which is the work of the Father, is also the work of the Son. Creation is *by him*, that is, by Christ,[31] because Christ is the creative Word[32] by whom God calls all things into existence. Within the Trinity, this is the role of the Son. When God said, "Let there be light," it is Christ the divine Word and fiat who brings light into existence. It is by Christ the Word that things are given their names. He in whom "all things hold together,"[33] not as an amorphous blob but in their separate identities, was the one who separated all things out in the first place, giving them form and name and significance. Since then, he has, by his Word, sustained them.

In the Book of Proverbs we read: "I [this is Wisdom speaking] was appointed from eternity, from the beginning, before the world began. ... I was there when he set the heavens in place, when he marked out the horizon on the face of the deep, when he established the clouds above and fixed securely the fountains of the deep, when he gave the sea its boundary so the waters would not overstep his command, and when he marked out the foundations of the earth. Then I was the craftsman at his side" (8:23–30). The Old Testament expresses God's creation with a series of verbs: "set in place," "mark out," "establish," "give boundaries." The psalmist speaks of the "moon and the stars" in the heavens as being "set in place" by "the work of [God's] fingers" (Ps. 8:3). To the separate elements of this complex work, the master craftsman gives names.

Paul understands the essential nature of creation as a beautifully structured and ordered cosmos when he speaks of the Father naming all the fatherhoods in heaven and earth and when he describes Christ as the Wisdom of God. Such structure is also evident in other Pauline terminology.

GOD CREATES BY MAKING HOLY DISTINCTIONS

The Creator/creature distinction determines the way God creates everything. From nothing God brought forth cosmic matter, the original "chaos."[34] God's work of creation consists in turning chaos into cosmos.[35] God creates by separating things out and making distinctions, giving things their place and function. This is the essence of what the Bible means by the act of creation. God *separates* the light from the darkness. God *separates* the waters above from the waters below.[36] God forms the great lights to *separate* the day from night.[37] God also creates the sun and the moon "to govern the day and the night, and to *separate* light from darkness" (Gen. 1:18).

God's acts of creative "separation" are related to the notion of holiness. The root meaning of holiness is not so much a moral concept as it is the fact of being in a specific place for a particular function. This is how God is holy. He is the only true and living God, who has his own place and his own form of existence. This is also true of creatures. For instance, God commands Israel: "You are to set the Levites apart from the other Israelites" in order to maintain temple service (Num. 8:14). Moses uses the same verb, "to separate,"[38] here in Numbers as he does in the creation account of Genesis. These Levites may enter the temple "because they are consecrated" (made holy, set apart).[39] To separate and make holy are clearly synonymous terms, a fact of great consequence,[40] essential to the worldview of the Bible.

Names and holiness are deeply related, as we see in Israel's special feasts. In Leviticus, God says to Moses: "Speak to the Israelites and say to them: 'These are my appointed [or called/named] feasts, the appointed [named] feasts of the LORD, which you are to proclaim as sacred assemblies'" (Lev. 23:2).[41] These were special assemblies, set apart by God, called "holy" by God.

One might say that creation as the separation and naming of its elements constitutes the sanctification of the cosmos. By separating things out and giving them specific names and functions, God is "sanctifying" what he makes. In creation, God places his holy stamp on what he makes, granting creatures place, function, and significance.[42] Having these things, creatures are holy as God is holy. They have their significant place just as God has his.

GOD CREATES BY SETTING IN ORDER

"God is not a God of disorder," says Paul (1 Cor. 14:33), yet under sin "the whole creation has been groaning as in the pains of childbirth right up to the present time" (Rom. 8:22). Sin will not be allowed to deconstruct God's handiwork completely. Paul describes the curses God placed on the creation[43] in the following way: "For the creation was subjected to frustration, not by its own choice, but by the will of the one who subjected it, in hope . . ." (8:20). Even when sin enters the world, God, the Creator of cosmic order, intervenes in an orderly way. He "subjects," or "sets under an orderly structure" (Greek, *hupotasso*) even the fallen creation, "in hope," that is, in the hope that one day the creation will rediscover its benevolent Creator and the good order the Creator intended. So Paul continues: "The creation waits in eager expectation . . . [to] be liberated from its bondage to decay and brought into the glorious freedom of the children of God" (8:20–21).

This verb *hupotasso,* often translated "submit," but meaning "set in an ordered structure," is one of the essential biblical verbs indicating the ordered nature of creation. God "submits" or puts into an ordered structure the fallen creation, because this is what he had already done in the nonfallen creation. He had "put everything under his [Adam's] feet: all flocks and herds, and the beasts of the field, the birds of the air, and the fish of the sea, all that swim the paths of the seas" (Ps. 8:6). The original work of the Creator is to set things within structures. Paul cites this psalm to describe the ultimate state of the cosmos, under the feet of the last Adam, and his use of the verb "submit" everywhere in his epistles shows how much this Old Testament view and this verb determines his view of the original creation. Paul actually juxtaposes "naming," which, as we noted, was one of his ways of describing how God creates in an orderly fashion, with the verb "submit." He says about Christ's future rule over the new creation, that Christ is "far above every name that can be named [that is, the whole extent of the created order] . . . and God placed everything [literally, submitted everything] under his feet" (Eph. 1:21–22).[44]

Everything God Created Is Good

Paul's View of the Flesh

It can appear that Paul, like the Gnostics, rejects the goodness of the physical creation. Paul was called by some in the ancient world the *apostolus haereticorum,* "the apostle of the heretics." The second- and third-century Gnostics found some of Paul's language amenable to their reinterpretations and allegorizations. And such interpretations continue today.[45] The depth and precision of Paul's thought can be enigmatic on a first reading. It can appear that Paul, like the Gnostics, rejects the goodness of the physical creation.

Many readers of Paul have come away thinking that this radical Christian thinker goes so far as to deny the goodness of the flesh, and thus of the created order. Many times he uses the term *flesh* as an image for sin. "Flesh" is the place of sinful passion;[46] he uses the term *fleshly* as an adjective describing the state of being in sin, "sold under sin";[47] thus the flesh is "incapable of pleasing God."[48] Paul further speaks of "the works" and the "desires of the flesh"; of "walking according to the flesh"; of "living according to the flesh"; and of "knowing according to the flesh."[49] How easy it might be to see here a pagan dichotomy between the upper and the lower natures, between our eternal spirits and our worthless created bodies.[50]

One must concede that the phrase "living according to the flesh" *sounds* very negative with regards to God's created order. But in the light of all the texts discussed above about God as Creator, there must be a better explanation.

For Paul, flesh was not created sinful, but is the *place,* the created reality, in which sin occurs. Thus, it becomes a kind of synonym for sin. The weakness of the flesh becomes the occasion for sin.[51] Though weak,[52] and needing God's constant attention and care, the flesh is not evil in and of itself. Paul makes many positive statements about the flesh. Jesus is "revealed in the flesh,"[53] and Paul boasts of "his kinsmen according to the flesh."[54] The term sometimes refers simply to physical life.[55] In these cases there are no negative connotations, as is also the case with the expression "flesh and blood,"[56] which means human existence as distinguished from the existence of God. In the final analysis, this phrase "flesh and blood" merely affirms the Creator/creature distinction, so essential to theism and to Paul's biblical worldview. Indeed, this must be so in the light of what Paul explicitly says about the goodness of creation.

Paul's View of "Good" Doctrine

Paul tells the young pastor, Timothy, that the battle against error is fought out at the level of doctrine.[57] Today's church, with its mantra of unification, puts feelings over doctrine. "Doctrine divides, the Spirit unites." Not according to Paul. He warns against the "doctrine of demons," and proposes in its place "sound doctrine" (health-giving doctrine, or hygienic teaching).[58] We too often want sound bites and video clips. Timothy is exhorted to "give attendance to reading, to exhortation, to doctrine," by which he will save himself and those who hear him.[59]

The "good teaching" that is opposed to "godless myths" and the "doctrine of demons" is not what we would expect. It is not, in this instance, the "trustworthy saying that deserves full acceptance: Christ Jesus came into the world to save sinners" (1 Tim. 1:15), good news though that is. It is that all created things are good.[60] The good doctrine includes a biblical doctrine of creation. The relationship between "good" teaching, "good" minister, and the "good" creation in this text should not be missed. Since they are all mentioned within three verses, Paul is implying a close relationship. Paul, apostle of the Christian gospel, locates the origin of his Christian teaching back at the beginning of the Bible, in the Old Testament revelation of God as Creator. This, he intimates, is where the gospel begins. Following the example of Moses, Paul gives a ringing endorsement of the Creator and his work. Six times in the first chapter of Genesis, God pronounces specific elements of the creation "good" (the same word Paul uses in 1 Timothy). The separation of light and darkness is good, as is the separation of sea and dry land, the creation of various forms of plant life according to their kind, the sun and the moon, animal life and livestock, and the creation of man and woman. Each element of the creation is good; and then, the seventh time God looks at *everything* and pronounces the whole creation "exceedingly good."[61] Paul says "amen" to Moses and, with virtually identical words, makes the same confession: "Everything God created is good" (1 Tim. 4:4).[62]

With this high view of creation, we expect a high view of man.

According to Paul, Who Is Man?

As Paul echoes Moses concerning the goodness of creation, he also singles out the creation of man with a citation from Moses: "The first man Adam became a living being" (1 Cor. 15:45, citing Gen. 2:7). This answers a fundamental human question—Who am I? Created or uncreated? Master of my own fate, or creature in God's image? There is no more important question anyone can ask. The answer is either a worldview of pagan perennial philosophy[63] or one of biblical theism. Both answers are ancient, but one is the truth and the other is the lie. Both cannot be true.

Harold Bloom, raised in a Jewish home, became a world expert on Shakespeare and a professor at Yale. Bloom chose paganism. As a young man in the 1960s, reading the ancient Gnostic texts, he remembers with relish the deep sense of personal liberation he had when he discovered that he was uncreated, as old as God![64] Buddhists make the same "discovery" of their uncreated mind. Bloom the Gnostic sees the importance of this: "It makes a considerable difference to believe that you go back before the Creation."[65] For him this revolutionary insight meant liberation from his Jewish upbringing and deliverance from the oppressive notion of being a creature. Bloom became a pagan monist.

Mary, a young Jewish girl who became the mother of Jesus, took the other position. "I am the Lord's servant," she declared at the visit of the angel. "May it be to me as you have said" (Luke 1:38). Taking this position, she confessed her faith in the God of biblical theism, allowing her freedom to be circumscribed by the plans and structures that the God of the Bible had determined were right and good for her.

The stakes are high. In this day of confusion, an understanding of these two mutually exclusive options is imperative. The discourse is not mere theory. Paul exhorts Timothy that in order to be a "good minister of Jesus Christ" he must warn believers of the pagan alternative.[66] We must see Paul's positive teaching on the nature of humanity in the light of its pagan counterfeit, ancient and modern. Paul was conscious of writing in a polemical context. That context has not changed.

The Old Testament View of Man

Just as Paul took his view of God the Creator from the Old Testament, he also found there his high view of man. According to the Old Testament, humanity is the highest created form. There are no extra-terrestrial, superintelligent beings. On the hierarchy of created life, man reigns supreme. The following majestic descriptions reflect this belief.

The psalmist exults before God: "What is man that you are mindful of him, the son of man that you care for him? You made him a little lower than the heavenly beings and crowned him with glory and honor. You made him ruler over the works of your hands; you put everything under his feet: all flocks and herds, and the beasts of the field, the birds of the air, and the fish of the sea, all that swim the paths of the seas. O LORD, our Lord, how majestic is your name in all the earth!" (Ps. 8:4–9).

Another, equally majestic and poetic expression of the glory of created human life is found in the prophet Ezekiel:

This is what the Sovereign LORD says: "You were the model of perfection, full of wisdom and perfect in beauty. You were in Eden, the garden of God; every precious stone adorned you: ruby, topaz and emerald, chrysolite, onyx and jasper, sapphire, turquoise and beryl. Your settings and mountings were made of gold; on the day you were created they were prepared. You were anointed as a guardian cherub, for so I ordained you. You were on the holy mount of God; you walked among the fiery stones. You were blameless in your ways from the day you were created till wickedness was found in you" (Ezek. 28:11–15).

This kind of laudatory appreciation of humanity is presupposed in Paul's description of Adam as "the first man."[67] Eventually, says Paul, humanity will rule, even over the angels.[68]

Paul's Understanding of Adam and His Name

In his inspired commentary on Genesis, Paul insists on naming the first man. The name *Adam* is not in Genesis 2:7. As we noted above, Paul supplies it because he wants to affirm that creation is not a process of impersonal forces. God, the namer, names Adam. This is the loving act of the personal God, granting significance to man. Adam is not the product of irrational chance, a fortuitous conglomeration of random particles cooking in some prehistoric potage. The first man has a personal name, given to him by the God who made all things. This specific name identifies him as a historical person, comparable to the historical person bearing the name "last Adam." This specific man has a specific identity. He is made in the image of God. "God created man in his own image, in the image of God he created him; male and female he created them" (Gen. 1:27).

ADAM HAS A CLEAR SELF-IMAGE

This is what the divine image *does not mean*:
Man is not God, even though he is made "in the image of God." He is not his own cocreator, nor will he ever be divine. Even without sin, man is finite and limited and owes his entire existence to someone else. In radical distinction from this human condition, God is *divine.* Thus theologians speak of God's "incommunicable attributes," which means the qualities that only God can have. The confusion between God and man has created a crisis of ignorance. People no longer know the God of the Bible, just as they no longer truly know themselves. God is not a heavenly Santa Claus, a faraway benevolent uncle in the sky, or a spirit that inhabits everything. God is profoundly distinct from us. Only God is self-existent,[69] unchanging,[70] infinite,[71] all-powerful and all-knowing,[72] perfect,[73] and filling all things.[74] Making a clear distinction between God and man is the very essence of biblical wisdom. Without it we become fools.

This is what the divine image *does mean*: Though man is not God and never will be, he shares some unique qualities with the Creator that other created beings don't have. Like God, man possesses a spirit, which makes spiritual life with God possible. He possesses an intellect capable of rational and creative thinking. Man has a moral sense that regulates life for the good in order to please God. Because man was created from the beginning in the image of God, he cannot be simply another stage in animal evolution. Man is the result of God's action and in no sense has any say in his creation. His dignity lies in the dignity of the character of God. This God is not the extension of human aspirations. He is not a divinized human, as in Greek mythology. God is totally other, complete in his Trinitarian being—Father, Son, and Holy Spirit. With this divine image man is able to enter into personal, intimate com-munion with his Maker, giving him his true identity, dignity, and sanity.

Knowing his limits, man knows himself. This is good news in a world of postmodern deconstruction where everything, including the self, has been undone—"un-created"—in the name of choice and freedom.

Take, for example the Gen-Xers' multiple choice "gender blur." On a cover of the left wing intellectual magazine, *The Utne Reader,* is a man in a business suit with female breasts. Behind him, in a dress, is a woman with a man's hairy chest. The title announces the theme: "It's 2 A.M. Do You Know What Sex You Are? Does Anybody?" The editor comments: "We can be one gender on the Internet and another in bed."[75] One bisexual writer declares: "I want to be a sexual being without defining myself solely or even primarily on the basis of my sexuality."[76] Two "very feminine" lesbians promote their "GLAM Manifesto." They explain: "Being GLAM is about looking fabulous. . . . It's taking people's preconceived notions about gender and sexuality and appearance and mixing them up. The result is that everybody has a lot more options."

They speak of the "limiting traditional binary opposition of gender," and describe how they break it down: "If I walk down the street in lipstick and a typically feminine dress and high heels, then kiss this girl or hold this boy's hand, people ask themselves, 'Who does she sleep with?' It gives us freedom to break down stereotypes."[77]

At this level, breaking down stereotypes clearly leads to moral breakdown and will surely lead one day to mental and spiritual breakdown. Since we are made in the image of God, according to his creational hard-wiring, such a disassociation from the divine pattern can ultimately lead only to *personal* disintegration.

The truth about man made in the image of God gives to human life clear identity, transcendent significance, and essential dignity. Since God the Creator is Father, Adam's relationship to him is that of a "son." Though the term is not used in the creation accounts, the special relationship of human beings to God in the Bible is often described as a relationship of son to father. The promised line is called "the sons of God."[78] God at the exodus calls Israel "my firstborn son."[79] The goal of

redemptive history is to make God's people to be "sons."[80] Paul sees
that goal realized in the church and calls all Christian believers "sons of
God."[81] This all fits with Luke's designation of Adam as "son of God."[82]

Adam as "son of God" underlines the high view of man to be found
in the Bible. Paul emphasizes that man has dignity because he is "first."
Three times Paul describes Adam as "first," and one more time by
implication.[83] It is an ascription of nobility, already found in the Old
Testament Book of Job. Eliphaz, one of Job's friends, asks Job to consider Adam's place of privilege: "Are you the first man ever born? Were
you brought forth before the hills? Do you listen in on God's council?"
(15:17).[84] Paul has much to say about Adam as first.

ADAM IS FIRST IN TIME

When he affirms that the "first man" became a living being, Paul is
clearly referring to the start of something big. Adam becomes the first
human "living being."[85] What does this phrase mean? Paul's Greek term
psuche zosa gives rise to much speculation. From *psuche* we get "psyche"
and "psychology," and much effort is spent speculating what Paul meant
about Adam's soul over against his spirit and his body. *Zosa*, "living,"
gives us terms like "zoo" and "zoology." The Contemporary English
Version, desirous to communicate eternal truth in the contemporary
idiom, translates the expression as "living person," thereby sacrificing
accuracy for personal immediacy and warmth. But this is not what Paul
said. He is citing Genesis 2:7, which the Old Testament Contemporary
English Version translates "the man started breathing."[86]

The New International Version is consistent between its Old and
New Testament translations of the phrase, giving us "living being" but,
like other translations, fails to exhibit consistency in the way it translates the underlying Greek term where it appears elsewhere in Genesis
1 and 2. Genesis uses the same term, *psuche zosa*, for the animals that
move on the ground. Adam was to "rule over the fish of the sea and the
birds of the air and over every living creature [*psuch-zosa*] that moves
on the ground" (1:28).

Paul is not speculating about personhood or souls. He is affirming
the physical, space-time creation of Adam. Adam is the first living,
breathing human creature made in God's image. *Human* history thus

has a real, space-time beginning whose reality lies solely in God's decision to create; and the dignity of Adam, in one sense unique, is eventually passed on to his progeny.

Adam Is First in Authority

In the psalm of David cited earlier, one phrase in particular catches the significance of Adam's incredible role in the creation: "You made him ruler over the works of your hands; you have put everything under his feet." (Ps. 8:6). As a steward in God's world, and viceroy in God's stead, man names the animals and cares for the garden. Adam is thus the first environmentalist. Responsible dominion over creation is God's intention for man, both male and female, both for Adam and Eve and for their posterity. God, in bringing the cosmos under Adam's feet, gave Adam the intelligence, scientific skills, logic, and sensitivity needed to do the job. The Creator causes the future of his own handiwork to depend upon Adam's faithful stewardship. The implications of this are enormous.

Even though Adam was not around when most of the creation was set in place, God entrusted to him the maintenance of the created order. The divine handiwork holds together as long as Adam exercises rightful dominion and subdues the earth. Adam rules creation like the ideal righteous king in Israel who "rule[s] from sea to sea and from the river to the ends of the earth" (Ps. 72:8).[87] Adam subdues the earth the way the people of Israel were to subdue the land.[88] This is why Paul applies Psalm 8 (which refers to the first Adam) to the last Adam. The phrase from the psalm, "you have put all things under his feet," is pressed into service to describe the lordship of Jesus at the end of time.[89] Seeing Adam's dominion in the light of the final glory of the last Adam's rule reminds us of Paul's basic conviction concerning the cosmic dignity and importance of humanity. The lordship of both Adams puts humanity in an ontologically different position from the rest of creation. According to the Bible, there is no reason to believe the modern myths about created beings of higher intelligence somewhere in outer space who have figured out how the universe works, and one day will enter our world to help us. Equally, there is no reason to believe the pagan myth, ancient and modern, that everything is divine, a myth that reduces humanity to the level of just another "divine" animal.

ADAM IS FIRST IN ROLE

Man as the representative head of the woman is not a favorite topic today. Indeed, some consider "patriarchy" to be the original sin. Could Paul be a member of Women-Church? "Women-Church," says its founder, feminist theologian Rosemary Radford Ruether, "represents the first time that women collectively have claimed to be church . . . this means that patriarchy is rejected as God's will. It is rejected as the order of creation."[90]

What does Paul say? "Adam was formed first. . . ." (1 Tim. 2:13). Paul does not back away from a discussion of male/female issues. But he brings to them the perspective of the original, created order. In his letter to Timothy, he uses his authority as a prophet like Moses to "tamper" with the Old Testament text, just as he did when, in Corinthians, he comments on Genesis 2:7. You will remember that in commenting on the Genesis text, Paul adds two words, "Adam" and "first" to his quote from Genesis.[91] In Timothy, he says that "Adam was formed first." Paul is teaching on the different roles of men and women. With the same kind of prophetic authority, he evokes the *first part* of Genesis 2:7, "God made man." In this case too, he adds *the same two words,* "Adam" and "first."[92] So instead of "God made man," Paul says, "Adam was formed first."

This time Adam is named and identified as first not with regard to Christ and to the final things but with regard to gendered role distinctions. Paul clearly seeks to show an intentional chronology in redemption in the theological order from Adam to Christ. On a different level, he seeks to show divine intentionality in the ordering of creational sexuality. In 1 Corinthians 15:45 Adam is specifically named and set first to make clear God's plan for the coming of the last Adam for the purposes of recreation. Here Adam is named and set first for the purposes of the creation. "Adam was formed first, then Eve."[93] Just as Adam and Christ in different ways are essential for redemption, so Paul here teaches, by this distinctive use of Scripture, that Adam and Eve, in different, divinely-ordered ways, are essential for the project of creation.

While the Bible teaches a distinction of roles, it is an economic not an ontological distinction; that is, it is a distinction that has to do with "function" in the pursuit of the creational mandate, not with human worth. The triumphal exclamation of Adam—"Bone of my bones and flesh of my flesh" (Gen. 2:23)—is a statement of equality explicit at the very beginning of the canonical record. This text is also a statement about the normativity of the heterosexual, two-parent family: "For this reason a man shall leave his father and mother and be united to his wife, and they will become one flesh" (v. 24).

Paul, who knows the Creator as a God of order, and sees significance in order, finds in the account of creation clear evidence for role distinctions in the couple, and in the family. In being formed *first*, Adam is called to exercise headship over his wife, Eve, and she is to submit to him.[94] Paul unswervingly affirms that this is the original, good, created state of affairs: "Neither was man created for woman, but woman for man" (1 Cor. 11:9).

Adam functions in the created world in an analogous way to God. God brings all the animals "to the man," says Genesis 2:19, "to see what he would name them; and whatever the man called each living creature, that was its name."[95] Unlike the theory of evolution, which postulates a world where things mysteriously and miraculously mutate into other things in a chain of monistic being, biblical creation affirms real, created distinctions, and celebrates labels—names. The biblical account of creation makes a clear distinction between animals and humans, because man is to rule over the creation and is specifically made in God's image.[96] Creation is brought to its culmination in the further and final distinction between male and female—"male and female he created them."[97] The implicit distinction inherent in this creational act is made clear when Eve is given a distinguishing name. Adam declares about his wife: "She shall be called 'woman,' for she was taken out of man" (Gen. 2:23).[98] Just as light and darkness have different names, so do the individuals that make up the first human couple. Their distinctive roles are not made to suppress the woman and elevate the man. Their gender distinctions are created to help them live out the creational mandate of dominion and fruitfulness. In their difference, the male and the female produce the blessing of procreation.[99]

The male/female distinction of creation is maintained in redemption. In a prophetic act, Adam renames his wife "Eve, because she would become the mother of all the living" (3:20).[100] The creational distinctions are seen as essential for the realization of both God's creational mandate and his future work of salvation. Eve will be the mother of the Messiah; and women will be blessed in the good, created function of childbirth.[101]

This, argues Paul, is the pattern for human, and especially Christian, marriages.[102] For Paul, this distinction of roles is written into the very fabric of creation by the God of order who, from his own divine wisdom, made all things according to his will and each according to its own kind.

ADAM IS FIRST IN LINE

Adam is not a little clone in an amorphous mass of humanity. He is a fabulously designed prototype—the first exemplar of the human species of breathtaking variety and complexity. He is not the result of one poor spirit being who fell into matter out of a crowd of spirits dancing in cloud nines of divine light. He does not sojourn in matter for a short period of time.[103] He is, rather, the intentional and innovative origin of the human species, the first of a glorious line that also includes Eve. The great calling of dignity and significance as God's viceroy over the rest of creation is also given to woman. There is a final nuance in Paul's addition of the word *first* in his citation of Genesis 2:7. Adam is first in relation to what comes later. The creation of Adam is not God's final or only significant act. Because there is a first, there is a concluding, last act. Because there is a first Adam, there is a last Adam, and with him a new or last creation.

John Calvin saw this. In his commentary on Genesis, he says, "The state of man was not perfected in the person of Adam; but is a peculiar benefit conferred by Christ, that we may be renewed to a life which is celestial, whereas before the fall of Adam, man's life was only earthly, seeing it had no firm and settled constancy."[104]

Paul uses "first" in the very next verse—"The spiritual did not come first, but the natural, and after that the spiritual" (1 Cor. 15:46). In the plan of God, the natural has priority. Paganism believes that humans were first spiritual and that they fell into the natural, physical world. By the realization of their original, spiritual nature they will be able to escape the natural. Paul proposes a very different scheme. Human existence and history begin with the natural, which one day God will glorify. In God's plan there are two kinds of life, the "protozoic" and the "eschatozoic," if I can coin a term or two. Both are valid expressions of God's handiwork. Thus, though nothing God does is "natural," the original creative work is but the first touch on the divine canvas. Because of Paul's organic, progressive view of God's work, future glory is in no sense a restoration to Eden. As we shall see, his vision ranges far beyond an earthly garden, however idyllic we might imagine Eden to have been. Eden is preparatory, not final. Eden is wonderfully first, but it is not gloriously last.

The Significance of Paul's Doctrine of Creation

The general organic progress and unity in Paul's thinking comes to a specific expression in the breathtaking density and brevity of 1 Corinthians 15:45. I suppose I may be playing favorites, but it seems to me that no other text in the Bible contains such a vastness of scope. Using a mere seventeen Greek words, the apostle takes us from the dawn of historical time, prior to the fall, to the future resurrected life and the coming of the new heavens and earth. In so doing, he touches on all the essential themes of his thought:

- *theology,* the study of God, for God is the implied author of both acts
- *protology,* the doctrine of first things, in the description of the creation of Adam, the *first (protos)* man
- *providence,* implied in Adam becoming a *living* being
- *anthropology,* the doctrine of man, in the reference to the two Adams
- *soteriology,* the doctrine of salvation, in the giving of resurrection life
- *Christology,* the teaching about Christ, in the last Adam
- *ecclesiology,* the doctrine of the church, implied in those who are represented by this new federal head
- *eschatology,* the teaching of last things, in the expression the *last (eschatos)* Adam
- *pneumatology,* the doctrine of the Holy Spirit, in the reference to the Spirit who gives life

- *special revelation,* the doctrine of the Scriptures of the Old and New Testaments, explicit in the phrase, "as it is written," and implicit in Paul's inspired commentary.

From this simple, basic Bible study of one phrase in one verse[105] we conclude that Paul is making a majestic affirmation of Adam's *physical* creation. He does not intend to exaggerate who Adam was, as his rabbinic past had taught him to do. The rabbis believed Adam was a superman, one hundred feet tall, capable of superhuman exploits. Paul sticks to the biblical record. Adam became a "living creature," no more, no less. In Paul's theology, Adam is the first human exemplar of God's original, "natural" creation. Paul downplays any speculative idealization of the original work of God, for he is setting up what is to follow in the divine plan.

As a pivotal expression of Paul's theology, this verse is significant in that it cites a text from Genesis that describes the situation *before the fall.* Is this a mistake? An unimportant detail? Or does it say something profound about Paul's view of creation? By speaking of the pre-fall creation, this verse proposes a perfect balance between the two majestic, historical acts of God—creation and resurrection, standing at the two extremities of human history. As we shall see, Paul is the most radical of futurists because he is the most traditional of creationists. The future and the past go together and cannot be separated. Verse 45 is structured that way. It describes two parallel, essential acts of God, on which everything else in the history of the cosmos is based. On the one hand, there is God's act of creation—"the first man Adam became a living being." The product of this act no one can deny. There is *something* rather than *nothing,* and the *something* is of incredible beauty and design. On the other, there is God's act of resurrection—"the last Adam [became] a life-giving spirit." The product of this second unique act of God's power, people often have denied; but the emptiness of Christ's tomb still defies the skeptics—this act of God responds to the desire of the human heart for something better in the future.

In a luminous, specific example of the general relationship of the Old and New Testaments, we see God's intentions in resurrection implicit in creation, and his goals in creation become explicit in the act of resurrection.[106] The physical creation determines what kind of resurrection we should expect—a transformation of the physical.[107] In the same way, resurrection reflects back on the comparable, original divine act of creation that was just as miraculous. It seems to me that these two great acts of God are the key to understanding Paul. He constantly moves from what God has done in the past in *creation* to what God does to creation in his second recreative act of *resurrection*. These are the outside parameters of Paul's worldview, the two bookends of his thinking.[108]

The final piece of evidence for the structural importance of the doctrine of creation in Pauline thinking is his view of the future of the physical universe. As we shall argue later, creation is not left to rot or be discarded and destroyed like a worthless garment, but will be glorified by the power of God and worn with pride, like the gleaming white robes at the marriage supper of the Lamb.[109] The final picture of creation in Paul's theology is not its destruction, as the Gnostics believe, but its liberation and transformation under the lordship and reign of Christ, the last Adam.[110] Thus Paul would doubtless agree with John's vision of the future kingdom: "Whenever the living creatures give glory and honor and thanks to Him who sits on the throne, who lives forever and ever, the twenty-four elders fall down before Him who sits on the throne and worship Him who lives forever and ever, and cast their crowns before the throne, saying, 'You are worthy, Lord, to receive glory and honor and power; for You created all things, and by Your will they exist and were created'" (Rev. 4:9–11 NKJV).

Even in heaven, in the renewed heavens and earth, God is worshiped day and night—as Creator. Paul in his own way joins this heavenly song when he speaks of God as "the Creator—who is forever praised. Amen" (Rom. 1:25). If this is what we will be doing in heaven, what should we be doing now on earth?

The rest of this book will suggest some answers to this question. For the present, note that the doctrine of creation is not merely theoretical. Before we see some of its implications, however, I would like to point out the vastly important logical function of the teaching on creation within the movement of Paul's mind-blowing theology.

In light of Paul's carefully-worked-out doctrine of God and man, the modern, apostate propositions for the "survival" of Christianity in the third millennium would deal a death blow to true biblical faith. For example, John Shelby Spong, a retired Episcopalian bishop of Newark, New Jersey (whose books are promoted by the Jesus Seminar), states without nuance: "Christianity is doomed if it continues affirming a supernatural God . . . the church must reject its 'pre-modern past' by admitting the Bible and Christian doctrine are first-century inventions now refuted by science."[111] His call to abandon "the theistic definition of God" is a call to embrace the paganism Paul's doctrine of God was meant to counter.

Chapter 7

The Death of Creation

The Fact of Death

Mick Jagger of the Rolling Stones says his song "Joy" is about the joy of creation and the love of God. It is unexpected and encouraging to hear such sentiments from a rock icon, but life is not so joyful sometimes. One August evening, the day before her first anniversary, my daughter-in-law gave birth to her first baby. Jonathan David Jones was born with birth defects and died only nine hours later. Nine months of pregnancy and hours of painful labor gave birth to the disappointed hopes and love of Jonathan's parents, and to a little boy who knew only nine hours of life. These heart-wrenching moments confronted our family as never before with objective grief and emotional pain.

One relative of a victim in the Concorde crash in Paris in 2000 could only say: "We're hitting the boundaries of human comprehension." Thousands echoed such sentiments after the World Trade Center massacre of September 11, 2001, their incomprehension even greater, because of the determined nature of an act motivated by human hatred and evil yet clothed in religious self-righteousness. Faced with horrors such as these, how can we sing for joy at the creation and the love of God? Life that can be so ecstatically enjoyable can also seem so arbitrarily cruel.

Yet there are two surprising things about our grief, which differentiates us from animals.

1. We hate death.

After about seventy years, our life ends in ugly death. Norman Mailer, the radical 1960s novelist, once admitted that he thought of death at least three times a day. The head-in-the-sand, "hakuna matata" explanation of life states that life is beautiful. Hollywood set it to music: "Zip-a-dee-doo-dah, zip-a-dee-ay, my, oh my, what a beautiful day . . . wonderful feeling, wonderful day!" Try singing that as you stand over the lifeless body of a loved one. Though many try to argue that death is a "normal" fact of life, it never seems normal. The reality of certain death for every human being is terribly depressing, as the existentialists of the last century recognized. Declaring the world absurd, they counseled suicide as the only courageous, human response. Their explanation of life was that there is no explanation.

2. We are deeply troubled by guilt.

Studies report that a high percentage of women who have abortions feel guilt.[1] Senator Bob Kerry, bothered by a long-held secret about a massacre he led in Vietnam, finally confessed. In a speech at a Virginia military academy, he said, "It was not a military victory. It was a tragedy, and I had ordered it. . . . Though it could be justified militarily, I could never make my own peace with what happened that night. I have been haunted by it for thirty-two years."[2]

Evolution explains our present state as a "work-in-progress," as we evolve from lower to higher norms, but it cannot explain guilt. Why should the successful species in the ruthless struggle for existence be troubled by moral doubt?

The pagan, spiritual version of evolution claims that we all are evolving naturally into "God" and must rid the world of guilt,[3] because everything is "natural." Real evil must be explained away, as does Neale Donald Walsch: "Hitler went to heaven . . . his deeds were mistakes not crimes. . . . The mistakes did no harm to those whose deaths he caused because they were released from their earthly bondage."[4] Walsch would probably object with "moral" fervor if someone tried to "release" him from his "earthly bondage." Such an explanation leads to moral mayhem.

Pauline Realism

Paul's picture of creation's idyllic beauty and harmonious structure does not lead him into flights of amoral sentimentality. His high view of creation seems to clash with his jarring description of the human condition. Things have gone terribly wrong. Human beings are "filled with every kind of wickedness" (Rom. 1:29): sexually immoral, idolaters, adulterers, male prostitutes, homosexual offenders, thieves, greedy, drunkards, slanderers, swindlers.[5] We "gratify . . . the cravings of our sinful nature and follow its desires and thoughts" (Eph. 2:3). This corruption is not true only of the godless nations, as the psalmist David, whom Paul cites, states: "There is no one righteous, not even one; there is no one who understands, no one who seeks God. All have turned away, they have together become worthless; there is no one who does good, not even one" (Rom. 3:10–18).[6] The root cause, says Paul, is that "there is no fear of God before their eyes."

A Moral Universe

The cause of human dysfunction and decay is not ignorance, human mistakes, or spiritual amnesia. It is wide-awake, eyes-open moral rebellion. According to Paul, the first human couple (and especially Adam, the first man), caused creation's death by their actions. In spite of the ideal conditions of life in which they lived at the birth of creation, they chafed under the life-promoting and sustaining structures of the divinely-sanctified cosmos. Paul does not describe Eden as a place where Adam and Eve floated on clouds and did as they pleased. He presupposes an ordered physical reality with laws and expectations.

God-designed distinctions, created into the fabric of the physical cosmos, constitute the very essence of the moral universe. There is no neutral fact or nonethical decision. Everything is sanctified by God and bears the stamp of his character. The first man, as a living being in God's image, knows this. He works in the fields, cares for and rules over the animals, oversees the garden community, loves and cherishes his wife as his equal and unique helper, and together they honor and worship the Creator in the calling of creational dominion.

Stay Off the Grass

In Eden, the focal point of worship and moral existence is the tree of the knowledge of good and evil. God's command not to eat its fruit reminds Adam and Eve, who are physical creatures, that while everything is fabulously good, not everything is expedient, for the present.[7]

The desirable fruit of nature quietly and clearly declares that there is no source of life and beauty apart from God—not nature, not man. Human beings, male and female, owe their existence not to themselves as superior "living beings" made "in the image of God" but to a transcendent Lord who is incomparably Other. This lone tree stands between heaven and earth, at the center of the garden, as a witness before the eyes of these beautiful, limited earthlings to the life-giving truth of the Creator/creature distinction.

The visible "sacrament" of the tree is accompanied by an *explicit* divine word of prohibition: "You must not eat from the tree . . . for when you eat of it you will surely die" (Gen. 2:17). The first "no" in the Bible is given in order to undergird the "yes" of the tree and to ensure that Adam and Eve would have knowledge of God's moral authority and their place in relation to it.

"Law" stands at the heart of a theistic, moral universe, because through it the Creator enters into a meaningful, personal relationship with his creatures. Through it, he establishes for them the conditions of life, both physical and spiritual, that are advantageous to their well-being. If "law" in Greek might suggest rules, its equivalent in Hebrew "Torah" implies a way of living. The created cosmos, sanctified by God's ordered structures and clarified in its nature by God's spoken commands to the original couple, constitutes the source and origin of God's other biblical laws. For Paul, law is a number of things: the structures set in place at the beginning by God the Creator; the moral law of the Ten Commandments;[8] the whole written Torah (Moses and the prophets), that is, the whole Old Testament;[9] moral principles in general,[10] and natural law, that is, "the work of the law written on human hearts," known by every human being.[11] All the commandments of God, says Paul, are "holy, righteous and good," and have, as their intention, to bring life.[12] Do them and you live. Break them and they break you.[13]

The Essence of Sin

The fall is the result of man, in his lofty place of dignity and trust, breaking God's law. It draws down upon him God's just and necessary moral punishment. God had declared in his revelation to Moses:

"You shall have no other gods before me" (Exod. 20:3). Paul, as a prophet like Moses, declares "the wrath of God is being revealed from heaven against all the godlessness and wickedness of men" (Rom. 1:18). The wrath of God against idolatry has its origin in the disobedience of Adam and Eve, who live in the very presence of God and fail to obey his warnings. The command seems arbitrary and the justice primitive, especially since Paul affirms, as we already noted in 1 Timothy 4:4, that "everything God created is good, and nothing is to be rejected"—including food![14] Why then reject this good fruit, all the more since Eve saw that "the tree was *good* for food" (Gen. 3:6)? Paul, in his "second Moses" role, once more throws light on what the original Moses says. His description of full-blown paganism clarifies the original temptation: "they exchanged the truth of God for a lie, and worshiped and served created things rather than the Creator" (Rom. 1:25).

Adam and Eve were the first to exchange the truth of God for the lie. They were the first to locate the source of ultimate truth in themselves, to achieve their own transformation. At the moment of the serpent's temptation they began to do what we have done ever since—fail to honor God as Creator and unique source of all life, and consequently fail to give him thanks. At that crucial moment in their probation, rather than worshiping and serving the Creator, who is blessed forever, trusting him to bring about the fullness of creation's project in his own time, in his own way, they worshiped and served the creature (nature and themselves). They took the place of God, made themselves to be as God, and became God in their own eyes, taking upon themselves the role of defining how creation would reach its state of glorification. This is the first unholy act of rebellion against creation's structures, as the first couple sought to define their own structures, claiming to know better than God. Indeed, like the Gnostics after them, they implicitly treated God the Creator as a liar.[15]

It is still a live option. The serpent's repetitious lie is alive in the halls of contemporary power, and continues to propose the same diabolical falsehood that God and his Word are not good, and that the human autonomous will to control and his god-status is all the world needs for its own salvation.

Adam and Eve-R-Us

Adam is both the "First Man" and "Everyman." As the prophet Isaiah put it, "Your first father sinned" (Isa. 43:27). We can identify with his humanity, but his historical uniqueness in being the first man, occupying such a lofty and significant function, gives him a unique place in the history of the race. Adam, the original man, commits the original sin. His sin, being the first, has dreadful consequences for his progeny. Because Adam sinned, humanity fell into a state of sin. Just as the father of seven children who commits a crime and is jailed causes misery for his whole family, so the consequences of Adam's sin are visited upon his offspring. This seems to deprive all the children of moral responsibility, and it is hard to grapple with the mystery of the consequences of evil. There is a complexity to the human being, created in the image of God.[16] Though we are born in a sinful state, we are not mere robots, rebelling because that is our inevitable destiny. Paul confronts us with our knowledge of the true God, the Creator. Our guilt-ridden consciences constantly confirm our personal, individual culpability before the holy God, Creator of heaven and earth.[17] According to Paul, we are all guilty because "we have all sinned and fall short of the glory of God."[18] Certainly in our lucid moments, we know we sin, we know we inflict evil on others in our selfishness, and we feel the power of objective guilt.

We all have a pagan default button. Even those of us raised in cultures deeply affected by the Bible live in subtly pagan ways. Those who live in other cultures will live out the effects of paganism more obviously. But in whatever form, human evil always seeks to justify itself, for though we are sinners, we never cease to be moral beings who cannot stand the sight of our own guilt. Our default button masks what is plain and clearly seen[19] about ourselves, about the world and about God, or, as Paul would say, we "suppress the truth in unrighteousness" (Rom. 1:18 NKJV). But this active misrepresentation of the true nature of reality (both by unrighteous thinking and by immoral acting) constitutes the essence of the fall. It explains the dysfunction of the world as we know it.

Against all reason and common sense, both Adam and Eve ate the fruit, and all hell broke loose.

Human Dignity in Sin

"Sin entered the world through *one man,* and death through sin. . . . many died by the trespass of the *one man.* . . . through the disobedience of the *one man* the many were made sinners" (Rom. 5:12–19). There is no equivocation in this passage. Blame is attached not to some blind Creator but fairly and squarely on the shoulders of humanity, and of one man in particular. Guilt is not attributed to all the fallen angels nor to the heavenly principalities and powers. It is not laid on Lucifer the prince of the air and the bearer of false light, nor on the billions of stars nor the endless number of earth creatures—none of them caused the cosmic fall. Only man, the bearer of God's image and the crown of creation, bears guilt for the fall. Only one man, whose calling it was to make known "the manifold wisdom of God . . . to the rulers and authorities in the heavenly realms," could cause the disaster of the cosmic fall (Eph. 3:10). Even in sin, humanity in Adam is associated with extraordinary dignity and significance. This biblical focus on man is not the expression of a primitive, geocentric view of the ancient universe, as modern liberals pretend.[20] It is a recognition that man is the only self-consciously moral creature in the entire universe, in whom is invested responsibility for the outcome of creation's supreme program. Adam was to rule creation like the ideal righteous king in Israel.[21] Alas, Adam does what unrighteous kings have done ever since. As the prophet Daniel says: "The king will do as he pleases. He will exalt and magnify himself above every god and will say unheard-of things against the God of gods. He will be successful until the time of wrath is completed" (11:36).

The Fall

When I hit a golf ball out-of-bounds, my weekly optimism freezes over, my psyche goes to jelly, and my whole round begins to disintegrate. This is a trivial and humorous example of meltdown. The fall was neither funny nor trivial.

Inevitably, the whole of the cosmos that had been placed in trust under Adam's feet now began to disintegrate as Adam stepped out of the bounds God had established for human, created life. A great rumbling, roiling spiritual earthquake hurtled down the great halls of the universe at the moment when Adam and Eve betrayed their Maker and presumed to walk on God's holy ground. As they broke the delicate Creator/creature distinction, all the other structures and distinctions, so carefully and artfully put in place by the divine craftsman, began to implode, and the structures of creation entrusted to Adam's oversight, one by one, came crashing down.

Little wonder theology has called this the fall! The serpent had succeeded in reproducing for humanity the disastrous fate he had already brought on himself: "How you have fallen from heaven, O morning star, son of the dawn! You have been cast down to the earth, you who once laid low the nations! You said in your heart, 'I will ascend to heaven; I will raise my throne above the stars of God; I will sit enthroned on the mount of assembly, on the utmost heights of the sacred mountain. I will ascend above the tops of the clouds; I will make myself like the Most High.' But you are brought down to the grave, to the depths of the pit" (Isa. 14:12–15).[22]

The penalty for breaking God's command—"the day you eat you shall die"[23]—is applied that very day. "God's wrath is revealed from heaven," and the Creator gives Adam and Eve over to the consequences of their fateful decision. The effects of this rebellion on the carefully-erected distinctions that constitute the created order are immediate and far-reaching.

The Fall of Creation's Structures

Paul says "they exchanged the truth of God for the lie." When Adam and Eve exchanged God's truth for the pagan lie, a real exchange took place; and it brought with it devastating consequences. The first humans gave up creational norms and distinctions, exchanging them for diabolical perversions and unions, the effects of which we are still feeling as we see their full-blown form in our day, after centuries of Christian dominance in the West. As the West looks to the East for light, we are assured that the blend of humanity and religion will "unitedly bring to an end the great heresy of separateness."[24] This union, this joining of the opposites, is at the expense of the divinely-appointed distinctions, and thus will only propagate the apostasy and destruction of the fall.

THE DESTRUCTION OF THE CREATOR/CREATURE DISTINCTION

The first thing Scripture tells us about man is that he is creature. God created him in his own image for personal communion.[25] The fall destroys this. Now Adam and Eve are banished from the garden. No longer will they know direct communion with the Creator but henceforth will live in a hostile world of thorns and thistles, excommunicated, so to speak, from the table of his immediate presence. Adam as the representative human being, by claiming autonomy for the created order, irremediably skews the relationship between the human and the divine and becomes the unwitting father of paganism. Cut off from its true source of life, nature begins its headlong plunge into falsehood and death.

The fall is in no sense an honest mistake. It is a breach of trust between man and God. In a very personal sense, man "offends" the Creator who has condescended to establish such a relationship in the first place. This rupture of the primary relationship between man and God brings brokenness to relationships with other human beings as well. There is no human relationship in the entire cosmos that is left untouched. The breach is seen immediately in the dysfunction between Adam and Eve as they accuse each other, and it quickly culminates in the crime of murder among their immediate offspring. Paul describes our race as full of "evil, greed and depravity . . . full of envy, murder, strife, deceit and malice. . . . gossips, slanderers, God-haters, insolent, arrogant and boastful . . . senseless, faithless, heartless, ruthless" (Rom. 1:29–31).

The destruction of this first, foundational distinction between the Creator and the creature causes a breakdown in all the other divinely established distinctions that depend upon it.

THE FALL OF THE CLEAR DISTINCTION BETWEEN TRUTH AND FALSEHOOD

Since the creation of the world, God's invisible qualities—his eternal power and divine nature—have been clearly seen. . . . but their thinking became futile. . . . Although they claimed to be wise they became fools. . . . They exchanged the truth of God for a lie (Rom. 1:20–25).

The fall is an intellectual misthink, to coin a phrase. Belief in theism is not a sacrifice of the intellect. Indeed, it grants to human thought its genuine transcendent point of reference. According to the Bible, we are not like a bunch of ants on an anthill in the middle of the continent of Africa who decide to invent an "ant-like" interpretation of reality, with no clue of anything beyond our own little anthill. Our thinking is meaningful, not because we invent our own meaning, but because the all-wise Creator allows us to share in his timeless wisdom. In spite of being ant-like in our relations to the whole cosmos, we get to understand something as big as Africa, so to speak, namely, the whole cosmos, thanks to the revelation God graciously gives us.

This is not to say that fallen man cannot think, create, and invent. Great civilizations have been built on man's incredible capacity to analyze and shape the building blocks of the created world into expressions of exquisite sophistication. Paul spoke out surrounded by the glory that was Rome. Anyone who has seen the remains of Roman structures in European towns today will be amazed at the human ingenuity that produced them. The technological achievements of modern medicine and cybernetics boggle the mind. God himself salutes the power of human achievement. As he watches the pagan activity in the construction of the tower of Babel, he says, "If as one people speaking the same language, they have begun to do this, then nothing they plan to do will be impossible for them" (Gen. 11:6).

But all human achievement after the fall is accomplished without reference to the capstone of ultimate meaning that makes it all possible and ultimately significant. It is "borrowed capital" from theistic reality. It *assumes* significance for human reasoning. We open our mouths and constantly claim to be saying true things—while denying any rational, moral, and personal origin to created life. For example, take the philosophical elaboration of Darwinian evolution. Endless amounts of rational intelligence are expended to explain the chance character of the universe and the irrational source of all things. But without reference to the One who alone gives meaning to everything, human discourse remains earth-bound, ephemeral, hopelessly relative, ultimately purposeless and finally irrational.[26] Such faulty reasoning facilitates irrational, dehumanizing behavior and even the bold boast of not "thinking straight." In the prophet Jeremiah we read: "every man's own word becomes his oracle [divine revelation] and so you distort the words of the living God" (Jer. 23:36). As in the time of the judges in Israel, when everyone does what is right in his own eyes, the result is not unity but social chaos.

The Fall of the Distinction Between True and False Religion

They . . . exchanged the glory of the immortal God for images made to look like mortal men and birds and animals and reptiles. . . . They . . . worshiped and served created things rather than the Creator (Rom. 1:23, 25).

True worship celebrates and honors the personal Creator within the legitimate boundaries of the created order. According to Moses, such worship took place through the sacrament of the tree in the middle of the garden by which Adam and Eve gave glory to God, Maker of heaven and earth. The psalmist exults: "O Lord, our Lord, how majestic is your name in all the earth! . . . From the lips of children and infants you have ordained praise" (Ps. 8:1–2). In this rightful worship context, man has his legitimate place as steward over all things, including animals. From there, he is moved to worship by considering "the work of your [God's] fingers" (v. 3). According to Paul, this aspect of worship has not changed with the coming of the New Covenant. *Forever* we will owe to the Creator worship and service.[27]

Made in God's image, man is hard-wired for worship. But with the fall, human adoration exchanges the true object of worship for the false. We are still wired for worship, but we move from honoring the tree as a symbol of the good Creator who made it, to hugging trees and worshiping them in place of the Creator. We celebrate the lie about reality, and worship and serve the creation. Paul's description of first-century idolatry reads like an upside-down commentary on Psalm 8, mentioned above. In the pagan worship of nature, everything is turned on its head. God the Creator is nowhere to be seen; and man, though worshiped, is actually dishonored. Reduced to the level of animals, confused with animals, rather than ruling over them, man is "worshiped" just like everything else. This is what Israel did when she turned from God to worship the golden calf, as the psalmist says with biting irony, using words Paul will pick up later to describe paganism: "They exchanged their Glory for an image of a bull, which eats grass" (Ps. 106:20).[28]

As we noted in chapter 2, Paul knew the significant place and function animals occupied in the mystery cults flooding into Rome in the first century. The cult of Isis included powerful animal figures, notably the jackal-headed god, Anubis, half human, half animal. In the religious feasts of the mysteries, the priests would dress as monkeys, crocodiles, ravens, and lions. "Such disguises," notes Robert Turcan, a recognized historian of the period, "altered the way in which the faithful viewed their humanity."[29]

Many twenty-first-century sophisticates feel that the Bible's teaching on true and false worship is obsolete. Even some leading contemporary "Christian" thinkers are unwilling to maintain Paul's black-and-white approach. According to a number of once-conservative Christian scholars, the religious challenge of our day is to replace the barbaric[30] and primitive ideas of Christianity with the more sophisticated insights of today's mature faith. According to Bishop Spong, as he is promoted by the Jesus Seminar: "Now the end of an era has come. Those doctrines and the mythology that houses them [the theistic view of God] have become obsolete . . . they have to be jettisoned and a new foundation laid."[31]

How new will this foundation be? Oddly enough, another star in the Jesus Seminar firmament gives the game away and argues that we should evolve backwards! Lloyd Geering, emeritus professor of religious studies at Victoria University, considered one of New Zealand's foremost thinkers, is described admiringly by Bishop Spong as a "Presbyterian heretic."[32] In imagining the spanking new future planetary religion, the maturing spiritual fruit of biological and human evolution, Geering predicts the return of the pagan goddess. "Mother Earth w[ill] be the consciously chosen symbol referring to everything about the earth's eco-system."[33] He notes that "the loving care of Mother Earth is in many quarters replacing the former sense of obedience to the Heavenly Father."[34] He goes on to say, "In the religion of the coming global society, the forces of nature, the process of evolution and the existence of life itself will be the objects of . . . veneration."[35]

We have come full circle. This new worship has morphed back into the pagan idolatry of ancient Rome. As noted above, the very modern Jean Houston calls for "a new alignment that only myth can bring."[36]

Through the rediscovery of pagan myth, "the Soul of the World, the *anima mundi*, is emerging."[37] For Houston, the transforming myth that will define our exciting future will be taken from the occult world of ancient Egyptian magic that took Rome by storm at the time of Paul.[38] If we become Isis and Osiris we will become full-fledged idolaters like Jean Houston herself. This medium, who was a confidant of a former first lady of the most powerful nation in the world, boasts a home full of ancient idols. She calls her idol collection "a fine complement of the gods of Egypt, . . . of Greece and Rome, of Tibet and Micronesia and of China . . . a mummy case in the dining room, Isis and Osiris in the living room, Thoth in the study." It has turned her suburban home into a veritable syncretistic pagan temple! And Houston worships her collection like the ancient Egyptians who "had no doubt the images . . . were alive."[39]

Twenty-first-century idol worshipers are no longer unusual.[40] You can buy your ceramic version of Osiris in your local mall. (If suppliers have not yet arrived in your area, just travel to California.)

The spirituality of this "new era" proposed by Spong, Funk, and Geering will lead both to existential despair and to the return of ancient, primitive, pagan mythology. Paul's analysis of fallen spirituality could hardly be more current or cutting-edge, proving once again that the real issues are not between the primitive and the modern, as Spong and others constantly claim, but between the worldviews of paganism and theism. I am reminded of Oliver O'Donovan's description of paganism's view of history as "a process which replaces the categories of good and evil with those of past and future,"[41] and nothing actually changes.

Paul does not see this kind of worship as the noble expression of the human search for God,[42] even if he does recognize the religious quest in every human soul.[43] He rather describes how this "exchange" of the true object of worship for the false produces spiritual confusion, as men and women are deceived to believe the lie. He calls it participation with demons.[44] His only answer is for people to understand that there is no fellowship between light and darkness, no harmony between Christ and Belial, no agreement between the temple of God and idols;[45] and, understanding that, to flee from idolatry.[46]

The Fall of the Male/Female Distinction

In the account of the creation of man, the first distinction noted is that between man and God. The second distinction God establishes at creation is between the male and the female. Inevitably, this distinction also is destroyed by the fall.

Adam

In his role as "first," Adam was to name, that is, to confirm and codify, the order God established in creation. This included his naming and interpreting the significant place of his wife as helper and mother of all life.[47] Nevertheless, at the moment of the great test in the garden, when the serpent appears next to the tree, Adam fails to fulfill his role and to name evil. Instead of denouncing evil, he participates in it. Instead of offering himself as an atonement for Eve's sin; instead of loving her and giving himself for her, as his role required,[48] he shifted the blame onto her and to God. Instead of being the spiritual leader and priest of his household, he is ready to make his wife the focus of God's wrath.[49]

Adam's work is related to his role. With the fall, his work of dominion as a royal gardener causing the earth to bear fruit[50] now becomes frustrated by a cursed earth of thorns and thistles, and work is "painful toil."[51] As the poet says, all is vanity and mortality and ends in dust. "'Meaningless! Meaningless!' says the Teacher. 'Utterly meaningless! Everything is meaningless.' What does man gain from all his labor at which he toils under the sun?" (Eccles. 1:2–3).

Because of Adam's representative role, tied to his gender (one of God's essential creational distinctions), Adam's sin is, for Paul, the "original" sin. It is Adam's sin, not Eve's, that condemns the cosmos to death.[52] It has to be a constitutive element of Adam's sin that he refused to fulfill the calling this distinct role imposed upon him, not simply that he committed the generic "human" sin.

Eve

Though the roles are different, Eve's is not just that of a helpless damsel in distress, a mere bystander with no significance. She looks more like the image proposed by modern radical feminists[53]—an inquisitive, independent woman seeking significance and liberation.[54] In both

Moses' and Paul's account of the fall, Eve is not a dithering ditz or a dumb blonde. She is a willing, powerful player. (Perhaps this is why some feminists like to claim her as a hero.) According to Moses, Eve was well-informed. She knew God's command, having learned it from Adam, and was able to cite it *verbatim* to the serpent.[55] So far, Adam had fulfilled his task and Eve had willingly submitted to her role. But at this point, she steps out from under God's protective commands and begins to give serious consideration to the serpent. Moved by the beauty of nature the tree represented, she began to desire wisdom on the devil's terms.[56] Too late, Eve confesses: "The serpent deceived me, and I ate" (Gen. 3:13).

Obviously Paul had carefully read these founding texts written by the hand of Moses. Twice he refers to this event. He notes that "the serpent deceived Eve by his craftiness" (2 Cor. 11:3 NKJV); that it was not Adam who was deceived but the "woman [who] being deceived, fell into transgression" (1 Tim. 2:14 NKJV). Paul is not speaking here of Eve's status as the weaker sex, nor is he inferring that she is morally undeveloped or spiritually inferior. Perhaps he is implying that she was open to such a temptation granted the role of submission she was called to fill. For both Moses and Paul, much of the fall has to do with gender role reversal. Just as Adam failed to fulfill his role, so did Eve.

Moses notes that Eve gave the forbidden fruit to her husband.[57] With such an action, Eve is clearly forcing the issue and taking the lead. As the woman in rightful, God-ordained submission, she is now seduced by the glittering promise of "liberation." In so doing, as the heretical Gnostics eagerly noted, she throws off her role and becomes Adam's teacher.

This desire, emerging at the occasion of the fall, constitutes for Eve a constantly frustrated desire after the fall. Eve's work, originally intended to be joyful maternity and glad participation with her husband in dominion, now becomes "painful" and conflictual,[58] a role she constantly will be tempted to resist. Describing the ensuing state of creation's disruption and deconstruction, God announces to Eve: "Your desire shall be for your husband" (Gen. 3:16b). God is not announcing to Eve some kind of playboy heaven on earth, where women will be forever-willing playmates for even more willing men. If that were the case, the second statement—"and he shall rule over you"—would make little sense. However, the phrase makes perfect sense if "desire" is taken to mean what it means thirteen verses later. Here Moses writes about the deep conflict with sin in the human heart. To Cain the Lord says: "sin lies at the door, And *its desire is for you,* but you should rule over it" (Gen. 4:7 NKJV). This desire is one for dominance in a context of unrelieved conflict. According to Moses, God predicts at the dawn of human history that while no one can eliminate the hard-wiring of sexual distinction, there will be a constant battle among the sexes over the issue of role. How appropriate is such an ancient description of our time, especially when woman's desire for autonomy presently has the upper hand and claims to hold the key to sexual peace. According to both Moses and Paul, neither women's liberation nor male chauvinism can ever bring an end to the war. The only path to peace between the sexes is rediscovering the creational norms and exercising them in the power of the Spirit, who raised Christ from the dead. Eve's woeful, illegitimate reach for the fool's gold of independence, as the Bible describes her action, is now proposed as *life;* but the message is manifestly false.

The outright rejection of the Bible's teaching is characteristic of our time. Such a rejection is even proposed as a serious option for Bible readers. However, those who propose such a "study" of the Bible do not pretend that the Bible makes no claims about role distinctions. Even radicals find this argument unworthy of serious scholarly interest.[59] They admit that the texts argue for role distinctions. They simply reject these arguments and encourage others to feel free to read "against the grain." You cannot eliminate such notions from the Scriptures, because both Moses and Paul see gender distinctions as a fundamental part of the separation and distinction pattern in God's original creation. The fall disrupted these patterns, which we need to understand and apply.

The Destruction of Distinctions between Heterosexuality and Homosexuality

"Therefore God gave them over in the sinful desires of their hearts to sexual impurity for the degrading of their bodies with one another. . . . even their women exchanged natural relations for unnatural ones. In the same way the men also abandoned natural relations with women and were inflamed with lust for one another" (Rom. 1:24–27). The fall produces sexual perversion and eliminates the normative character of heterosexuality. Again, Paul does not read like a boorish primitive. Indeed, the simultaneous contemporary rise of religious paganism and homosexuality make Paul read like the morning newspaper. His explanation needs to be heard in today's collapsing culture. For Paul there is a deep relationship between pagan religion and sexual perversion. If worshiping the creature rather than the Creator represents a theoretical undermining of a biblical worldview of God, then the destruction of biblical sexual boundaries produces not merely theoretical rebellion but also practical transgression, with the attendant breakdown of society.

Little wonder, in a day when the same kind of paganism is on the rise, a popular book on pedagogy among teachers of religion in America has the provocative title: *Teaching to Transgress: Education as the Practice of Freedom.*[60] The "state of breakdown," which Jean Houston notes and applauds, is a breakdown of authority, civility, and morality. In the sexual revolution of the sixties, "If it moves, fondle it" became the "liberating" mantra of sexual freedom. Radical feminists demanded their sisters be "sinarticulate," have the "courage to sin," and to "liberate the inner slut." Elinor Gadon, in *The Once and Future Goddess* refers to "erotic feminist" Deena Metzger, who states that we must "engage in two heresies . . . first, return to . . . the neolithic, pagan, matriarchal perception of the sacred universe itself . . . second, re-sanctify the body." She confesses to a certain angst: "We often feel as though we are defying God in the act of seeking the divine. . . . We must allow ourselves whatever time it takes to re-establish the consciousness of the Sacred Prostitute."[61]

The pagan agenda seeks to break down the normativity of creational structures, and nowhere is such a breakdown more obvious than in the practice of homosexuality. In the seventies, homosexual and feminist advocates, using ridicule, demonstrations, and intimidating power plays, forced the American Psychological Association to rescind its long-held ruling that homosexuality was a behavioral disorder. One of the outraged psychiatrists then present wrote: "The board of trustees has made a terrible, almost unforgivable decision which will adversely affect the lives of young homosexuals who are desperately seeking direction and cure. That decision will give them an easy way out."[62]

In Romans, as we have noted, Paul describes how idolatry in the mind gives rise to idolatry with the body.[63] Sinful thinking is solidified in sinful bodily action. Though all sins are equally sinful, Paul calls sexual sins "sin against his own body" (1 Cor. 6:18). The entire person, body and soul, is thus involved in sexual transgression. Sexual sins are deeply habit-forming and come to represent the entire person. This is surely part of what Paul means by the "hardening of hearts," or "God giving them over." Sexuality is integral to who we are, so sexual perversion becomes a defining element of personal identity. This is why denouncing sexual perversion is immediately taken as an attack on the person. Even here, though all sin is sinful, there are gradations, and more or less powerful, practical consequences. If heterosexual adultery and fornication might be considered a kind of practical heresy,[64] homosexual activity is practical apostasy, for it is the most complete expression of the pagan distortion of the Creator's intention for humanity, the crown jewel of his work. The exchange seems to work this way:

Monists tell us to complete the circle by looking into ourselves. Your self sits at the center. Spiritual understanding dawns when you eliminate distinctions and rational controls to take your place in the unity of all things. Such mysticism eliminates guilt and everything associated with the real, physical world of the creation, defined and controlled by the law of God. For example, Islam, a Christian heresy, maintains a certain form of theism and disavows homosexuality. However the monist variant, *Sufism*, which is certainly growing in popularity in the West, allows a different practice. A pro-gay Muslim makes this interesting observation: "Religious gays in the realm of Islam . . . would have to take recourse in the antinomian Sufism (mysticism) . . . [where] all that counts is union with the divine through mystic exaltation. On that level it becomes immaterial whether a believer is hetero- or homosexual."[65]

The physico-theological mechanism seems to function as androgynous persons, whether homosexual or bisexual, express within themselves both sexual roles and identities. As in classic monistic spirituality, they have, on the physical plane, joined the opposites, proving and experiencing that there are no distinctions. "Something in our gay/lesbian being as an all-encompassing existential standpoint, . . . appears to heighten our spiritual capacities," says J. Michael Clark, professor at Emory University and Georgia State University, and a gay spokesman.[66] For spiritual inspiration, Clark turns not to Paul or to biblical teaching on sexuality but to the paganism of Native American animism. Specifically, for Clark, the *berdache,* an androgynous American Indian shaman, born as a male but as an adult, choosing to live as a female, constitutes a desirable gay spiritual model, for the *berdache* achieves "the reunion of the cosmic, sexual and moral polarities,"[67] or the "joining of the opposites." How interesting that the *Berdaches* were known as "sacred Balancers," unifying the polarities to "nurture wholeness."[68]

Paul's analysis is on the money. He teaches that a human society that adopts pagan religion will eventually fall into the most unspeakable sexual perversions. This was not theory. He saw it in Nero, the emperor who ordered his execution. Elsewhere I have documented that sexual perversion of androgyny is not an incidental footnote of pagan religious history, of mere passing interest, but represents one of its fundamental ideological commitments.[69] This is seen in the fact that the pagan *priesthood* is identified, across space and time, with the blurring of sexual identity via homosexual androgyny. Such evidence indicates, beyond a doubt, the enormous priority paganism has given in the past, and continues to give in the present, both to the undermining of God-ordained monogamous heterosexuality, and to the enthusiastic promotion of androgyny in its varied forms.[70]

The Fall from Probation to Judgment

God descends and pronounces judgment: "Because you have done this, cursed are you" (Gen. 3:14). Justice will be meted out, and Adam and Eve are banished from the Garden of Eden, cut off from the tree of life. Paul's analysis of the situation does not flatter us. Rather it tells us the truth: "Men are without excuse" (Rom. 1:20). Adam and Eve stand guilty, and in their deep sense of guilt, hide from God's presence.

The whole pagan enterprise is to avoid the fundamental human problem of guilt. But how *do* we deal with evil? Do we embrace it, accept it, come to love it? This is the pagan solution, especially pernicious in its pseudo-Christian form. The "Jesus" of *A Course in Miracles* soothingly reassures us: "You cannot blame yourself . . . this is why blame must be undone. . . . Come wholly without condemnation . . . to God's altar. . . . It is guilt that has obscured the Father to you."[71] But without guilt, is there any wonder kids take guns to school and in cold blood execute their friends?

"The heart is deceitful above all things and desperately wicked," says the Lord to Jeremiah. "Who can know it? Only I, the LORD, search the heart, I test the mind" (Jer. 17:9–10 NKJV). The pain of cancer throughout the body cannot be calmed by aspirin. It needs drastic treatment. In the same way, guilt is an objective reality that cannot be silenced by pagan myths. "Whatever the law says, it says to those who are under the law, so that every mouth may be silenced and the whole world held accountable to God" (Rom. 3:19). According to Paul, we are accountable, guilty, and without excuse, for at least two reasons:

1. Because of our knowledge of God the Creator

Paul says we all know there is a divine Creator, responsible for the beauty and order all around us. He makes this point to the spiritual elite of Athens who, to cover their bets, also worshiped An Unknown God.[72] This God "gives all men life and breath and everything else" (Acts 17:25). He is the Savior/benefactor of all men,[73] whose existence is "clearly seen . . . from what has been made" (Rom. 1:20).

In our day the great *excuse* is evolution. Belief in a chance universe of timeless duration without any need of outside, divine intervention seems to get people off the hook. But if you are hanging here, you had better take a closer look. There are all kinds of problems with this excuse. Chance can *never* produce purpose and meaning, and these notions are essential to present human life. If the physical universe has a beginning, as most physicists now believe it did, there is not enough time, by chance mutations, to account for the immense complexity we see around us. Rational personhood describes who we are as human beings. Impersonal chance cannot produce persons, nor can irrational chance produce rational beings. The cause must contain the results that eventually appear. The cause of my computer is a computer mind in the head of someone who works at Hewlett-Packard. Only this is an adequate explanation of what I have before my eyes. Moreover, our very existence in the present depends on things functioning in a consistent way, and not according to the principle of chance. How could people build the computer I am working on, and how could I use it, if it was all a matter of chance?[74]

If the process (the life we now lead) works that way, the beginning must have worked that way too. So we are constantly driven back to the God Paul says we all know—a God of "eternal power,"[75] that is, a God capable of producing the whole of created reality, and a God of "divine nature,"[76] that is, a God who, though personal like us, transcends our creaturely nature.

"The heavens declare the glory of God; the skies proclaim the work of his hands. Day after day, they pour forth speech; night after night they display knowledge. . . . Their voice goes out into all the earth, their words to the ends of the world" (Ps. 19:1–4). On the basis of God's nature apparent in the nature around us, Paul says that men are without excuse.

2. Because of our knowledge of God the Lawgiver

As the crown and jewel of the creation, human beings bear the image of God, especially as that expresses the sense of morality. There are many forms of the law (see above) so that human beings "know God's righteous decree."[77] Knowing this decree "that those who do such things [immoral acts] deserve death, they not only continue to do these very things but approve of those who practice them" (Rom. 1:32). In Paul's book, approval is just as bad as doing. We sin knowingly, but we also have a conscience that warns us of our immoral actions. Lady Luck cannot account for our keen sense of justice, which we apply, mercilessly sometimes, to those who do us wrong, while often failing to be anywhere near as sensitive to our own wrongdoing against others. Paul argues that people "show that the requirements of the law are written on their hearts, their consciences also bearing witness, and their thoughts now accusing, now even defending them" (Rom. 2:15). Paul is merely proving that our excuses, and our accusations of other people, demonstrate our own inconsistency, but also the fact that we cannot live with others without the rule of morals and law. The present moral universe in which we make all our moral judgments of others must have a moral beginning. So once more we are faced squarely with God, the Lawgiver.

Conscience is a precious thing, for moral pain is the God-given alert system to bring us to our senses. Dulling this alert system is a major preoccupation of the pagan myth, and it can be very sophisticated. In our contemporary psychologized, Freudianized world, we are experts in making excuses. In his defense, an attorney in my local community, charged with the murder of his mistress, said: "I didn't decide to kill her. . . . I just kept pulling the trigger. I didn't decide it. I just kept doing it."[78] This fifty-two-year-old professional of the law cannot confess his wrongdoing, admit his guilt, and accept justice like a mature human being. We all have become experts in making excuses for every fault we commit. In a society without sin, where no one, except perhaps "the government" or multinational companies, is responsible and shame is considered a behavioral pathology,[79] Paul's declaration hits like a bolt out of the blue: "They are without excuse." Like the diagnosis of an illness, the accusation of guilt, though at first blush negative, calls us back to our roots and appeals to the truly human within us. The chance to admit guilt and declare "I did it," is good for the soul, as all parents know who have seen the release when their child finally admits to wrongdoing and clear channels of communication are reestablished. And to be deprived of the reality of one's own sin and one's objective sense of guilt is, in an odd way, profoundly dehumanizing.[80]

Before the law, "every mouth [is] silenced and the whole world [is] held accountable to God" (Rom. 3:19).

The Fall of Creation into Death

According to Paul, the destruction of these creational distinctions does not produce a better life on earth, but results in condemnation and death. The most irrational exchange of all is the choice of death: "For when you eat of it you will surely die" (Gen. 2:17). This choice appears to be a choice for human freedom, but it is actually a choice for the inevitable application of the righteous "wrath of God." God's wrath is revealed, both as woeful present degradation but also as present and future punishment for disobedience.[81] In other words, the choice involves grave implications. The "letter" of the law "kills,"[82] for it is the written document of the dispensation of death,[83] of accusation and rightful condemnation.[84] There is a day of accountability, "for we must all stand before the judgment seat of Christ" (2 Cor. 5:10). The law that declares: "In the day you eat you shall die,"[85] must be judicially applied as the inevitable consequences of human disobedience. This commandment, which is "holy, righteous and good,"[86] intended to bring life, actually brings death. Sin leads to death,[87] or "works death,"[88] hence the phrase: "The wages of sin is death" (Rom. 6:23). This dread consequence of sin is both spiritual and physical: the unregenerate are spiritually "dead in their trespasses and sins,"[89] but this death is also physical: "The corruptible cannot inherit the incorruptible,"[90] so death is "the last enemy."[91] And for those in its clutches, "There will be trouble and distress for every human being who does evil" (Rom. 2:9).

This cold analysis has one more chilling aspect: We can do nothing about our plight. Adam and Eve could not fix their situation or undo their sin. They couldn't go backwards in time to the point where sin didn't exist. As Paul says, "Flesh and blood cannot inherit the kingdom of God" (1 Cor. 15:50). There are no human resources.

We are "dead in our trespasses and sins."[92] There is nothing humanity can do. Flesh, the expression of human weakness, is incapable of pleasing God.[93]

Even law-keeping does not help, for "all our righteousness is as filthy rags."[94] As the old, politically-incorrect hymn says: "Guilty, vile and helpless, we . . . ." Our situation is without hope. We are without God and without hope in the world. There are no inner resources, no going within the self or the powers of the created order to lift the curse from humanity's shoulders. And the sting of that curse is death, physical and spiritual.

But evil will not have the final say.

Chapter 8

The Rebirth of Creation I: The Life and Death of Jesus Christ

I should like to know why Christ is termed by Paul the Second Adam . . . unless it be that a human condition was decreed him, for the purpose of raising up the ruined posterity of Adam.

JOHN CALVIN

From Generation to Degeneration to Regeneration

The rebirth of creation began in the oddest and most obscure of places—the womb of an unmarried teenage virgin, in the far-flung Roman province of Judea. You may find Christianity unbelievable, but you have to admit its amazing consistency. Just as the Holy Spirit "hovered" over the original creation to bring it to life, so he "overshadowed" this Jewish girl to give birth to "the Son of God," bringing about the rebirth of creation.[1] Even the creational roles of male and female are reengaged to bring about final redemption. Woman, according to the plan and wisdom of God, bears the Last Man. The first man, Adam, and his wife Eve, the "mother of all the living,"[2] find their *redemptive* counterparts in Jesus and Mary. The Creator employs what he already made to produce what will be. God is the master of ecological efficiency. He reuses the good structures, intact in spite of creation's fall, to accomplish creation's regeneration. He will do the same with the dead body of Jesus.

This account of creation and redemption has been the historic teaching of the gospel message from the very beginning, but today people strenuously object to its implicit exclusivism. Politically and religiously correct propaganda encourages the general public to dismiss orthodox Christians as narrow-minded, bigoted, and intolerant. Orthodox Christian belief is dismissed as narrow-minded bigotry. The Bible's good news of Christ's cosmos-transforming birth, hailed by the angelic multitude as the beginning of peace on earth, is now rejected as intolerance and as the cause of war.

On the campus, Western academics—once willing exponents of the culture of Christendom—no longer measure history using B.C. (before Christ) and A.D. (*anno domini*—the year of the Lord). They now employ the more inclusive but meaningless B.C.E. (before common era) and C.E. (common era). That Christ no longer serves as the great signpost of human history would be proof enough that we live in a "post-Christian" era, in which history has no truly significant events. In this post-Christian era, signposts are no longer needed. There is no drama of salvation, and gripping plots give way to special effects. All events are merely "common"!

Whatever our culture chooses to do with Christ, there is no question that, for Paul, Christ stands at the very center of God's plan for the cosmos. Christ is the microcosm of creation. According to God's plan, what happens to Christ determines what happens to the entire universe. In his birth, death, and resurrection, Christ recapitulates the whole story. Like the first Adam, the last Adam is unique. Miss this and you miss the whole point of New Testament Christianity. This follows, not because of bigoted thinking, but from the Bible's account of creation. If, as we have sought to show, the creation plays an essential role in Paul's description of redemption, then God's original plan to place the moral fate of the created order on the shoulders of one man necessarily requires that the salvage of that destroyed order depends upon the faithful obedience of one man. Since history began with one man, it will be brought to its conclusion by one man. As Paul reasons, since death came through a man, the resurrection of the dead comes also through a man.[3] There is exclusivism here, but it is inevitable if the moral character of the universe is to be maintained.[4]

Morals depend on persons. The trust between the person of God and his personal creature, Adam, constitutes the very key of the moral universe, giving everything else ultimate significance. There is no other satisfactory explanation to the existence of morals in our world. Animals make great pets but disappointing colleagues and unthinkable marriage partners. They have neither conscience nor moral sensitivity. Human beings do—even those who believe in a chance, impersonal origin of the cosmos. Many such individuals spend their lives prodded by conscience, trying to decide which things are moral or immoral, just or unjust, and often getting upset with people who do not agree with them. According to the Bible, as we have already noted, the personal God, at the beginning, entrusts the whole fate of the cosmos to one individual: a morally accountable, historic person, Adam. With his failure, the cosmos falls into death. For the cosmos to relive, another man must replay the role of Adam and sets things right. The birth, death, and rebirth of Christ recapitulates both the history of Adam and that of the cosmos, redoing what Adam failed to do and restoring what Adam lost, which was nothing less than God's original, beautiful, creative work. In Christ's birth, the creation is reaffirmed as a thing of value; in his atoning death, creation is cleansed; in his rebirth, creation is transformed and glorified.

One day we will regret getting rid of B.C./A.D., if it is not until the day when, according to Paul, every tongue will be obliged to confess that Jesus is the center of history and Lord of the cosmos.[5] For the moment, the culture has chosen another worldview, so Christian believers must confess the truth wherever they can, "shining," as Paul says, "like stars in the universe" before "a crooked and depraved generation" (Phil. 2:15).

The Birth of Christ—The Reaffirmation of Creation

Just as B.C./A.D. are ceding to B.C.E./C.E., Christmas is giving way to "Winter Break," and Easter to "Spring Break." Instead of marking our calendar in relation to the events of the Christian story, we now celebrate, as pagans have always done, the predictable cycle of the year and nature's circle of life. But our calendar switch is not merely a name change. Without Christ as its reference point, life loses its significance and history its drama, for the "rites of spring" will never produce anything like Handel's *Messiah*. Paganism offers a hybrid pagano-"Christian" *Missa Gaia*, a celebration of "interspecies ecumenism," in which celebrants howl like wolves, giving their rendition of the "Howlelujah Chorus," claiming to redeem the Earth from the Fall![6]

History without significant events produces a depressing Western culture for tomorrow, as described by the contemporary English social observer, Theodore Dalrymple: "Thus are the young condemned to live in an eternal present, a present that merely exists, without connection to a past that might explain it or to a future that might develop from it. Theirs is truly a life of one damned thing after another."[7]

The only breaks young people get from a relentless procession of meaningless events are empty celebrations associated with winter and spring.

Christmas As the Celebration of the Incarnation

A "white Christmas" sounds especially romantic to those who live in southern California and who do *not* play golf! But such sentimentality is absent from what the Bible declares to be a unique, historical event that took place at a specific moment in space and time. At the center of history, on "Christmas Day," God the Creator took on the form of a human creature in order to defeat death, Nature and Man's implacable enemy. The event was long in coming and much anticipated. Even its promise brings "light." So the prophet says: "The people walking in darkness have seen a great light; on those living in the land of the shadow of death a light has dawned" (Isa. 9:2).

The amazing claim of the early Christians was that a young Jewish construction worker, who became a religious teacher at the age of thirty, and who was executed by the Romans for treason three years later, is the divine Creator of the universe. Paganism claims that we are all divine; Christianity says that by a divine miracle, only one man is divine. The incarnation is unique. It never happened before, and it will never happen again. No wonder Christmas has been such a big deal in Western history ever since. It celebrates the world-changing event of the incarnation (the in-fleshment) of the divine Son.

Paul uses "Son" or "Son of God" to evoke Christ's status and role. Generally he uses the name "Jesus Christ" ("Jesus" being Christ's given name, and "Christ," though an office or role, tending to function as a second, proper name). However, the term *son* brings out the deep mystery and richness of Christ's person by showing:

1. *Jesus' divinity:* Christ is God, the second person of the Trinity, as in the phrase, "Father, Son, and Holy Spirit";
2. *Jesus' humanity:* Christ is a real human being, as in the phrase, "Adam, the son of God" (Luke 3:37).

The two meanings of "son" represent how Paul teaches the great truth of the incarnation. But when Paul focuses on Christ the Son, placing him at the center of everything, this automatically also places God the Father, the Creator, at the very center of the event of redemption.

CHRIST THE DIVINE SON

We have already noted that Paul sees Christ, the second person of the Trinity, as the divine agent of creation. Christ is "the image of the invisible God,"[8] acting within the Godhead to bring about the great work of the created universe. Paul confesses "one Lord, Jesus Christ, through whom all things came and through whom we live" (1 Cor. 8:6). Of Christ it is appropriate to say: "All things were created by him and for him."[9] What Paul is assuming here is Christ's divine "preexistence" within the Trinitarian person of God. Such preexistence can be expressed as equality of nature (Christ was "in very nature God," possessing "equality with God"[10]) or as a special relationship of belonging ("God . . . sen[t] his own Son,"[11] or "God sent [literally: sent out] his Son, born of a woman."[12]) As in the Philippians account, Christ is sent out on a mission from the preexistent being of God. The "Son" existed prior to being born of a woman. This absolute use of "Son" is doubtless present also in the phrase, "the gospel . . . regarding his Son,"[13] for Paul then begins to recount the earthly life of Christ. Here as well, divine preexistence precedes Christ's earthly life of service.

The divine nature of Christ is clouded in mystery. How does God join the divine Creator/human creature distinction? How are these two natures brought together while remaining distinct? How does the divine not overshadow the human? Paul does not tell us. By his teaching concerning Christ's divine nature, Paul underlines that the act of redemption is *God's* gracious provision for the human plight. It is divine salvation, not human self-help. In Christ, "*God* demonstrates his own love towards us" (Rom. 5:8). In Christ, "because of his great love towards us, *God*, who is rich in mercy, made us alive with Christ" (Eph. 2:4). The incarnation is an act of God.

The great emphasis in Paul's teaching is on Christ as human.

CHRIST THE TRUE HUMAN SON OF GOD

Christ is also the human "son of God" just as all Christian believers are "sons of God,"[14] as Adam was the "son of God,"[15] and as were the Old Testament heroes[16] and Israel.[17] As the last Adam, Christ is truly and completely human. "Son" in this sense carries the notion of being a chosen, created human being, obedient to the Father's will. Because of this, Christ, the human son, serves as the model of believers, who are to be "conformed to the likeness of his Son, that he might be the firstborn among many brothers" (Rom. 8:29). In his humanity, Christ is the firstborn, the prototype of many brothers. Paul develops the parallel even further. We know sonship with God the way Christ, the human son, knew it. "Because you are sons, God sent the Spirit of his Son into our hearts, the Spirit who calls out, 'Abba, Father'" (Gal. 4:6). Christ and the believer, all sons, equally call God "Abba, Father." Paul prays that the church will "reach unity in the faith and in the knowledge of the Son of God and become mature, attaining to the whole measure of the fullness of Christ" (Eph. 4:13). He is not praying that we will become divine, but that we will reach the fullness of Christ, the human son. This is the kind of sonship Paul is describing when he speaks of Christ "who through the Spirit of holiness was declared with power to be the Son of God by his resurrection from the dead" (Rom. 1:4). At the resurrection Christ is not adopted as the divine Son, the second person of the Trinity. It is not his divine nature that is being recognized. The resurrection vindicates him in his human nature, as the true and faithful last Adam, the first human son, the first "newly created" being, transformed by resurrection power.[18]

The Fact of the Incarnation

By juxtaposing the notion of eternal, divine Son with the notion of earthly, human son, Paul demonstrates his belief in the great miracle of the incarnation. Unlike other New Testament writers, Paul does not describe the details.[19] He merely states the fact with "simple" phrases like: "God sent his Son";[20] "Who, being in very nature God, . . . made himself nothing, taking the very nature of a servant, being made in human likeness" (Phil. 2:6–7); "Christ Jesus came into the world . . .";[21] "the appearing of our Savior, Christ Jesus."[22]

The incarnation explains why Christ occupies center stage in Paul's theology. This miraculous happening is the determining event of cosmic history. Specifically, the incarnation confirms the value of creation by showing that God considers it worthy of redemption. In the incarnation God declares that he has not abandoned his original work. God could have caused creation to implode, and started again from scratch. He did not. The British theologian, Oliver O'Donovan, of Oxford University, expresses God's love for his creation well:

"... the Christian Gospel ... proclaim[s] that God has made himself at home in the world, that the Word has become flesh.... The Created order has been vindicated...." [By] the message of the incarnation . . . we learn how, through a unique presence of God to his creation, the whole created order is taken up into the fate of this particular representative man at this particular moment of history, on whose one fate turns the redemption of all.[23]

Creation is taken up, both its good parts and its bad. The bad is judged and cleansed, and with the good is then transformed.

This "taking up," this transformation of creation, causes Christ's humanity to dominate Paul's theology, which hinges on the doctrine of God the Creator. Though his divinity is always in the background, Christ's humanity is everywhere in the foreground, because the fate of this one man is tied inextricably with the rescue of the cosmos. Jesus Christ relives Adam's original probation, as Paul makes abundantly clear, and passes the test, paving the way for the redemption of all: "For if, by the trespass of the one man, death reigned through that one man, how much more will those who receive God's abundant provision of grace and of the gift of righteousness reign in life through the one man, Jesus Christ" (Rom. 5:17). "As in Adam all die, so in Christ all will be made alive" (1 Cor. 15:22).

Like Adam, Christ experiences the fullness of created reality and exercises his calling to have dominion as God intended. Unlike Adam, his probation and vocation are lived out not in a garden utopia of vegetal abundance, but in a threatening wilderness of thistles and thorns; not in a pristine, pre-fall world, but in the fallen, dying ruins that resulted from Adam's sin.

The incarnation refers not simply to the moment of Christ's miraculous birth, but to the whole of his human experience in this fallen world. We will examine the range of these experiences through the themes of: his human nature, his obedience to the law, his experience of sin, and his tasting of death.

Christ, a Real Human Being—Born of a Woman[24]

Some years ago, critical orthodoxy declared that Paul was not interested in the Jesus of history. The apostle's only concern was to raise up the "spiritual" Christ, preached by the church after Jesus' death.[25] These same scholars found little of theological significance in Paul's theology of God the Creator. While it is true that Paul does not set himself up as a source of knowledge of the historical Jesus (respecting the specific role of the Twelve), his theology demands a historical incarnation and his writing gives importance to the earthly Jesus, especially as model of believing faith.[26]

Three times Paul calls Christ "the man Christ Jesus,"[27] explicitly highlighting his humanity. Paul knows in great detail the historical events of the Last Supper;[28] he knows the simplicity and poverty of Jesus' earthly life,[29] the events of Jesus' trial before Pilate, the specific details of his execution[30] and burial.[31] So important is the humanity of Christ that Paul denounces those in Corinth, doubtless proto-Gnostics who, in ecstatic utterances, denied the historical reality and significance of the earthly Jesus.[32]

The new man is not a new creation *ex nihilo* nor yet a disembodied spirit, new in the sense of being liberated from Adamic flesh. The last Adam bears the flesh of Adam so that he can redeem it from death. God sent his son "in the likeness of sinful flesh . . . [to] condemn sin in the flesh" (Rom. 8:3 NKJV). The first Adam did not exist until God created him, and then he "became" a physical human being. From nothing, he became a physical human creature. The last Adam began as a physical human creature and "became," through the resurrection, spiritual.[33] In other words, his incarnation was the miracle that made him part of the first, Adamic humanity that God created at the beginning. There was a time when the last Adam shared the same flesh as the first Adam. It was not a special body, the prototype of a newly-created superflesh for the world to come. In God's plan for the cosmos and for Christ, the physical had to come first.[34] Just as we "have borne the likeness of the earthly man,"[35] so did Christ. The last Adam takes on the "likeness of sinful flesh";[36] he takes on the "lowly body of Adam."[37] Taking on Adamic flesh is an integral part of the redemptive plan within human history, and this really happened in the space-time event of the incarnation. "When the time had fully come, God sent his Son, born of a woman, born under law . . ." (Gal. 4:4).

Born under the Law

"Born under the law" is a huge theological statement. It implies that the human life of the last Adam, like that of the First, was one of moral probation. During his earthly sojourn, Christ is on trial. At every moment his moral commitment is being tested. As a Jew he was required to keep the law,[38] knowing the biblical principle of probation that "the one who does these things will live by them."[39] For the law, "which is holy, righteous and good,"[40] was "intended to bring life,"[41] though it brought death to sinners. Paul does not set himself up as a historian of the life of Jesus and gives no account of Christ's temptation by the devil in the wilderness,[42] or of Jesus' constant struggles with demonic attacks.[43] However, Paul makes many normative statements about the function of the law and often describes the moral struggles every believer faces.

The law is a schoolmaster[44] not only for us, but for Jesus himself. If we struggle with the demands of the law,[45] so did Jesus. If the law causes sin to become "exceedingly sinful"[46] (for "the power of sin is the law" [1 Cor. 15:56]), Jesus surely experienced that gruesome reality, a fact that makes his own moral triumph all the more heroic.

If the believer is able through the Spirit to fulfill "the just require-ments of the law,"[47] it is only because Jesus fulfilled them supremely, for Paul exhorts believers to "follow the example of Christ" (1 Cor. 11:1). What Adam and his progeny failed to do, Christ did. Sin is the desire to affirm one's autonomy over against God the Creator, pre-tending a right to existence and a right to define that existence. This Christ never did. Rather he did "the things of the law," and by doing them merited life.[48] Christ was not simply under the law. In his moral perfection, he was the *telos* or goal of the law.[49] He became the embodiment and final version of the Law, what Paul calls "the law of Christ."[50] He passed the Adamic probation and fulfilled by his active obedience all the obligations of the original "covenant of works," thus meriting life. However, this was not to be.

Christ and Sin

Christ's moral victory, unique in history, is all the more astounding when we realize that he overturned the failure of the first Adam in the context of a deeply sinful world. In order to "condemn sin in the flesh,"[51] Christ had to be in the closest proximity with sin, though remaining morally pure. As the author of Hebrews says, to be a true "high priest," one who deals effectively with sin, Jesus had to be "tempted in every way, just as we are—yet was without sin" (Heb. 4:15).

To describe the mystery of Christ's incarnation, Paul says Christ took on the likeness of sinful flesh.[52] Even though Christ's birth was miraculous, Paul gives no reason to think that Christ's body or flesh was a unique prototype, already fitted for the world to come, or even a special version of human flesh, made just for Christ. Paul says that human flesh is weak.[53] To "condemn sin in the flesh,"[54] the flesh Christ took on had to be real, Adamic, weak, sin-stained flesh. This is surely what he means by the "lowly body,"[55] or "this body of death."[56]

Some might argue that "in the likeness of sinful flesh" means that Christ looked like a man, but that his flesh was not sinful. But when Paul uses the term *likeness,* he means "in the form of something."[57] Paul affirms that Jesus took on sinful flesh without sinning. He knew no sin,[58] says Paul categorically. However, the last Adam suffers all the effects of sin—fatigue, thirst, suffering, and death. As was predicted, it was in such a body and in active obedience to the Father's will that Jesus "bore our griefs and carried our sorrows,"[59] being "obedient to death—even death on a cross!" (Phil. 2:8).

It is nearly impossible for us to imagine a perfect human being. What would it be like to meet a completely unselfish person? Someone without any hidden agenda, arrogance, false motivations, hypocrisy, or pretense; whose inner thought life would never entertain a suggestion of dishonesty; who would look into the human heart with deep and unrestrained sympathy; whose eyes would speak utter goodness; who would, in the presence of sin and injustice, express pure, righteous indignation; who would denounce evil without concern for personal comfort; who would give the clothes off his back and his whole life to alleviate suffering and evil. The Son of God was just such a human being. Only a person on that level of moral and spiritual purity could undo the effects of Adam's fall. It is a part of the great irony of history that the life of such a person, the only person who never sinned, would be snuffed out by sinners.

Paul gives the measure of Christ's moral perfection and selflessness when he says: "Very rarely will anyone die for a righteous man, though for a good man someone might possibly dare to die. But God demonstrates his own love for us in this [here we see demonstrated the ungrudging, unparalleled self-sacrifice of Christ]: While we were still sinners, Christ died for us" (Rom. 5:7–8).

We have begun to broach the subject of the powerful, incredible, world-changing, creation-cleansing event of Christ's God-willed death.

The Death of Christ—The Cleansing of Creation

Paul has so much to say about the death of Christ that he calls his gospel "the message of the cross" (1 Cor. 1:18). But the first question is: "How can someone's death be such good news?" The answer depends on the uniqueness of Christ. His was the only human death that was truly undeserved. If "the wages of sin is death,"[60] and "the mind of sinful man is death,"[61] then Christ should never have died! He had no sin for which to pay wages, and his mind was never tainted with a wicked thought. Having kept the law, Christ merited life. Having passed probation, he had earned immortality. However, God chose Christ's death as the only way to cleanse the cosmos of the stain of Adam's sin.

Apostate Gnostic "Christians," whether ancient or modern, are consistent. Just as they deny significance to the fleshly Jesus, so they deny meaning to his physical death. For the ancient Gnostics, there is no contamination with created flesh at Christ's "birth" and therefore Christ's death is also a meaningless concept.[62] If the Gnostics are right that the incarnation did not happen, then Christ's atoning, physical death could not have happened either. The Gnostic Apocalypse of Peter explains what really happened at Calvary. Jesus died on the cross, but the *real* Christ sat on the branch of a tree, watching and laughing: "He whom you saw on the tree, glad and laughing, this is the living Jesus. But the one in whose hands and feet they drive the nails is the fleshly part which is the substitute being put to shame, the one who came into being in his likeness."[63]

The First Apocalypse of James makes the same affirmation: "The Lord said, 'James, do not be concerned for me. . . . I am he who was within me. Never have I suffered in any way, nor have I been distressed.'"[64]

Modern Gnostics say essentially the same thing. Marcus Borg of the Jesus Seminar believes the cross is only "an extraordinarily rich image" of dying to self—it is not the act of God on my behalf.[65] Borg states that there is nothing in earliest Christianity "to suggest that Jesus' death had a positive or redemptive significance."[66] In a different key, the Voice (supposedly Jesus) who possessed Dr. Helen Schucman, a Jewish atheist and psychologist, in 1965, exhorts believers: "Do not make the pathetic error of clinging to the old rugged cross. . . . Your only calling here is to devote yourself with active willingness to the denial of guilt in all its forms."[67] The radical lesbian feminist who was once an evangelical, Virginia Ramey Mollenkott, admits: "I can no longer worship in a theological context that depicts God as an abusive parent and Jesus as the obedient trusting child."[68] Dolores Williams, Professor at Union Theological Seminary, offered a classic of theological precision when she reasoned: "I don't think we need a theory of atonement at all. . . . I don't think we need folks hanging on crosses and blood dripping and weird stuff."[69]

What these "imaginative" modern Gnostics offer is in complete contradiction with the early Church confessions.

Christ's Death—An Essential Creedal Affirmation

When we discuss the significance of the death of Jesus Christ, we are not dealing with footnotes. The death of Christ is *the first statement in the earliest creed in the history of the Church,* a creed composed in Palestine in the late thirties or early forties of the first century, as virtually all scholars admit.[70] Paul says he received this creed from others who preceded him and passed it on, in classic rabbinic style, to the Corinthians, not as an archaic oddity but as a fact of vital and primordial significance for their salvation.[71] Christ's death was believed by the entire early Christian church. Here is how Paul puts it: "For what I received I passed on to you as of first importance: that Christ died for our sins according to the Scriptures" (1 Cor. 15:3). Without this affirmation, there is no Christianity. With less creedal formality, Paul constantly reaffirms this confession: "We believe that Jesus died" (1 Thess. 4:14); "we are convinced that one died for all" (2 Cor. 5:14).[72] So important is the death of Christ that Paul can even say: "I resolved to know nothing while I was with you except Jesus Christ and him crucified" (1 Cor. 2:2). So important is the death of Christ that it summarizes Paul's entire message: "We preach Christ crucified" (1 Cor. 1:23). So important is the death of Christ that it defines the preaching of all the apostles, as Paul explicitly states—"Whether it was I or they [Peter and the other apostles], this is what *we* preach, and this is what you believed" (1 Cor. 15:11).

Why is the death of Christ primordial?

Christ's Death Is the Only Answer to the Human Predicament

A doctor who tells you to take aspirin twice a day when your pain is from a serious blood cancer is no doctor at all, but a killer.

The cosmos is dying, not evolving to higher and higher forms, as apostate theological doctors tell us. The biblical prognosis from Doctor Paul is straightforward: the righteous law is killing us,[73] for it is the written document of the dispensation of death[74] and condemnation.[75] The original law, which Paul cites—"In the day you eat you shall die"[76]—judicially applies the inevitable consequences of sin. This "holy, righteous and good"[77] commandment, "intended to bring life," actually "brings death."[78] "Sin leads to death"[79] or "works death,"[80] hence the statement, "The wages of sin is death" (Rom. 6:23). Fallen, sinful human beings are "dead in their trespasses and sins"[81] because "no one is righteous," all are responsible, "and without excuse."[82] All must stand before the judgment seat of Christ[83] on the day "when God will judge men's secrets through Jesus Christ" (Rom. 2:16). This dread consequence of sin is both spiritual and physical. This is why "the corruptible cannot inherit the incorruptible."[84] As human beings, we are always faced with the result of sin, the implacable "last enemy,"[85] death.

Doctor Paul tells us that there is nothing humanity can do about its fatal disease. "Flesh and blood cannot inherit the kingdom of God" (1 Cor. 15:50). Our situation is without hope. This is still true, in spite of the giddy intoxication of our sophisticated twenty-first century, which believes in the coming of a new world order of justice and liberation. Human optimism has never been more ill-founded. Our sex-obsessed, over-entertained, emotionally- and morally-crippled culture has no inner resources to bring on utopia, even if such were a human possibility. Only some outside force could bring about an ideal global community. Alas, past history and a dose of realism indicate that such dreams, if imposed by power-hungry global leaders with technological and occultic-spiritual resources, would inevitably produce a moral, spiritual, and social nightmare.

No inner resources, no going within, no dreams of empire (however global and sustainable), no ordinary power can lift the moral curse from humanity's impotent shoulders. Says Paul, we are "powerless."[86] We need outside help from a source outside creation, namely the power of God the Creator, to conquer the immense power of sin and death. According to Paul, "The message of the cross . . . is *the power of God*" (1 Cor. 1:18).

Isaac Lichtenstein, after working for forty years as a dedicated Hungarian Jewish rabbi, was finally moved by "the greatness and *power*" of the gospel message. In 1909 he wrote, after having read the New Testament for the first time: "All seemed so new to me and yet it did me good like the sight of an old friend. . . . I had thought the New Testament to be impure, a source of pride, of selfishness, of hatred, and of the worst kind of violence, but as I opened it I felt myself wonderfully taken possession of. A sudden glory, a light flashed through my soul. I looked for thorns and found roses; I discovered pearls instead of pebbles; instead of hatred, love; instead of vengeance, forgiveness; instead of bondage, freedom."[87]

This is how the first-century rabbi, Paul, saw it too.

Christ's Death for Us

For Paul, Christ dies not primarily as a stirring example of individual fortitude, a quality sometimes found in ancient rabbis.[88] He died supremely as a substitute. He passively submitted to God's righteous judgment and was "made a curse *for us,*"[89] "made to be sin *for us.*"[90] Paul's whole argument is based on the fact that death as a noble example does us no good. This is why he says: "When we were still powerless, Christ died *for* the ungodly" (Rom. 5:6). He cites a word from the historical Jesus at the Last Supper: "This is my body, which is *for you*" (1 Cor. 11:24). In Old Testament language, Paul declares that "Christ, our Passover lamb, has been sacrificed"[91] for us. These two small words, *for us,* occurring in nineteen phrases describing the death of Christ, embody the towering truth at the heart of the gospel and at the center of a theistic worldview.

Modern pagan spiritual leaders offer another perspective: "Only by *reinventing ourselves at a profound level* will we release the Earth Community from its present impasse."[92] For these naïve souls, the salvation of the planet rests on *human* capability. The coming utopia will be a *human* achievement. These two views of human capacity are diametrically opposed. Only one can be true. I take the biblical approach. If we did not create the world, we certainly cannot save it.

"While we were still powerless,"[93] says Paul, God acts *for us.* The creedal statement noted above includes the reference to Scripture and the phrase *for our sins.* The God of the Old Testament "demonstrates his own love *for us* in this: While we were still sinners, Christ died *for us.*"[94] Marcus Borg's denial of Christ's death as "the act of God on my behalf"[95] flies in the face of the earliest statement of the Christian gospel and the whole point of the Bible's message, expressed so poignantly in the Book of Hebrews: "By the grace of God he ... taste[d] death *for everyone*" (Heb. 2:9).

Christ's Death—Justice Served

Since the true human problem is moral offense against the Creator, all autonomous human projects for global unity and justice only compound the problem. Our utopian projects are covered with the fingerprints of sometimes well-meaning but always sinful, selfish, fallible human beings. Such structures will *always* implode. Any hope for setting the cosmos right depends on righting the original, specific wrong. Since God established the universe under a moral agreement between himself and Adam and Eve, the redemption of creation must respect that structure. The righteous God who set up the moral structure of the universe this way must solve creation's deep problem in a moral, law-abiding way. Because the universe has a moral character, reflecting the character of God, Paul's theology of cosmic redemption is full of legal terminology. In his saving of creation, God cannot do it any old way. He had to do it in a particular way. In the words of Paul, God had "to demonstrate his justice . . . so as to be just and the one who justifies" (Rom. 3:26).

The early creed states that Christ died "according to the Scriptures." In the Old Testament, God promises to "swallow up death forever."[96] He promises to "blot out your transgressions . . . and remember your sins no more" (Isa. 43:25). God's Servant would be a "guilt-offering"[97] who would be "pierced through for our transgressions, and crushed for our iniquities,"[98] and would "bear the sins of many."[99] As in everything, the New Testament clarifies the Old, for in the gospel this old promise becomes reality. The psalmist reminds the Lord: "With you there is forgiveness" (literally, "atonement").[100] Paul sees in Christ's death the goal of the Old Testament's sacrificial system. "God presented him as a sacrifice of atonement."[101] The addition of the phrase, "in his blood," refers to the Old Testament background of the Day of Atonement[102] where innocent blood covers sins. It is in Christ that this sacrificial system reaches its great and effective fulfillment.[103] We are "justified through his blood."[104] On the cross Christ "canceled the written code, with its regulations, that was against us and that stood opposed to us; he took it away, nailing it to the cross" (Col. 2:14).[105] By his death, Christ "condemned sin,"[106] so that "there is therefore now no condemnation" (Rom. 8:1). On the Day of Atonement the priests were to "sound the trumpet throughout your land" (Lev. 25:9). Paul assures us that there is a "last trumpet,"[107] signaling Christ's defeat of "the last enemy," death.[108]

Christ's Death—True Relationships Restored

Adam's sin shattered the relationship between God and creation, thus abusing God's trust and confidence. That rupture brought down God's righteous, divine wrath[109] and produced a relationship of enmity instead of intimacy. In our sinful state we are "God's enemies"[110] and our minds are "hostile to God."[111] Hostility to God the Creator, who is the true source of life and peace, creates "the dividing wall of hostility"[112] between creatures, particularly the hatred between Jews and pagans. Because Christ's death solves the first, essential problem between sinners and God, it can also respond to the second—broken relationships between sinners. Our human offenses are against the Creator, and we need reconciliation *with* the Creator, not liberation *from* the Creator. It is the Creator/Father who provides this reconciliation through his Son.

PEACE

Christ's death brings about the end of hostilities between the Creator and the creature. "When we were God's enemies, we were reconciled to him through the death of his Son . . ." (Rom. 5:10). In spite of God's righteous wrath, Paul calls him "the God of peace"[113] or "the Lord of peace,"[114] and his message "the gospel of peace."[115] The message is that Christ's death "has destroyed . . . the dividing wall of hostility[116] by making peace through his blood, shed on the cross."[117] "For he himself is our peace."[118] The "dividing wall"[119] is not only between Jews and Gentiles, but also between God and the sinner, because Christ preaches peace both to Jews and to pagans.[120]

The restoration of communion with God the Creator through Christ's death is the necessary event that restores the relationships between fallen human beings among themselves. "Christ has made the two [antagonistic enemies] one."[121] The effect of being reconciled to God produces reconciliation on the level of human relationships. Peaceful living together in the body of Christ becomes a genuine possibility and thus a major emphasis in Paul's application of the gospel to the life of believers.[122]

ACCESS

By removing hostility, the death of Christ restores *access* to God. Adam and Eve were ejected from God's presence. Through Jesus Christ, the door is open again. Through him "we have gained access by faith into this grace in which we now stand" (Rom. 5:2). "Access" also evokes the notion of the Holy of Holies in the temple, the place where God's Spirit lived, where only the high priest could go, once a year, covered by the sacrificial blood, to meet with God and to plead before him for the people. The Book of Hebrews develops this theme to show its fulfillment in the death of Christ. The author exhorts believers: "Therefore, brothers, since we have confidence to enter the Most Holy Place by the blood of Jesus, . . . let us draw near to God with a sincere heart in full assurance of faith" (Heb. 10:19, 22).

Knowing the dangers of entering God's holy presence, how can believers have "assurance" or "confidence"?

CONFIDENCE FROM A CLEAR CONSCIENCE

Because of the death of Christ, God can be "just and the one who justifies."[123] It is because God justifies that we can have peace with God and access into his presence. The great statement of the gospel is the confident declaration: "We have been justified."[124] We are accounted righteous because of Christ's righteousness, as if we had never sinned. Though we cannot "establish [our] own righteousness," we are given "the righteousness that comes from God"[125] as a "free gift."[126] Being justified or cleansed is the gift that grants us confidence to approach God, by his Spirit. We have confidence to be who we are in the world God made. We have confidence to address God as Father and believe that God hears our prayers. Here is a great Trinitarian declaration of the new status God grants: "Through him [Christ] we both have access to the Father by one Spirit."[127]

In order that the fallen universe may be transformed one day, it first must be cleansed and purged. The cross is thus a necessary moment in God's plan of redemption. We must conclude that Christ's death is

God's gift for the cleansing of creation. As Paul says: Christ "reconciles to himself *all things*, whether things on earth or things in heaven, by making peace through his blood, shed on the cross" (Col. 1:20).

With Christ's innocent blood falling from the cross and covering the earth, something immense had to happen—and it did!

Finished?

When Jesus cried out on the cross, "It is finished," and expired, there was a sense in which his earthly work was finished; but there was a part of it that was a long way from being finished. His active obedience to death on a cross was finished. Perhaps a good analogy is a woman in childbirth. When the baby arrives and the hard work of bearing that child is done, a huge sense of accomplishment and relief pours out of the mother, "It's finished! The baby's here!" However, she knows that she must now rear the child to maturity. In Jesus' case, his work on the cross was something like the birthing of the new creation. But redemption still had to see the child mature.

The irony of Jesus' death was that the last enemy apparently had won, for Jesus died a sinner's death bearing the sins of the world upon himself, doing what both Moses and Paul wished they could do, namely take the punishment of the people. As Paul put it: "I . . . wish that I myself were cursed and cut off from Christ for the sake of my brothers" (Rom. 9:3). What neither Moses nor Paul could do, God did by making the sinless Son to be sin for us.[128]

For redemption to be finished and applied to Adam's race, the last Adam had to be saved from sin and death. Before the resurrection can be of any import to the sons who would follow, it had to rescue the last Adam. Only when the first of many brothers was raised could it be significant for believers and the whole creation. As in his death, so in his own resurrection, the last Adam is the representative man. We need now to see how the resurrection is significant for Christ before it can be significant to raise the fallen cosmos.

In a very real sense, Christ is the first Christian.

Chapter 9

The Rebirth of Creation II: The Resurrection of Jesus Christ

Paul's message to pagans, ancient and modern, is stunning—*Utopia is coming, and I have seen it*. While "no eye has seen nor ear heard what God has prepared" for future utopian life,[1] Paul has seen the resurrected Jesus[2] and from the revelation of the Spirit, understands something of that reality.[3] Nothing in pagan philosophy or spirituality prepared Paul's world for such an announcement.[4]

Paul proposes the resurrection not as a religious myth or stirring poem. The Greek term *gospel,* which Paul always uses,[5] means "news story." The early Christian creed appeals to eyewitnesses[6] of an objective event that changed history. Addressing a Roman public official, Paul declares: "I am not insane, most excellent Festus. . . . What I am saying is true and reasonable. The king is familiar with these things. . . . none of this has escaped his notice, because it was not done in a corner" (Acts 26:25–26).

Paul lays before the court contemporary, provable events that would be reported on your local televised newscast. The news story is not the "simple" fact that someone walked away from a grave. This story is the ultimate scoop, the one event that brings the end of history as we know it. The resurrection of the man Jesus is a real, objective event, but it is also earth-shaking and unique—as unique as the original creation that got history going in the first place.

The resurrection is not *primarily* about Christians being spiritually raised with Christ, true though that is. It is not *primarily* an important element of a new, systematic description of the plan of God to save the world. It is not *primarily* a doctrine of how to live in this world. It is rather the declaration of a new, future utopian reality that has already come into existence at the moment of Christ's resurrection. In other words, all the terms that describe "resurrection life," even those that describe present Christian experience, actually describe, first and foremost, life in the new heavens and earth. Only in a secondary and partial sense do they relate to Christian living in the here and now. Quite simply, the gospel is the declaration of the certainty of God's coming cosmic utopia.

Pagan notions of utopia, whether a this-worldly utopia established by human ingenuity and deep spirituality, or the dream of the Elysian Fields that entranced Maximus of *Gladiator* fame, or the Buddhist notion of the future as absorption of the self into the divine—all clash with the reality of the creation and the intractable problem of human sin.

One can certainly identify with hopeful views of the future. We all want life to work out. As the French say, imitating the English, we all want life to have a "appy ending." Unfortunately, such optimism does not take into consideration humanity's overwhelming moral problems or the unavoidable reality of death. Ironically, the solutions from the radical left are in no way radical enough. The truth is, Christianity seems far too radical to believe.

We need to assert the radical message of Christianity in light of what is often alleged about it. Richard Grigg, the Roman Catholic theologian cited above, and author of the book *When God Becomes Goddess*, argues that traditional Christianity has gone "private." He claims that it is limited to the domain of personal experience and no longer speaks to the great issues facing humanity today, like war, hunger, ecology, scientific advances, and multiculturalism.[7] On the basis of this accusation, he calls for a new religiosity based on the goddess, one that focuses on a this-worldly utopia. In other words, he calls for the paganization of Christianity.

By emphasizing personal experience and personal salvation, modern Christianity has defined itself as an affair of private spirituality. For many, the gospel offers only the simplistic "Jesus and me." But if Christianity is not to be marginalized in a culture seduced by worldly utopic dreams, it must speak about more than personal experience. The essence of the Christian message is the radical transformation of this physical cosmos. A theologian of a century ago, Gerhardus Vos of Princeton Seminary, described with great clarity the true nature of the gospel: "Paul exhibits the resurrection as that towards which everything in Christianity tends; . . . Ours is a religion whose center of gravity lies beyond the grave in the world to come. . . . the thirst for the world to come was of the very substance of the religion of [Paul's] heart. He felt deeply that the believer's destiny and God's purposes with reference to him transcend all limits of what this earthly life can possibly bring or possibly contain."[8]

We need to understand the phenomenon of the resurrection in its proper, biblical context, as God's final creative act, producing utopia.

Resurrection: God's Second Creation Act

With the resurrection we are not dealing with a peripheral subject. Paul directly mentions the theme on fifty-six different occasions. Notable in Paul's vocabulary is the fact that he uses the verb "to raise" forty times, and thirty-nine of those times the verb is in the passive voice ("was raised"). This indicates that Paul deals with the resurrection from the perspective of the last Adam, that is, Christ, the true man. It is not Christ the divine Son raising himself from the dead, but God raising Jesus, the last Adam. God does not crucify Jesus. That is done by the rulers of this world.[9] God's great work is to raise Jesus from the dead, and thus begin the creation of a new humanity.

Resurrection: God's Creative Act

God as the active and transcendent Creator of all things is a classic confession of the Old Testament Scriptures. We read in the psalms: "For all the gods of the nations are idols, but the LORD made the heavens" (Ps. 96:5)[10] We find the same teaching in Paul.[11] God has acted to produce the cosmos. But in a similar vein, as Paul insists on thirty-nine different occasions, God is also the one who raises the dead. In both acts of creation—out of nothing and out of death—God is at work as the great author of life. This is equally the work of God the Spirit.

There is much written on the Spirit that is of great value, but there is one question that must not be avoided, namely, "What is *the* great contribution of the Spirit?" Ecstatic speech? Altered states of consciousness? The fruits of the Spirit? Spiritual enthusiasm in general? However partially right these various answers may be, the correct answer must surely be the Spirit's work of resurrection, the bringing into being of the new creation. Just as the Spirit was the agent of the original, physical creation,[12] he is also the one who brings into existence its future, glorified state. He is the "glory" and "power" of God who raised Christ,[13] and will raise us.[14]

In both epoch-changing events (creation and resurrection) God is the sovereign author who deploys his great power to bring about life. By its character as a cosmos-changing event, through the direct intervention of God, resurrection is comparable to creation.

Resurrection: The Goal of Creation

Resurrection is not an unforeseen or newfangled idea with no relation to creation. It is not a new plan by which God starts all over again, having seen the failure of creation through Adam's sin and devised plan B. On the contrary, Paul sees it as the necessary and final stage of God's intention for the physical cosmos, which Adam's sin only complicates.[15] In this case, God will not allow Adam's sin to "uncreate what God created . . . man's rebellion has not succeeded in destroying the natural order to which he belongs."[16] But creation was never God's final word, even without the event of Adam's rebellion. This is surely what Paul means when he says: "The spiritual [read "resurrectional"] did not come first but the natural [the original created order],[17] and after that the spiritual" (1 Cor. 15:46). The world order of creation was to be followed by the world order of the new creation. As a number of scholars note, Adam's testing in the garden was surely not to go on forever.[18] A successful passing of the test was to be rewarded by some sort of transformation. The last adam did past the test. In a context of sin, in the hostile wilderness rather than a perfect garden, he successfully went through the temptation[19] and was finally rewarded by resurrection.

Resurrection flows organically out of creation as its final state of being. Thus Paul says the "mystery," which is the divine revelation concerning resurrection, "was for ages past kept hidden in God, who created all things" (Eph. 3:9). The mystery is hidden in the Creator, so Paul finds the mystery deeply embedded in the Creator's work. Thus he cites the Genesis passage on the pre-fall establishment of marriage to teach about the work of Christ.[20] In other words, here, as in so many ways, the Old becomes patent in the New, just as the New is latent in the Old. The radical transformation of the creation in the case of the body of Jesus and the demonstration of its future possibilities is rooted in its glorious, miraculous creational beginnings.

One particular text of Paul, which we have already examined, says this better than any other—1 Corinthians 15:45, "And so it is written, 'The first man Adam became a living being.' The last Adam became a life-giving spirit" (NKJV).

We look again at this text because its elements stand like two book-ends, embracing the full extent of God's plan for the universe. In these two lines Paul evokes both creation and resurrection, as represented by the two Adams. Our text comes at the end of a letter that Paul sent to a troubled church. Every chapter, except the last, deals with problems; and the fifteenth chapter deals with the greatest of them, the Corinthian view of resurrection. In verse 45 in particular, Paul gives a definitive answer to the Corinthians, who are tempted to adopt a pagan view of God and the world. Paul challenges them by confronting them with the biblical revelation of God, Creator and Redeemer of heaven and earth.

By "living being," as its other uses in the first few chapters of Genesis indicate, Paul is referring to created, physical animal life.[21] This term, "living being," is another form of the expression "natural" found in the immediate context, verses 44 and 46,[22] so it refers to natural, created life. Adam "became" what he previously was not. He went from nonexistence to existence.[23] So in the first phrase Paul is speaking about the coming into being of human, natural life at creation.

In the second part of the verse, about the last adam, there is no verb, which has led a number of translations to supply one, often giving the rendering "the last Adam *is* a life-giving spirit."[24] This translation makes Paul refer to Christ as the unchanging Son of God, the one who always *is* a life-giving spirit. Unfortunately, such translations miss entirely what Paul is saying. In focusing on the two Adams, he is speaking about the *history of humanity*. Though not repeated, the verb is unambiguously and clearly presupposed. The verbal phrase is, literally, *became into*. *Became* is lacking in the second phrase, but *into* is repeated. An English stylistic equivalent would be: "One of the twins *went into* the drug store, the other *into* the bakery." To translate this sentence the way some scholars translate 1 Corinthians 15:45, we would have to say, "One of the twins *went into* the drug store, the other *is in* the bakery." When we put *became* back into the phrase, Paul's teaching is very clear. He is teaching that, like the first Adam, who "became a living being" at a moment in time, so the last Adam also "became" something, specifically, "a life-giving spirit," at a particular moment in time.[25] For the first Adam that event was creation. For the last Adam that event was the resurrection. When Paul says he became a *spirit*, he is presupposing his statements about the resurrection body in verses 44 and 46, which tell us that the body is raised "spiritual." In other words, the future, resurrected state of the body is "spiritual."

This verse thus teaches that God is the author of two complementary foundational events that determined the lives of the two representative Adams. Each gives rise to life, one to this-worldly created human existence and the other to resurrected human existence in the eternal presence of God. As Paul shows in the next verse,[26] this was God's intention all along. The *physical* was first, then the *spiritual.*

Resurrection: A Bodily Reality

Paul describes the resurrection the way the French eat a good meal.

Most memorable French meals are accompanied by a mouth-watering, rich and creamy sauce. No Frenchman would commit the culinary heresy of eating such a meal without bread. The bread means that there will be *nothing* left of the meal when he is done. The plate will be as new, totally empty. This is the way Paul describes God's act of resurrection. The radical act of resurrection leaves no remainder. There is nothing left on the plate. There is no embarrassing body in the tomb.

Paul's language does not suggest that the spiritual *eliminates* the physical. In no sense does he imply that God discards the physical and starts again by creating a brand new spiritual reality. Much of modern biblical scholarship wants you to believe this, dismissing the bodily resurrection of Christ as an example of the primitive and legendary faith of the early church. According to the most influential New Testament scholar of the twentieth century, Rudolf Bultmann, "The resurrection, of course, simply cannot be a visible fact in the realm of human history . . . [Paul thinks] he can guarantee the resurrection of Christ as an objective fact by listing the witnesses who had seen him risen. But is such proof convincing?"[27]

This deep confession of skepticism, rejecting Paul's arguments out of hand, rang through the halls of learning of the twentieth century, producing generations of Bible teachers in lockstep with their skeptical mentors.

The contemporary spiritual child of such teaching is the *Jesus Seminar*, which has declared its opposition to bodily resurrection: "Informed Christians know that the Easter narratives in the Gospels are not literal accounts of historical events that supposedly took place during the six weeks after the crucifixion. They also know the 'resurrection' did not happen on the morning of Easter Sunday, or on any other day in time."[28]

At their meeting to study the resurrection, Jesus Seminar scholars agreed that the body of Jesus undoubtedly decayed in the usual way.[29] Such a conclusion about the resurrection automatically makes Christianity into a "privatized" religion, since each believer is free to define "Christ" by some amorphous spiritualized principle rather than being reconciled to God, as Paul says, "by Christ's physical body through death."[30] Having destroyed the universal objectivity of Christ's resurrection, these scholars then accuse Christianity of being a privatized religion.

The certitude concerning the impossibility of Jesus' physical resurrection is based on two arguments: (1) the "legendary" character of the Gospel accounts of the empty tomb, and (2) the absence of the "empty tomb" in Paul's writings.

The first argument is based upon a subjective judgment about the Gospels and flows from antisupernatural presuppositions about the world. The second argument proves superfluous if Paul arrives at the same conclusions about the resurrection without mentioning the words "empty tomb." Paul adds weight to the resurrection with his own, creative support, making two arguments in favor of Christ's physical resurrection rather than just one. Does the fact that Paul fails to mention Mary and the virgin birth mean he rejects what the Gospels affirm about the incarnation? Hardly. We know he does believe in the miracle of the incarnation, but he gets there by a different route.

Paul does not mention the empty tomb;[31] but if the resurrection is the fulfillment of creation, and is its very goal, then creation cannot be "left behind." If reconciliation means reconciliation with the Creator, then creation is restored, not destroyed. Numerous are the ways Paul makes this point. The resurrection body is related to the physical body[32] the way the full-grown plant is organically connected to the seed.[33] "The mortal puts on immortality."[34] "The perishable clothes itself in imperishability."[35] Wolfhart Pannenberg, a German liberal systematic theologian, argues that "according to Paul, the transformation will occur to the present mortal body," because the corruptible body will put on incorruptibility.[36] The resurrection consists of giving life to a mortal body, not leaving it in the grave. This organic relationship, like that of a chrysalis to a butterfly, arises because the same God who creates the physical universe will also recreate it. Thus "the spiritual is not first, the physical is."[37]

Utopia Has Arrived: The Resurrection of Jesus Christ

The originating event of creation is stupendous. What little we now understand about the vastness of the physical universe makes the notion of the "time" before its creation and the power that brought it about mind-boggling. But if resurrection is creation's goal and fulfillment, then we have a second creative act of God that is just as baffling and mind-bending. Paul presents the resurrection of Christ as the first and decisive event in this final transformation of the universe. Christ's resurrection is prototypical of all other resurrections, so if we can say anything generally about resurrection, it has to based upon this partic-ular, defining event. Christ, the last Adam, is the federal head of the new humanity and the firstborn among many brethren, who represents all of humanity in this first step for humanity into the new existence. His new humanity determines the humanity of those represented by him, as well as the fate of the whole universe. Thus, the crucial question for Christian theology and for cosmology is the significance of the last Adam's own resurrection.

What happens to the last Adam at his resurrection? The Bible gives us some very specific answers to our question.[38]

What I am about to develop in this chapter may strike you as odd, but notice the underlying logic: *Everything on the Easter Sunday side of the resurrection is an aspect of life in the new heavens and the new earth. It is gained by Christ, either in fullness (in his case) or by anticipation (in the case of believers).* That is to say, new birth, adoption, redemption, justification, sanctification, baptism in the Spirit, and glorification are not primarily descriptions of the present state of believers. They are categories of the future, transformed universe that made its first appearance when God raised the physical body of Jesus from the dead. Only in a secondary sense are they then categories of present Christian experience. To put it another way, all that the believer presently experi-ences "in part," "by faith," the last Adam, at the resurrection, experienced "by sight" and in full measure.

Paul develops just such an argument in Ephesians. He thanks God for blessing believers "with every spiritual blessing in the heavenly realm."[39] Notice! They already have everything, but they have it "spir-itually," by faith. He then prays that the "eyes of your heart may be enlightened . . . that you may know . . . the riches of his [the Spirit's] glorious inheritance . . . and his incomparably great power . . . which he exerted by raising Christ from the dead" (Eph. 1:18–20). In other words, Christ's resurrection, produced by the power of God, is the objective source of these blessings. It is the utopia for which we long. This inheritance contains all the spiritual blessings we now have by faith and one day will have by sight, in fullness. The basic logic of his thought is expressed in the following example: since Christ, through the resurrection, was seated at the right hand of God, it can be said that *in Christ* believers also are seated in the heavenlies.[40] In what follows we intend to unpack the full implications of this programmatic statement.

Utopian Home: Christ's Resurrection as Adoption

Can we ever speak of the adoption of Christ without falling into adoptionist Christology? According to this heretical belief, the purely human Jesus of the Gospel accounts, with no relationship to the pre-existent Son, is adopted after his death into the Godhead as a divine being and at that specific moment "becomes" for the first time the Son of God. Though this heresy has existed nearly as long as the church, it also finds support among liberal exegetes of modern times who have claimed to see such an idea in the teaching of Paul. They read Paul's statement that at the resurrection Christ is *declared Son of God*[41] and argue that Paul thus "hellenizes" and "divinizes" the simple Jewish prophet to bring Christianity into line with the myths about "divine men" that are typical of the pagan mystery religions.

In Paul's thinking, however, adoption has a very different meaning, one totally foreign to such pagan notions, rooted instead in the Bible's view of reality. Adoption is put in the context of God and creation. God is Father and Creator, while humanity is his special creation. Adam is God's "son."[42] At the fall, Adam loses his status as "son" and becomes the original "prodigal son," banished into the exile of a far country east of Eden.[43] One of the earliest public statements of "adoption" is God's command to Moses: "You shall say to Pharaoh, 'Thus says the LORD,' "Israel is My son, My firstborn""" (Exod. 44:22 NKJV). This special, renewed relationship of sonship marks the Bible's vision of final salvation. The prophet Jeremiah declares that God's saving purpose is to be Israel's Father, and for Israel to be God's "first-born,"[44] a prophecy Paul sees fulfilled in the church.[45] To the church in Galatia, Paul declares: "Because you are sons, God sent the Spirit of his Son into our hearts, the Spirit who calls out, 'Abba, Father.' So you are no longer a slave, but a son; and since you are a son, God has made you also an heir" (Gal. 4:6).

In Romans, he repeats this idea: "You received the Spirit of adoption by whom we cry out, 'Abba, Father'" (Rom. 8:15 NKJV).

By this notion of adoption as son and heir, with the legal right to inherit a fortune, Paul directly evokes resurrection, for a few verses later on the fortune received by the heirs is defined as the resurrection of our bodies, which Paul also calls "the adoption of our bodies."[46] Our mortal, sin-stained bodies will be *adopted* by the Lord, the Creator, into the spiritual, heavenly realm, transformed into a state perfectly adapted for eternal life in the direct presence of the Lord.

What will happen to our bodies has already happened to the body of Jesus. His human flesh was "adopted" at his moment of resurrection. In other words, when Jesus was raised, the incarnate, corporeal reality of human existence that he took on in order to deal with sin was transformed—adopted—into the heavenly reality for eternal sonship in the presence of God the Father. He went on in, beyond the veil, "the author and finisher of our faith," as Hebrews 12:2 says. During his earthly life, the true Son, the last Adam and the faithful Israelite, was (like Israel) publicly declared to be God's chosen one, his "beloved son."[47] But at the resurrection that position of sonship is solidified and becomes a definitive reality. This is why Paul uses the phrase: "declared to be the Son of God with power . . . by the resurrection from the dead" (Rom. 1:4 NKJV).[48] What Moses in a veiled, prophetic manner foresaw,[49] Paul, in his statement about "adopted" Israel, declares triumphantly, publicly, and finally to the Roman world of his day.

In the person of Jesus, God has finally readopted creation. Those who claim to see adoptionistic Christology in this text, have failed to note that Paul is speaking about Christ's *human nature*.[50] It is Christ's human flesh, descended from King David, that is being *adopted* into the ultimate filial relationship with the Father that resurrection makes possible. What happens to Christ as firstfruits means that created humanity is adopted into a new, eternal utopian relationship with the Creator.

What is the pagan alternative? Go within, find our inner divine spark, wait to shed our fleshly shells, and then fly off as pure divine spirits to become one with the great divine Spirit inhabiting all things. But if there is a Father/Creator, he must do a work of transformation. His miraculous act of resurrection both adopts our bodies for endless life with him and yet maintains them as part of our individual identity. They thus remain as signs throughout eternity of the necessary separation between the Creator and the creatures in which creatures always will find their true bliss. We will always be sons; he will always be Father—a structure the Bible constantly holds out as the great purpose of God.

Utopian Beginnings: Christ's Resurrection as New Birth

I grew up from my infancy in a church in Liverpool, England, where my dad played the organ and led the choir and where my mom was number one soprano and chief tea maker. I felt envious of really notable sinners. These colorful souls gave sensational testimonies of a life of past sin (including lurid details of wine, women, and song), and of a dramatic experience of grace. They encountered the miracle of the *new* or *second birth* and would cite Paul's well-known text: "If anyone is in Christ, he is a new creation: old things have passed away; behold, all things have become new" (2 Cor. 5:17 NKJV). As a kid who remembered no "pre-faith" life, I would wonder how such a deeply marking experience could ever be true for me. Oh to be "born again" in such a conclusive and convincing way! I longed for my "old things" to be really bad and for the "new" to be truly pure.

Like all believers, Christ had a "second birth," not as the eternal Son,[51] but as the "incarnate" last Adam. His first birth took place in the year 4 B.C.,[52] when he was "born of a woman,"[53] "born of the human family of David"[54] in the fifteenth year of the reign of the Roman emperor, Tiberias Caesar.[55]

He was "born again" at the resurrection. On the cross he died. He was so dead, says Paul, that he was buried.[56] At the moment of his resurrection, he "became a life-giving spirit"[57] and "the first-*born* of many brothers."[58] Notice the radical change suggested by these verbs. While it might sound strange at first to speak of Christ being *born again,* this is exactly what Paul says, citing an Old Testament psalm: "You are My Son; today I have begotten You," and then adds this commentary: "God has fulfilled this . . . in that He has raised up Jesus" (Acts 13:33 NKJV). Thus the spiritual *new birth* of the believer—"if anyone is in Christ"[59]—depends so much more on what happened physically to Christ at the resurrection than on any subjective, even dramatic personal experience of grace in the life of the believers.[60] I wonder if the millions of "born-again" Americans understand this. The "new creation" may not be limited to personal experience. It is the state of affairs brought on by the first, decisive change in the old creation that occurred on Easter morning, when, as one popularized translation puts it, "Jesus busted out of the grave." This is what Paul means when he uses the term "new creation" elsewhere.[61] The "all things have become new" evokes not human decisions and sensational behavior changes, nor even, in the first place, the objective event of personal spiritual regeneration, but God's mighty act of raising the dead body of Jesus from the grave, and thus producing the total, history-changing *new birth* transformation of the last Adam.[62] The empty tomb is the first crack in the physical universe, announcing its glorious transformation. God acted in *birthing* Jesus at the incarnation. He acted in *rebirthing* Jesus at the resurrection. Only on this divine generation can we depend. Christ's "new birth," like the first lark of spring, is the first exemplar or the prototype of the "new heavens and the new earth."

Utopian Perfection: Christ's Resurrection as Redemption

Pawn shops still exist. In the movie the *Music Box* a lawyer/daughter defends her father, an American Hungarian immigrant who is accused of past crimes against humanity during the Nazi occupation of Hungary. Acquiring by chance a thirty-year-old pawn ticket, she pays the pawn shop owner the amount borrowed—as a matter of fact a piddling sum—and *redeems* a Hungarian music box. To her horror, it contains all bad news. She discovers, tucked inside the box, damning photos of her father as a Nazi executioner.

Christ's redemption is all good news. Paul describes the death of Jesus as the paying of a sum of money to redeem people stuck in the pawn shop of sin. In other words, salvation can be described as deliverance by the paying of a ransom.[63] Oliver O'Donovan's comment is helpful here: "When we describe the saving work of Christ by the term 'redemption' we stress the fact that it presupposes the created order. Redemption suggests the recovery of something given and lost. When we ask what it is that was given and lost, and must now be recovered, the answer is not just mankind, but mankind in his context as the ruler of the ordered creation that God has made. . . ."[64]

This is doubtless why Paul calls the final act of God "the day of redemption."[65] Interestingly, the future resurrection of believers is also described as a the *redemption* of our bodies.[66] The resurrection is the getting back of our bodies, redeemed out of the sinful state in which they are presently held. That our bodies are redeemed tells us something about the resurrection of Jesus.

Since Christ is the representative head of many brethren, "the first-born from the dead"[67] in his resurrection, Pauline logic suggests that if our resurrection is the redemption of our bodies, then so is the resurrection of the body of Jesus. His body was made to be sin and needed to be bought back, redeemed out of death. In the case of Christ, his holy life pays his own ransom price. This payment covers us too—because of God's condescending love.

The gospel is the most amazing thing you've ever heard. The Creator of life becomes the firstborn from among the dead. This shows to what length God will go to show his love to us, in order to redeem us from death. *In a monistic universe there is no condescension.* It is strictly a DIY culture: "Do it yourself." Everything and everybody are divine; so everybody deserves everything, and no act is an act of condescension.

Only in a theistic universe does loving condescension have any meaning. The only solution to human problems, the only demonstration of constraining love, the unique declaration of unmerited favor/grace—these are to be found only in a theistic universe. "Going within" will not find them. "Going within" the self to find one's own divinity is not only foolish, but it does not work. "The heart is deceitful . . . and desperately wicked. Who can know it?" (Jer. 17:9 NKJV). "Going within" is folly of titanic proportions.

Our access to God depends entirely upon him and his act of redemption for us. The soul who goes within goes astray. The gospel of the new spirituality is sugar-coated poison. Our flesh is weak;[68] no good dwells in it;[69] it is a slave of sin;[70] it cannot please God.[71] This is loving condescension. "What the law was powerless to do in that it was weakened by the sinful nature, God did by sending his own Son in the likeness of sinful man to be a sin offering" (Rom. 8:3).

Redemption emphasizes the theme of God's acting for us. Provision is made for us of a ransom price we could never pay. This is an arrangement one can hardly resist, for at the end of the transaction we get something we could never afford—resurrected, redeemed bodies in a utopian life with God.

Utopian Justice: Christ's Resurrection as Justification

The Bible promises a life with no tears, no sighing, no bad conscience, no nights of moral agony, but rather a life of peace and love with God and man—all this because of justification. It is true that one of the essential affirmations about Christian experience is the gift of justification. Paul says it better than anyone: "Therefore, since we have been justified through faith, we have peace with God through our Lord Jesus Christ" (Rom. 5:1). But there are good reasons for thinking that Jesus' experience of being justified precedes ours and has to do with the Spirit's work of raising him from the dead.[72] But in what sense?

In what is doubtless an early confession of the church, incorporated by Paul in his letter to Timothy, we read about Christ that "He appeared in flesh; He was justified by the Spirit or in the spirit."[73] Since these two phrases are parallel, with the same prepositions "in" (Greek, *en*), since he appeared *in* the flesh, then it makes more sense to read, "justified in the spirit." Since the domain of the Spirit is resurrection life, it suggests that we understand Christ's justification as the result of the resurrection. This is how it works.

By the resurrection God effectively declares Jesus as truly "just." The resurrection vindicates him in the manner of the righteous sufferer of the Old Testament who waits on God: "He who vindicates me is near: who then will bring charges against me?" (Isa. 50:8). Thus the Lord promises his chosen ones: "'No weapon forged against you will prevail, and you will refute every tongue that accuses you. This is the heritage of the servants of the LORD, and this is their vindication from me,' declares the LORD" (Isa. 54:17).[74] In this way, the resurrection justifies or vindicates Jesus. He who was identified with sinners and died under the curse is by the resurrection declared to be who he really is, the truly righteous one.[75] Resurrection is his reward for a righteous life but is also the cleansing of a body that had been made to be sin.[76] The sermon of Peter five weeks after the resurrection and a fifteen-minute walk from the empty grave says it all:

this man, . . . you crucified and killed by the hands of wicked men. But *God raised him up, having freed him from death, because it was impossible for him to be held in its power.* David says concerning him, "For you will not abandon me to the grave, or let your Holy One see decay." . . . Fellow Israelites, I may say to you confidently of our ancestor David that he both died and was buried, and his tomb is with us to this day. . . . David spoke of the resurrection of the Messiah. . . . This Jesus God raised up, and of that all of us are witnesses (Acts 2:23–32).

What we could not merit, Jesus did. This is what the Christian gospel declares. Our justification and right to resurrection depend entirely on Christ's merited justification and hard-won resurrection. In order to be "the first born from the dead,"[77] he had "to reconcile to himself all things . . . by making peace through his blood shed on the cross" (Col. 1:20). Christ's death and his resurrection constitute the essence of the Christian gospel. The paid penalty and the incredible reward come with no points, no upfront fees, no commercial sweet-talk, no hidden costs. The fine print pledges a divine lifetime guarantee, no strings attached.

God could raise Jesus because he was just. On the contrary, we stand no chance. Our sinful, mortal bodies must rot in the grave. They can only be raised by being covered by Christ's justice, which is exactly what the gospel declares. "He [Christ] was delivered over to death for our sins and raised to life for our justification" (Rom. 4:25). When you think about it, only theism has really good news—a utopia of true justice.

The resurrection is thus the great event of divine theodicy, that is, the moment where God is shown to be the good and just Creator and Redeemer. While it is true that in the resurrection of Christ "the moral order was publicly and cosmically vindicated by God,"[78] it is also true that by this same event God himself is vindicated. The fallen world seems to vindicate the Gnostics who call the Creator evil. The resurrection vindicates God as "just and the justifier of all those who have faith in him."[79]

Utopian Intimacy: Christ's Resurrection as Reconciliation

From the divine glory and the trinitarian intimacy of heaven, the eternal Son humbles himself to take on the form of a human servant, "even death on a cross."[80] He comes to "seek and save those who are lost," those who are "without God and without hope in the world," in the far country of death, reaching out to publicans and sinners where they are.[81] Humanity, says Paul, is at enmity with the Creator;[82] and in his identification with sinners, Christ goes so far as to be so identified with sin so as to become "an object of wrath,"[83] incurring the wrath of God against sin.[84] Thus, in the cross, he is forsaken by God and communion with his Father is broken.[85]

At his resurrection he achieves *reconciliation* with God so that "we now have access to the Father":[86] "But now *in Christ Jesus*, you who once were far off have been brought near . . . reconciled . . . to God" (Eph. 2:13, 16). Paul speaks about "being with Christ which is far better,"[87] even when compared to present Christian experience.

This access for the believer *in Christ Jesus* is possible because such reconciliation is first experienced by Christ himself. Christ "was raised from the dead and seated at his [God's] right hand in the heavenly places."[88] If we are "seated in the heavenlies,"[89] with "boldness of access,"[90] it is because Christ already has gained it. "Seated at God's right hand" means, in the first place, that the last Adam has been given access to the Father and knows the joy of personal communion. Christ as the last Adam suffers no loss of individuality in the experience of resurrection. He is not spiritually absorbed into eternal nothingness. He has a place at God's right hand, in God's presence. As with all believers, the resurrection gains uninterrupted access for him into the presence of the personal God of the Bible.

At his resurrection Christ achieves both his own reconciliation and "the reconciliation of all things."[91] As the last Adam he delivers all things from the vanity of the fall; and in him they are reconciled, that is, brought back to God in a new and glorified form of utopian peace and intimacy.

Utopian Union: Christ's Resurrection
as Baptism in the Spirit

We so often have things backwards. We immediately identify the Spirit
with exotic, "spiritual" phenomena. Some have found the measure of
the Spirit's work in manifestations of uncontrolled laughing, shaking, or
barking. Some look to sensational emotive expression and mystical
states of altered consciousness. In this realm, pagan spirituality has as
much to offer. On a less exotic level, Christians often identify the Spirit's
work with enthusiasm, great piety, holy living, or individual regeneration. We forget—and some have never been told—that the greatest
work of the Spirit was in the creation of the physical world and in its
transformation through the resurrection of Jesus Christ. In this work,
pagan spirituality has nothing to offer. The physical resurrection must
be the starting point of Christian teaching on the Spirit. Just as the Spirit
is the agent of the old creation, he is equally the agent of the new.[92]
Every other work of the Spirit in the present, however it may be defined,
is but a limited foretaste of the great power already deployed by the God
who made the heavens and the earth, in the raising of Jesus. This power
will one day be deployed in the raising of our mortal bodies.[93]

The Spirit is not only the divine *agent* who causes resurrection to
take place. At another level the Spirit empowers the *mode* of resurrection life. The Spirit's own character determines how human beings will
live in God's utopian world. Gerhardus Vos noted that Paul's enigmatic
statement that Christ was raised from the dead "according to the Spirit
of holiness" had to do with the *mode* of the resurrection. *Flesh* and
spirit "were two successive stages in [Christ's] life."[94] He noted that in
this text Paul makes two strictly parallel statements. He is recounting
how Christ was "born *out of* the seed of David *according to* the flesh,"
and then how, literally "*out of* the resurrection, he was declared Son of
God with power *according to* the spirit of holiness."[95] If *flesh* marked
the character of the earthly life the Savior led, then *holy spirit* describes
the character of the life of the resurrection.[96]

In support of this is another text of Paul we have already examined,
which speaks of Christ as the one: "who was manifested in the flesh,
vindicated in the spirit."[97] *Flesh* and *spirit* are the two domains in which
the humanity of the last Adam, in the history of redemption, has taken

up his abode, the latter, *spirit,* in a definitive sense. This is confirmed by how Paul describes the future life as compared to the present physical life. He calls it "the spiritual."[98] Enveloping as it does the whole of future existence, just the way "the natural"[99] envelops the whole of created existence, again suggests that *spirit* evokes the kind of utopian resurrection life of the future. This same idea is present when Paul speaks of the new life as lived "according to the spirit,"[100] in comparison to the old life lived "according to the flesh."[101] Is this also what Paul means when he states that at the resurrection the last Adam "became a life-giving spirit," a prototype human being of the new creation?[102]

Having examined Paul's texts, we conclude that if the Spirit is the manner of life of the resurrection, then the future life is the true domain of the Spirit. From Paul we learn about the Spirit's present activity and about the character of "life in the Spirit." But these expressions are only pale reflections of utopian, spiritual life with God. Life in the Spirit now is already power, a sound, renewed mind,[103] holiness, purity, wisdom, righteousness,[104] light,[105] joy, peace, patience, goodness, gentleness, self-control, and the reality of a new mature man in the image of Christ, imbued with the mind of Christ. If we already know this sharper reflection of the image of God, then what will we be like in the utopian life? We will truly be like Christ, who, in his resurrection is the first example of a glorified man. How unthinkably glorious will be the intensification of our heavenly, resurrected spiritual life.

Utopian Destiny: Christ's Resurrection as Sanctification

It is appropriate to note, in thinking about the Spirit as agent and mode of the resurrection, that we have to do with the *Holy* Spirit, and that it was the *Spirit of holiness* who raised Jesus from the dead.[106] In other words, holiness and sanctification are an essential part of the resurrection.

What is holiness? Our thinking about holiness is another place where we tend to have it all wrong. We see saints as people who, over the long haul, with monumental personal effort, give proof of a marked, even unusual degree of commitment to living for others.

People like Buddha, Gandhi, and Mother Teresa come to mind. Most religions can boast of a few such people.

However, the definition of sainthood is much stricter in the Bible. In fact, its definition is so strict that not even Mother Teresa has a chance. In fact, God recognizes only one saint, Christ. He is the uniquely sinless one, the only human being never to have sinned.[107] Even the evil spirits address Jesus as "the Holy One [Saint] of God."[108] Though on this level, the Bible reduces the number of saints to one, on another level it gives the name "saints" to all who belong to Christ. Christians are called "those who have been sanctified";[109] Paul describes the Corinthians as those "who have been washed, . . . who have been sanctified."[110] The moral character of many in the Corinthian church makes this label particularly surprising. How can Paul give the name "saints" to people involved in in-fighting, sexual immorality, spiritual pride, and denial of the resurrection? Paul is not crazy. He is consistent. He can call Corinthian believers "saints" because he teaches that the whole of the Christian life derives from the work of Christ. Holiness is a gift. Nothing, including sanctification, is merited. To these same Corinthians Paul states that Jesus Christ has "become to them holiness/sanctification."[111]

Sanctification is not a gradually acquired set of holy actions that finally tips the scales in our favor. The generic meaning of the term, expressed already in the Old Testament, is the idea of setting things or people apart for *special use* by the Lord. So the holy vessels in the Jerusalem temple are not more clean or more golden than the vessels on King David's table in his palace. They are holy because they are set apart for God's special use in the temple rituals.

Certainly, Christ was set apart by the Father for his earthly ministry, and in his sinless life he demonstrated his holy character. But the resurrection marks a radical and definitive "setting apart" of Christ for his service to God.

Paul argues this in Romans: "Since Christ was raised from the dead, he cannot die again; death no longer has mastery over him. The death he died, he died to sin once for all; but the life he lives, he lives to God" (Rom. 6:9–10). Where is Christ now? He is in God's presence, and as the last Adam, is living for God. Before Christ's resurrection, death reigned over Jesus, since, in his human nature, he lived within the domain of sin, and was, in the flesh, subject to death—as his own death proves. However, the resurrection changed everything for Christ. At his resurrection, Christ was totally liberated from sin and death. At his resurrection, Christ's humanity was entirely and completely set apart for eternal life with God in the new domain of glorified humanity.

At the resurrection, God takes back what is his by resanctifying creation. Christ's redemptive work on the cross and in the resurrection places him as head over all things. As head, he subjects all things, sets all things in their rightful and reconciled places, "each in his own turn: Christ, the firstfruits; then, when he comes, those who belong to him" (1 Cor. 15:23). God will not allow the original order to be destroyed. At the end, with man in his rightful place, God's order will be restored and transformed.[112] In other words, as head over all things, the last Adam sanctifies, or rather resanctifies, the cosmos into its rightful place of "submission" to the will and design of God. The restoration of creation includes not just humanity but, as we shall see, humanity as it originally was, as ruler "over the works of your hands."[113] Thus the general resurrection and final transformation represent the complete sanctification of the cosmos, where everything finds again its rightful and ultimate place. The biblical utopia is a holy place.

Utopian Dominion: Christ's Resurrection as Ascension

The incarnation is God's condescension into a state of humiliation. The resurrection is man's ascension to a state of exaltation. God raises humanity in Christ to newness of life and cosmic dominion. "Jesus Christ . . . was raised to life . . . at the right hand of God" (Rom. 8:34). We have seen that the phrase "at the right hand of God" implies a place of personal intimacy in the presence of God, but it also expresses the notion of delegated dominion. The psalmist David prophesies the Messiah's lordship within the reality of the fall: "The Lord says to my Lord: 'Sit at my right hand until I make your enemies a footstool for your feet'" (Ps. 110:1).[114] The notion of dominion joins "sitting" with the idea of things subjected under one's feet. It picks up the great declaration of Adam's dominion over creation before the fall: "You made him ruler over the works of your hands; you put [or placed] everything *under his feet*" (Ps. 8:6). Adam shares something of the lordship of his maker, of whom it is said: "He parted the heavens and came down; dark clouds were under his feet" (Ps. 18:9).

Interestingly, this statement about Adam's and humanity's place in the first creation is used on three occasions by Paul to describe the new creation and the lordship of the new humanity, restored from its lost position in the fall. It is difficult to avoid the notion that something lost is being restored and glorified. In the great chapter on the resurrection, 1 Corinthians 15, Paul works out the implications of the resurrection for the future of the cosmos by citing the same Psalm 8—"For he 'has put everything under his feet.'"

In another text Paul cites this psalm, joining it with the notion of "being seated" and "being raised" to make the same point: "He [God] *raised* him [Christ] from the dead *and seated him at his right hand* in the heavenly realms, far above all rule and authority, power and dominion, and every title that can be given, not only in this present age but also in the one to come. And God *placed all things under his feet* and appointed him to be head over everything . . . who fills everything in every way" (Eph. 1:20–23).[115]

What is thoroughly amazing about these texts is that they apply the reality of universal lordship not to Christ as second person of the divine Trinity, but to Christ, the last Adam. With the dominion and rule originally granted to Adam and Eve,[116] Christ, the last Adam in his kingly role, submits all things to God's holy order.

In this sense, the resurrection elevates Jesus as cosmic judge. At Athens, Paul juxtaposes resurrection and judgment.[117] Death is not the end. After death there is the judgment. The books will be opened, wrongs will be righted, and sin will be punished. And he who went through the judgment, bearing sin, is appointed by God as the final Judge. Judgment will surely happen because a man has been found who has come through death and can judge with righteousness. "We must all," says Paul, "stand before the judgment seat of Christ."[118]

What is equally amazing is that Christ, being the first human being of the coming new order, shares his dominion with those united to him. In this kingly role of dominion, seated at the right hand of God, far above all principalities and powers, Christ is the prototype of a renewed humanity. He is the first born from the dead, the first born of many brothers. Here the last Adam becomes the first of a new humanity, and shares that reign with the people of the Messiah. Says Paul: "And God raised us up with Christ and seated us with him in the heavenly realms in Christ Jesus" (Eph. 2:6). This dominion is communal. The new humanity is also a community of many, not a collection of lone individuals. Thus says Paul, the saints will judge the earth and angels.[119] Christ as the true man, the last Adam, is our present and future model. When the cosmos is renewed we will fully share in that universal lordship, as the prophet Daniel announced long ago: "Then the sovereignty, power and greatness of the kingdoms under the whole heaven will be handed over to the saints, the people of the Most High. His kingdom will be an everlasting kingdom, and all rulers will worship and obey [or be given their rightful place beneath] him" (Dan. 7:27).[120]

BEYOND THE DOMINION OF ADAM

It is important to note that the last Adam is endowed with lordship that reaffirms but exceeds that exercised by Adam. The phrase, "all things under his feet," is expanded in the notion of the lordship ascribed to Jesus in the Christ hymn of Philippians. The rule of Jesus is not merely terrestrial. "At the name of Jesus every knee should bow in heaven and on earth and under the earth" (Phil. 2:10). This Adam will destroy "all dominion, authority and power.[121] In him is all God's fullness, and through him God will reconcile to himself all things, whether things on earth or in heaven."[122]

The phrase "all things" makes the same point. In redemption Christ achieves "the reconciliation of all things."[123] "All things" should be taken here as a reference to the created universe, not to some totally new things created from nothing. According to Paul, God is the Creator of "all things,"[124] and the first verse of the Bible makes clear what that is: "God created the heavens and the earth."[125] "All things" is "the heavens and the earth." As to the future, God's redemptive plan is to "bring all things in heaven and on earth under one head, even Christ" (Eph. 1:10). In this text, "all things" and "heaven and earth" joined together show that the object of resurrectional transformation is the entire universe of the original creation.

What Adam did for the earth, the last Adam will do for the entire cosmos. To emphasize the cosmic reach of this notion, Paul speaks of the "fullness of Christ."[126] In the Old Testament "fullness" (πλήρωμα) refers to totality[127] and the enormity of creation and of God's lordship over it. "The heavens are yours, and yours also the earth; you founded the world and all that is in it" (Ps. 89:11). The Creator Lord declares: "I know every bird in the mountains, and the creatures of the field are mine. . . . the world is mine, and all that is in it" (Ps. 50:11–12). Paul cites the well-known psalm of David: "The earth is the LORD's, and everything in it" (1 Cor. 10:26, citing Ps. 24:1). Thus the church that will share one day in this cosmic dominion is described as "his [Christ's] body, the fullness of him who fills everything in every way" (Eph. 1:23). To the church, Paul declares: "In Christ all the fullness of the Deity lives in bodily form, and you have been given fullness in Christ, who is the head over every power and authority" (1 Cor. 15:23). Christ, with the church, the end-time Adam and Eve, fills the universe the way the original Adam and Eve were to fill the earth.

We stand amazed before the vast scope of redemption, filtered through the theological mind of the apostle Paul and written down by the inspiration of the Holy Spirit of truth. But here is the great significance of the spatial sense of redemption and resurrection, as one scholar, with great depth perception, describes it: "It is *this* hostile, threatening space that Christ himself has invaded and occupied. . . . In its vertical and its horizontal dimensions, this alien space is converted into the Father's house, a place fit for human habitation. Since Christ fills this space and there is no space unoccupied by him, to dwell within this space is to be in Christ."[128]

In other words, this "space" is the original creation over which the last Adam now reigns. This is not some newly created space, known only to God. It is the original heavens and earth that God created *ex nihilo*, "from nothing." The new creation is not *ex nihilo*. It is the redemption of the old, brought back into submission to man and God and gloriously transformed.

God Overturns Vanity

The continuity of creation and resurrection has the following important consequence. The resurrection of Christ and his empty tomb is the first expression of God's reestablishment of ownership of the cosmos, retaking what is, in fact, rightfully his own, but lost through the fall. Over this "threatening space," even in the fall, God remains in control. Paul teaches that God subjected (the same verb which means "to set in its right place")[129] the fallen world to *vanity*.[130] Thus the curses of Genesis 3 are God's action to limit the effect of sin in a world that he still controls. In a sense, Christ's redemptive work is to participate in this vain subjection to vanity, for he bears the curse,[131] is subject to sin, is placed "under the law,"[132] and tastes this vanity for us all. But there is the hope of a renewed creation, subjected to the will of God, without vanity, where God is seen, without impediment, through the creation-claiming work of Christ as Lord of all. At the heart of this reclaiming and reordering of the cosmos is the resurrection, on which our own resurrection depends. The resurrection is the way in which everything is brought under divine lordship, as Paul explicitly says: Christ "who, by the power that enables him to bring everything under his control [*hupotasso*], will," by that same power, "transform our lowly bodies so that they will be like his glorious body" (Phil. 3:21).

God Reasserts Lordship over Creation

God owns the creation because he is its source and because he formed it to reflect his character of order and distinction. The new order established at the resurrection is the old order transformed.[133] In his saving act, God retrieves and restores fallen creation from the clutches of evil and death, and he transforms it through the obedience and resurrection of Christ. This way of looking at creation is what Paul teaches throughout his writings, and it has the strong support of Scripture. The Letter to the Hebrews says: "It is not to angels that he has subjected [set in its rightful place] the world to come, about which we are speaking" (2:5). It is to Christ as the last Adam. For the Hebrews text immediately adds: "But there is a place where someone has testified: 'What is *man* that you are mindful of him, the *son of man* that you care for him?'" (v. 6).

The final state must approximate the beginning. Adam is a vice-regent. God the Creator is the true King. Thus the picture of creation reoccupied and renewed, with things in their rightful place, is finally complete when the Son, as true man, sets himself in his rightful place in relation to God the Father.[134] "When he has done this," says Paul, "then the Son himself will be made subject to him who put everything under him, so that God may be all in all" (1 Cor. 15:28).

Before this majestic statement of completeness, one cannot avoid the sense that all will be right, all will be holy, all will be in its proper place, and the original good creation will be glorious.

Utopian Glory: Resurrection as Glorification

Glory means a state of utter perfection relative to what someone or something was meant to be. At the resurrection, Christ is raised in glory[135] by the glory of the Father.[136] His shining humanity reflects God's great intention for the race. Paul saw God's glory in the face of Christ.[137] In that face is to be seen the shimmering beauty of redeemed humanity reflecting the originating glory of God the Creator; man in God's image, transformed by resurrection power. As Paul would say, "raised in glory, imperishable, immortal, powerful, spiritual."[138] Paul cannot find enough body language to express this change from a "lowly body" to a "glorious body."[139] Just as created bodies have different glories,[140] so also will the body of the new creation, a body appropriate for a transformed, glorious universe where humanity is in right relationship with God and everything is in its rightful place.[141] This Jesus calls "the Kingdom in power,"[142] just as Paul calls the last Adam at his resurrection "Son of God in power."[143] This is the power of what is right, finally appropriate, and wonderfully glorious. At the resurrection this took place for Christ. He is the guarantor that it will take place for the entire cosmos.

When everything is finally in its rightful place, then the transformed cosmos will know its true and final glory, what Paul calls "the freedom of glory."[144] Delivered from vanity and purposelessness—the failure to bring glory to God[145]—the creation will serve its original, glorious purpose, of giving glory to God, the sovereign artist and Creator, "the Father of glory."[146]

A fabulous southern Californian sunset can only hint at the coming glory of the cosmos. If you have ever seen pictures from the Hubble telescope, you catch a glimpse of the glory of the created universe as it now is—millions of galaxies, each one as big or bigger than our own. Now try to imagine the glory of a transformed universe. It boggles the mind, but that is future glory!

The resurrection is the unique disclosure of the ultimate, optimistic truth about the nature of the universe. If anyone can deliver utopia, it is God the Creator through Jesus, the last and new man. He is the only perfect substitute, the one on whose shoulders the fate of the world turns. Only he can remove the stain of sin. Only he has been raised from the dead, the down payment of the transformed cosmos. If this is exclusivist, so be it.[147] Myths, wishes, half-truths, fallible human projects and programs for global justice, mixed with downright lies are impotent to bring about a true utopia. How foolish we would be to lose the certain hope of a real utopia by settling for temporary, sin-cursed human unity, or for feeble fables that promise the moon and deliver dust sandwiches.

Chapter 10

Utopia Now?

If utopia has already come with the resurrection of Jesus, why not utopia now? Why does the church have to live through what Paul calls "the last days," or "the evil days,"[1] marked by heresy, blatant sin, suffering, and persecution? Surely we are now living in the very opposite of utopia?[2]

Paul gives us an answer that doesn't sell very well in our culture of instant gratification. That answer is "wait." Ultimate pleasure is deferred. While utopia is now for Jesus, it is still future for the church. Would Paul have felt advertising pressure, were he announcing his message today? I doubt it. Throughout history, people have tried to put a falsely positive spin on Christian experience, but Paul knew his message would not be accepted, even in Roman times. He says to the Corinthians that if Christians are wrong about the future, then they get the worst possible deal in the present.[3]

When Paul was alive, many considered the Christian message sheer stupidity.[4] However, it had one thing going for it: it is true. For the Christian, the present is a time of deferred utopia, for there are important and essential things God still needs to do. Specifically, God must

- call a people
- form that people to be fit for the utopia to come
- empower that people in this world
- make that people a present witness of the utopian world to come.[5]

God Calls a People

The triumph of the last Adam would be hollow if he were the only beneficiary. But the last Adam is, like the first, the head of a race, and his victory gives rise to a new humanity. That is why Paul calls Christ "the firstborn from the dead" or "the firstborn of many brothers."[6] In the words of Hebrews, Christ "brings many sons to glory"[7] because he became "the source of eternal life to all who obey him."[8] Jesus came to announce utopia, to "seek and to save the lost."[9] The whole project of redemption depends upon making it known.

A vault of free money at the local bank is of no use unless people know about it. If there is phenomenal news that affects humanity about the coming utopia, then that news must be made known. The early church, beginning with its founder, was remarkably intentional about this. Jesus went around declaring: "The time is fulfilled, and the kingdom of God [his term for utopia] is at hand" (Mark 1:15 NKJV). Paul makes the great announcement: "Now is the time of God's favor, now is the day of salvation" (2 Cor. 6:2). Paul can say this because Jesus had already declared the same message to Zacchaeus, the Jewish apostate tax collector: "Today salvation has come to this house" (Luke 19:9). Indeed, Jesus began his ministry by announcing the fulfillment of Old Testament prophecy: "The Spirit of the Lord is on me . . . to proclaim the year of the Lord's favor" (Luke 4:18–19). Paul's expectation that every tongue will one day confess Jesus as *Lord* explains why he spends the greater part of his ministry going from city to city in the ancient world, from Jerusalem to Illyricum, which is modern Yugoslavia,[10] "preaching the good news about Jesus and the resurrection."[11] He wants to preach the gospel in Rome;[12] he plans to go to Spain;[13] he wants to go everywhere where the gospel has not been preached[14]—because to him was given the task of opening up the whole world to the gospel message. As the apostle to the pagans,[15] he headed the world-wide mission, already commissioned by Jesus, of "mak[ing] disciples of every nation."[16]

If this mission goes on longer than anyone expected, it is, in part, because of the forbearance of God.[17] Knowing the goodness of God, Paul says that God "wants all men to be saved and to come to a knowledge of the truth" (1 Tim. 2:4). If this is what God wants, if this is what Paul does, then this is surely a high priority for the church. According to Jesus, this announcement of utopia is to continue "until the end of the age."[18] Thus Paul exhorts the Ephesian believers to have their "feet fitted with a readiness to announce the gospel of peace."[19] These shoes are meant for talking! We are to speak the gospel everywhere and any-where. Paul's exhortation to the Ephesians mirrors the prayer request he has for them about his own ministry. Cooped up in a Roman prison, he says, "Pray also for me, that whenever I open my mouth, words may be given me so that I will fearlessly make known the mystery of the gospel, for which I am an ambassador in chains. Pray that I may declare it fearlessly, as I should" (Eph. 6:19–20).

"Woe to me," he says elsewhere, "if I do not preach the gospel."[20]

God's call announces that utopia is coming for those who believe, promising them an assured, eternal future, and a present foretaste of the good things to come. As the good news of utopia goes out in the world, people respond "by faith" as God's Spirit convinces them of their sin and need and includes them in the community of the justified, redeemed, adopted, Spirit-filled, sanctified, and glorified. Paul explic-itly affirms to the believers in Ephesus: "You also were included in Christ when you heard the word of truth, the gospel of your salvation" (Eph. 1:13). To be thus included in Christ means to be enrolled in the coming utopia Christ has brought into existence at his resurrection. In this time of mission and forbearance, such ones are "added daily" to the church, sometimes in the thousands.[21]

Clearly, in these "last days," evangelism is a present and major gospel priority, but its goal is not just numbers.

God Forms a People

There is a "calling of the pagans" for the purpose of "the sanctification of the pagans." Paul's goal is not only to reach as many pagans as pos-sible but to bring them to "the obedience of faith."[22] "This is the will of God," says Paul to his pagan converts, "your sanctification."[23]

Certainly Paul goes to Jews because the gospel is for the Jews first and foremost[24] and because the new people of God, made up of both Jews and pagans, demonstrate the momentous fact of reconciliation. The equivalent today would be reconciliation between Israelis and Palestinians. However, the decisive inclusion of the pagans in the people of God (which, in the plan of God, occurs after the all-Jewish event of Pentecost), and their subsequent sanctification, allows Paul to give the most complete account of the work of Christ. The pagans are in an extreme state of hopelessness—"without God and without hope in the world."[25] Their marked and obvious moral perversity[26] and their universal location (the ends of the earth)[27] enable Paul, to whom is entrusted the articulation of "the gospel of the Gentiles,"[28] to provide the most complete account of the depth and the breadth of divine redemption.

Paul's ministry as the apostle to the pagans has as its goal "that the Gentiles might become an offering acceptable to God, sanctified by the Holy Spirit."[29] Specifically, for pagans, sanctification is both the cognitive acquisition of the Bible's worldview[30] and also living it out in practical ways. God's forming and refining of a people is expressed in the biblical notion of *testing*.

The Fact of Testing

The Bible teaches more than love and peace. It contains tough demands. God is interested in how we live; and in a very real sense, his people are on probation. The psalmist David knows this and calls on the Lord: "Test me . . . and try me, examine my heart and my mind" (Ps. 26:2). Paul uses this same basic term *test* some thirty times. The faithful, mature Christian, who has "stood the test," is the one who has God's "approval."[31] There are many ways this process is described: reaching maturity;[32] growth from childhood to adulthood;[33] growing up into Christ;[34] running for the prize;[35] attaining to what lies ahead;[36] being built up into maturity;[37] and imitating Christ.[38] This process that Paul calls "every man's work," God tests by fire.[39]

It is surely an indisputable fact that testing is part of God's present plan for his people.

The Nature of Testing

God refines and tests his called-out people in two distinct ways: (1) through the hardships and difficulties inherent in this fallen world; (2) through their willing obedience to his laws.

HARDSHIPS AND DIFFICULTIES

I have a good friend who is a most competent lawyer, a natural athlete, a wonderful father, a successful "best-selling" fiction writer, and a mature and dedicated Christian. Recently he learned his youthful body had been invaded by a vicious, deadly cancer. As I worked on these pages, I received a call that another elder in our church has just finished his test, leaving his lovely widow to face her own, perhaps harder, test. Two years ago my own newborn grandson lived only nine hours before his testing was finished, leaving behind brokenhearted parents and family members who must put their faith to the test because of losing him.

Anyone who believes that becoming a Christian means the end of difficulties and hardships and the beginning of unending health and wealth does not live in the world I know, and has not read the Paul I read. "Suffering," says Bible scholar Thomas Schreiner, "was not a side effect of the Pauline mission; rather it was at the very center of his apostolic evangelism . . . demonstrating the truth of the Gospel."[40]

Not only did Paul live a life of constant suffering, but, without the least hint of sadomasochism, he made it his goal to share in the sufferings of Christ.[41] This was not something to be avoided. On the contrary, he actually sees suffering of one sort or another—sickness, famine, poverty, persecution—as an essential part of the growth in Christian maturity, and thus of the testing process. Finding one's comfort in God in the midst of suffering, Paul argues, is an essential element of Christian fellowship, for it gives others encouragement and comfort.[42] Individual suffering is the testing process that reveals the spiritual quality of "perseverance," which, says Paul, produces "character," literally faith that has stood the test. Such character then produces "hope," the sure expectation of participation in utopia.[43]

GOD'S LAW AND TESTING

In 1980 a Christian author wrote a book with an intriguing and insightful title: *A Long Obedience in the Same Direction*.[44] If the subtitle, *Discipleship in an Instant Society,* was already appropriate a generation ago, how much more is it relevant today, in our culture of lightning-fast personal computers and the instantaneous, far-reaching World Wide Web? A program of "long obedience" fits awkwardly with contemporary society's love affair with instant gratification.

With the subject of obedience, we raise here the much-debated question of the role of the law in the life of the Christian.[45] If we are freed from the law,[46] how can it be said that we must still obey it? There are also two versions of the law, the law from God the Redeemer and that from God the Creator.

The Law of Christ the Redeemer

In the history of redemption, Paul argues that law was given to make sin more obvious, and thus to bring Israel to Christ.[47] In the death and resurrection of Christ, believers are freed from the law that accuses us[48] but have become slaves to righteousness.[49] But what is righteousness? By what ethical standard do Christians regulate their conduct? Paul calls it "the law of Christ,"[50] or the "law of the Spirit."

Jesus declared that he had come to fulfill the Mosaic law,[51] which is what Paul says too: Christ "is the end [or goal] of the law."[52] This law, now liberated from the narrow context of the Mosaic theocracy, appears, in the teaching of Jesus in the Sermon on the Mount, as an ideal intensification of the law of Moses: "You have heard that it was said to the people long ago, 'Do not murder.'... But I tell you that any-one who is angry with his brother will be subject to judgment" (Matt. 5:21–22). This is the new law of the coming kingdom. Thus, for Jesus, the deep emotions of the heart, like anger and lust, break the law. Those of complete honesty and selflessness fulfill it. The same approach is found in Paul. The "desires of the sinful nature"[53] break the law; "gentleness, self-control,"[54] and "love"—these "fulfill the law."[55] Finally we have to say that the law given to Moses has become personified in Christ's sinless life. His moral achievement establishes a new and final publication of the law, "the law of Christ." As the ultimate expression of selfless love, Christ is the implied subject of 1 Corinthians 13, the biblical chapter on love. Thus in his person, he sums up the entire law of Moses, for Paul says: "The entire law is summed up in a single command: 'Love your neighbor as yourself'" (Gal. 5:14).

This end-time understanding of the law means that Paul will derive moral principles from the law of Moses, while not taking over the whole time-specific Mosaic economy. This he shows is the "proper" use of the law—"We know that the law is good if one uses it properly" (1 Tim. 1:8). In defending the payment of church leaders, Paul argues from Deuteronomy. He states: "For it is written in the Law of Moses: 'Do not muzzle an ox while it is treading out the grain.' Is it about oxen that God is concerned? Surely he says this for us" (1 Cor. 9:9–10). Used in this way, we uphold the law.[56] He cites[57] the fifth commandment of the Decalogue, "honor your father and mother,"[58] even reproducing the promise of long life on the earth; but he omits the phrase specific to the Mosaic theocracy—"[the land] the Lord your God is giving you."

Just as God gave the law to historical Israel through Moses for the purpose of redemption, so, through Christ, the Second Moses, that law is reinterpreted and republished for the new Israel of God, the church, which is under the obligation to live by it.

The Law of Christ the Creator

Through his death and resurrection, Christ is Savior. In his divine nature, Christ is Creator. Thus the reconciliation he achieves through his incarnation achieves nothing less than the reconciliation of fallen creatures with the Creator. This has enormous implications for present Christian living, since obedience to the structures of creation is part of the way God tests us and refines us.[59]

The sanctification of the Gentiles makes this abundantly clear. The Gentiles are those who are "without God,"[60] that is, without the Creator God of the Old Testament. This God the pagans do not know, or rather choose not to know, for they "do not honor" him nor do they "give him thanks"[61] as Creator. As we have already noted, Paul's great project is not only to preach the gospel to the Gentiles, but also to bring them to "the obedience of faith"[62] in order to present them as the people of God, as a pure virgin, holy, and without blemish, to Christ.[63] Moral and ethical purity is now demanded of those who once were the sexually immoral, idolaters, adulteresses, male prostitutes, homosexual offenders, thieves, greedy, drunkards, slanderers, swindlers,[64] involved in acts of creational distortion, who worshiped and served the creature rather than the Creator,[65] who "lived with lustful passion, like the Gentiles who do not know God"[66]—not just God the Redeemer but also, and perhaps primarily in this context, God the Creator.

Since redemption involves present reconciliation with the Creator and future transformation of the creation,[67] this present Creation has

eternal significance. Thus what is now done "in the body"[68] counts forever. Because creation is good[69] and will get better, Satan has always,
from the beginning, sought to overturn its structures. The first sin was
against the Creator, in the body, and it overturned creation's structures.
Those who are new creatures in Christ Jesus seek to bring glory to God
the Creator in their mortal bodies. Part of the moral, ethical, and spiritual demands made on the believer is submission to the creational
orders in the areas of sexuality, the family, work, and the state. Paul
refers to the normativity of creation by a general reference to "the
law,"[70] citations of texts from the first three chapters of Genesis,[71] general appeals to "nature,"[72] and overwhelmingly, by a consistent appeal
to God-established order in the world.

The Law of the God of Order

There is a word group in Greek—*tass*—that means "structure, order."
Its verbal form signifies to "set in a fixed or appropriate place, ordain,
fix, determine."[73] It is not without interest that Paul uses this term and
its cognates on no less than seventy-six occasions. A particularly clear
example is his instruction concerning the believer's responsibility relative to the secular state.[74] In the first five verses of the passage in which
he discusses this issue, Paul uses five forms from this *tass* group. Paul's
argument is that everyone must "set himself under [or subject himself
to]" the governing authorities who are "set in place" by God. All who
"set themselves against" this order are finally "setting themselves
against" God.

Is Paul's insistence on this word a chance occurrence, a matter of
style, or a theologically significant repetition? Is this text an isolated
case, or is it illustrative of a theological and systematic thinking? Why
does it appear in Paul's teaching on the role of women, where he uses
the same word, "set under," which we translate "submit"? Is this an
expression of rabbinic chauvinism that Paul has not quite brushed off,
or is it part of a coherent understanding of the way reality is structured?

Paul's thought here is not haphazardly expressed. He is teaching us
about the character of God and the nature of his work. Such teaching
is an essential part of Paul's program for the moral restructuring of the
deconstructed Gentiles.

As we noted in chapter 6, God, the Creator and Redeemer, is the one who, by his sovereign word, turned chaos into cosmic order, and, in so doing, left his imprint of intelligent ordering and vast variety on all the things he made.[75] Paul merely reproduces what the Old Testament already affirmed: "the heavens declare the glory of God, and the firmament shows His handiwork" (Ps. 19:1 NKJV). In the classic text about man in creation, God's creative action is described as subjection, "setting under": "You have set all things under his feet."[76] In the history of redemption, the same imagery is maintained. In the fallen world, God symbolically reclaims that lordship for Israel in the promised land, "setting the nations under our feet."[77]

Given its Old Testament use, we should not be surprised to see Paul using the "setting under" term to "restructure" the thinking and acting of converted pagans. Paul teaches that after the fall, God *subjected* the creation to vanity,[78] implying that the curses of Genesis are God's action to limit the effect of sin in a fallen world over which he still retains control.[79] But there is the eschatological hope of a renewed creation "subjected to the will of God *without vanity.*" Thus, during the ministry of Jesus "the seventy returned with joy, saying, 'Lord, even the demons are *subject* to us in Your name'" (Luke 10:17 NKJV). They witness by anticipation the final arrangement of things in the transformed universe when God "subjects all things under his [Christ's] feet"[80] as the victorious last Adam, head of the church, the new humanity. How interesting that the description of the new creation contains the classic definition of the old. It is surely on the basis of God's structuring/subjecting activity in creation that Paul can argue concerning the creation: "All flesh is not the same: Men have one kind of flesh, animals have another" (1 Cor. 15:39–41)—birds, fish, heavenly bodies, the sun, the moon, the stars. He is making the point that since creation is this way, the new creation will follow suit. "All will be made alive, but each in his own turn or order."[81]

If both old and new creations are structured this way, it is not surprising that present Christian living would be marked by the same order. Just as we either give our members as slaves to righteousness or unrighteousness, so Christ does not deliver the creation *from subjection,* but from *the subjection to vanity.* Present Christian "freedom" is the rediscovery of freeing subjection to God's cosmic order.

Because God is the subjector, redeemed creatures have nothing to fear and everything to gain. Submission is asked of everyone in all the spheres of God's ordered universe. As we have seen, political and civic power is *ordained* by God.[82] For this reason one must submit to civil authorities.[83] Likewise, in the church, Paul exhorts Christians to "submit" to its leaders,[84] who have "set" themselves in the ministry of the saints.[85] In the other domains of life, Paul calls upon Christians to submit to the creational structures—in work and employment,[86] in the family,[87] and in marriage.[88]

Paul's teaching on these matters is based on what God commands.[89] With the same divine authority[90] Paul himself gives commands to the church[91] concerning all kinds of matters, and he does so with specific instructions that such commands are to be respected not only in particular situations, but in all the churches.[92] Some things Paul teaches by concession, not command, but when he has a command of the Lord,[93] he uses it. Paul's own gospel[94] and his apostolate[95] both come through a divine command.[96]

Everything, then, is established by God. Therefore, a mark of the sinful mind is that it does not "submit to or set itself under God's law."[97] This includes the Jews who did not *submit to* the righteousness of God.[98] Thus, the one who opposes ("sets himself against") God opposes[99] what God has "ordained."[100] Those who refuse to work are not simply lazy. They are without creational structure.[101] Willful sinners are rebels, without a spirit of submission to God,[102] exchanging the glory of the immortal God for man-made images and worshiping the creature.

Christians, even Gentile pagan Christians, have understood submission, since it is exemplified by their Savior, Christ, who in his earthly existence "submits" to his parents,[103] and in his glorified state "submits to the Father."[104] The faith of Christians is called "the submission of their confession to the gospel."[105] They submit one to the other.[106] But since creation is differentiated, so is the submission required. Christ, every human being, all Christians, church members, Christian women, Christian employees/slaves, Christian children— each one has particular areas of submission in order to worship the one

true God, Creator and Redeemer to whom all things are finally submitted. God is a God of peace, not of disorder.[107] Thus everything
should be done in a fitting and "orderly" fashion,[108] so Paul congratu-
lates the Colossians on their good order.[109]

It is within these structures of God's created order that we live out
our sanctification. Submission to the structures of creation is part of
present testing, because that was the way Adam and Eve were required
to live before they fell.

The Reason for Testing: Probation

God placed Adam on probation to prepare him for the coming utopia
of what Scripture calls the great Sabbath rest.[110] Adam failed the test
because he thought he knew better than God. God called Israel his son,
and, calling him out of Egypt, tested him in the wilderness. Israel failed
the test when the grumbling people thought they knew better than
God. Jesus, the last Adam, was led by the Spirit into the wilderness and
was tested. He passed the test, citing God's Word to the devil, with
Scripture taken from Deuteronomy. Paul compares the present church
to the generation under Moses in the wilderness.[111] In both
1 Corinthians 10:11 and Philippians 2:12, Paul argues that the generation under Moses is the one generation in the history of the people of
God of the Old Testament that is "typological" of the church. The trek
in the wilderness through both times of testing and blessing, being led
by the Spirit in the period of the "already" of deliverance from Egypt
and the "not yet" of entry into the promised land, is taken by Paul as a
prophetic description of the time of the church "trekking" between the
resurrection and the second coming. Indeed, he says quite clearly that
it was written for us. The present time is a time of divine appointment
that takes its noble place in the history of redemption according to the
express will of the Father.

All that was written about the earlier people of God is written
about us and for our benefit, says Paul.[112] Thus, Moses, in revealing to
Israel the grand purpose behind the wilderness wanderings, actually
divulges God's purpose for the church in these last days, "those on
whom the ends of the age have come."[113]

In the texts that Jesus cited during his wilderness testing,[114] Moses reveals the purpose of the divine testing of his people:

Remember the long way that the Lord your God has led you these forty years in the wilderness, in order to humble you, *testing you to know what was in your heart, whether or not you would keep his commandments . . . to humble you and to test you, and in the end to do you good.* Do not say to yourself, "My power and the might of my own hand have gotten me this wealth." . . . *But remember the Lord your God, for it is he who gives you power* to get wealth, so that he may confirm his covenant that he swore to your ancestors, as he is doing today.

Moses lays down for the people of God a program of sanctification that leads to blessing, to be lived in the light of God's saving grace so that the reality and validity of the Old Covenant believer's faith might become evident. As Israel walks free from the Egyptian prison house of slavery toward the promised land, God is testing Israel's heart.

It is the same for the new Israel, trekking from the past saving event of Christ's resurrection toward the coming utopia of cosmic transformation. Paul, a second Moses, agrees with Moses. "No doubt there have to be differences among you to show which of you have God's approval" (1 Cor. 11:19). In other words, in this wilderness period, the true believers will emerge. Like Moses, Paul believes that in the present "God . . . tests our hearts."[115] This is why Paul, as Christ's ambassador, writes to the church in Corinth—"to see if you would stand the test and be obedient in everything" (2 Cor. 2:9). This earthly pilgrimage "in jars of clay to show that this all-surpassing power is from God and not from us" (2 Cor. 4:7). These trials, says the apostle Peter, "have come so that your faith—of greater worth than gold, which perishes even though refined by fire—may be proved genuine" (1 Pet. 1:7).

Only tried and tested, genuine faith will inherit utopia.

The Goal of Testing: Glorification

Paul endures suffering and sickness endemic to this preutopian life because he knows a big day of rewards is coming. He sees a shining prize with his name on it, what he calls a "crown of righteousness,"[116] a "crown that will last forever."[117] Like Jesus who despised the difficulties of this life for the great joy to come,[118] Paul knows nothing in this present life can compare to what is coming.[119] He believes with great confidence that "the Lord, the righteous Judge," will recompense him "and all who have longed for his appearing" (2 Tim. 4:8). Thus he reassures believers: "You will be counted worthy of the kingdom of God, for which you are suffering" (2 Thess. 1:5). Paul presently "shar[es] in his [Christ's] sufferings … to attain to the resurrection from the dead" (Phil. 3:10–11). This is the crowning event, the glorification of God's original handiwork.

James expresses in clear terms what Paul so evidently believes. This fellow apostle and blood brother of Jesus pronounces a benediction on all those who remain faithful in testing: "Blessed is the man who perseveres under trial, because when he has stood the test, he will receive the crown of life that God has promised to those who love him" (James 1:12).

But a question remains. How do you do it? How do you remain faithful in testing? How do you reconcile yourself with the Creator's moral demands and keep his covenant? Is future reward a sufficiently powerful motivation?

God Empowers His People by His Spirit

It can only be done in the power of the Spirit. Energized by the Spirit, fired by the afterburn of Christ's powerful exit from the claws of death, sustained by all the spiritual blessings that flow therefrom, we can make it, according to Paul. The reason is that Christians are those who have "tasted of the powers of the age to come"[120] through the coming of the Spirit. So the church is not caught off guard by the delay of the coming of utopia, because the period immediately following the resurrection is understood and indeed experienced as the time of the coming of the Spirit. As the apostle Peter declares in the first Christian sermon ever preached, these "last days" prophesied by the prophet Joel involve the powerful presence of the Spirit in the church.

The Spirit is himself a gift. He is "the promise of the Father"[121] and the gift of the Son.[122] But this gift comes bearing gifts.[123]

The Gift of the Church

One of the great spiritual blessings in the present time is the church.[124] The church is *Christ's* and it is *his body,* but it is born with the coming of the Spirit,[125] through the ministry of the Spirit. The present reality of the future utopia is lived in communion, in the church. The life of the church does not grow out of the simple human need for friendship or encouragement. The church is not a country club or a humanitarian organization. It is not a human institution, created by power-hungry male bishops of the second century.[126]

The church arises from the two-Adam schema of creation and recreation. In creation we are *in Adam*.[127] In recreation we are *in Christ*.[128] Paul uses the phrase "in Christ" eighty times, and for him it defines Christian existence. In everything the Christian does, he is conscious of this new and all-encompassing reality. The new reality of being "in Christ" is materially and specifically experienced in the communal reality of the "body of Christ," the church. One cannot be a Christian and ignore the church. Paul uses the term *church*[129] sixty-one times. Paul bears with the many sufferings that accompany his apostolic ministry "for the sake of his body, which is the church."[130] The church is also the locus of real reconciliation, both between man and God and between antagonistic peoples, in particular Jews and Gentiles.[131] The church is the place where Christians build one another up, share one another's burdens, and serve Christ with their various gifts.[132] In the church, through the pastoral office[133] and the teaching of the Scriptures, the *word of Christ dwells richly*[134] and Christians come together for God-centered worship in spirit and truth.[135] It is here that Christians grow up in love into the full maturity of Christ.[136]

The Gift of the Spirit-Inspired Word

The people of God are also empowered by the "word of God." Paul indicates the Spirit's role in bringing this word to the church by associating "word" with "power." The word of God is "the sword of the Spirit."[137] The word Paul preaches, the gospel,[138] is "the word of God in its fullness,"[139] and the "power of God for salvation."[140] So the word is accompanied by the Spirit's power.[141] The word is defined as the apostolic word, and is not the "word of men, but . . . actually . . . the word of God, which is at work in you who believe" (1 Thess. 2:13). The word effects changed hearts and "works," because it is powerfully inspired and applied by the Spirit. Thus Paul claims that he is teaching with

"truthful speech and in the power of God; with weapons of righteousness in the right hand and in the left" (2 Cor. 6:7). A claim to truth, a
rock on which to stand, "the rock on which Christ builds his church,"
empowers Christ's people to be more than conquerors.[142]

The Gift of All Spiritual Blessings

When Paul makes the grand statement about God's people, who are
called, tested and "blesse[d] . . . with all spiritual blessings in Christ,"[143]
we must not miss the force of the word *spiritual*. All these blessings
come from the Spirit. One of them, "adoption as sons through Jesus
Christ,"[144] evokes the Spirit who is behind all these blessings, for in
another letter Paul describes the Spirit as "the Spirit of sonship . . . by
whom we cry, 'Abba, Father.'"[145] These are clearly some of the "blessings" that flow from Christ's resurrection triumph.

When Paul uses the term *spiritual*, he does not refer to the pagan
kind of spirituality that promotes irrational mysticism. For Paul, the
Spirit's work concerns the mind and involves the thinking process.
Paul speaks frequently of the "understanding" and its involvement in
the believer's spiritual faith. "We have not received the spirit of the
world," he says, "but the Spirit who is from God, that we may *understand* what God has freely given us" (1 Cor. 2:12). His prayer for the
Colossians is "that God [would] fill you with the *knowledge* of his will
through all spiritual wisdom and *understanding*" (Col. 1:9). For the
Ephesians he prays that God "may give you the Spirit of wisdom and
revelation . . . that the eyes of your heart may be enlightened in order
that you may know the hope to which he has called you, the riches of
his glorious inheritance in the saints" (Eph. 1:17–18). These are the
spiritual blessings that result from the resurrection of Christ. The
Spirit makes us understand what the future holds for those who are
included in Christ.

This action of the Spirit and the knowledge that the Spirit reveals
changes us. But note! The locus of transformation in the present time
is "the inner man," not "the outer man," which is wasting away.[146] By
the resurrection power in the "spiritual" domain, we are being changed
from glory to glory "which comes from the Lord, who is the Spirit."[147]
The present place of meeting with God is through the Spirit,[148] and the

language used is prayer by the Spirit.[149] Thus the present struggle is "spiritual,"[150] and in that struggle, we see exhibited the "fruit of the Spirit."[151]

The Gift of Christ

Christ was physically present during the incarnation and the time of the resurrection appearances. One day he will return with that same resurrection glory. In the meantime, believers are not orphans. By the Spirit, through the word, Christ is present in the church as the firstborn of many brothers.[152] There is a necessary and beneficial confusion between Christ and the Spirit. Paul calls the Spirit "the Spirit of Christ,"[153] or "the Spirit of his [God's] Son."[154] The Spirit is the seal that marks us as belonging to Christ.[155] Christ dwells in us,[156] just as the Spirit dwells in us.[157] In a mysterious way, by the Spirit's ministry, the living, resurrected Christ is made present to believers, so that we come to know not an idea of power, but a person.[158] Through the Spirit, we come to love Christ in a manner that is deeply personal.[159]

Pastor Tim Keller of Manhattan captures this well. The proof that Christ was present in the church is that early Christians lost track of his grave. He compares the situation to parents constantly upbraiding their son for his messy room until the moment when the boy is taken from them in a fatal car accident, and then the messy room becomes an untouchable shrine. Nothing is picked up because in the experience of deep loss, the chaos on the floor reminds them of the time when their son was so obviously present. Because Christ remained present in the church after his crucifixion, early Christians had no instinct to make his grave a shrine.

To know Christ in this way is to live in the power of the resurrection and to face the future with undaunted faith.[160]

The Gift of Faith, Hope, and Patience

Someone who deeply and optimistically believes in the future will have an indomitable spirit. In Paul's view of the world, the true believer lives with such faith, which is a gift of God.[161] By it, the objective work of Christ is appropriated subjectively for the individual believer.[162] Coming from God, it is part of the utopian event of salvation, so that

Paul speaks of the coming of faith;[163] and the message of the gospel regarding the future is called "the word of faith."[164]

Only in Christianity is such faith possible. Pagans of all sorts, whether ancient or modern, "Christian" or non-Christian, do not believe in a transcendent God; and they have no sense that God has acted on their behalf. The liberal Muslim scholar, Abdullahi An-Na'im, states that "religion is what we make of it."[165] This is a different kind of faith—faith in the self. Liberal Christian scholar, Elaine Pagels, Harrington Professor of Religion at Princeton University, is of the same opinion. Pagels, in her highly acclaimed books on Gnosticism and Satan,[166] is committed to pluralism as the highest good. In her historical work, she seeks to show that original Christianity was not monolithic, but was made up of all kinds of views of reality, including that of pagan Gnosticism.[167] With a deep commitment to finding truth in all religions, she considers Buddhism useful.[168] Her statement about the essence of Christianity is telling: "I think belief is way overvalued in Christianity. Christianity became defined as a set of beliefs or propositions that are completely unprovable, instead of explorations of the spiritual and articulations of certain kinds of intuition and hope and love and ethical sensibility."[169]

Pagels sees religion as techniques for spirituality and human unity. She does not believe that the transcendent, personal God of the Bible acted to raise Jesus from the dead and bring about utopia. Her research is ideologically slanted to demonstrate that orthodoxy was a later development. A further extension of this view of "religion" is to see it as a useful stress reducer in harrowing times. Therapy comes through Buddhistic mindfulness meditation, which eliminates conflict and judgmentalism and teaches people to believe the best about themselves and to make choices that fit their tolerant beliefs.

It is easy to imagine how the distinction-making judgments of Christianity are seen as dangerous stress inducers that should be eliminated from public discourse for the psychological health of the population. It is important to recall that the first four major "founders" of Christianity had no political ambitions, but were assassinated by the state—John the Baptist, Jesus, Peter, and Paul, a fact that may well be unique in the annals of religious history. Jesus said he came not to bring peace, but a sword, the sword of truth.[170] There have been many historical periods when the truth was not appreciated, and those times could return.

Paul's writings are among the earliest Christian texts we possess. They demonstrate that biblical faith is not spiritual technology, intuition, a means to unite all the religions of the world, or a therapy to reduce mental stress. Pagels's statement that "belief is way overvalued" indicates how this woman, brilliant as she is, has failed to understand the essence of biblical faith. In Paul, Christian faith depends upon belief. Belief is the firm conviction of the truth that God has actually and objectively done something *for* humanity in time and space.

Such faith gives rise to hope.

A scrawny kid walked towards me in the fitness center. We clearly had different reasons for frequenting the same establishment! As he passed, I saw on the back of his sweat-drenched t-shirt the words: "Expect Victory." Whether he ever reached victory in his body-building exploits I will never know. But I do know how hard it has been for me to expect victory in my attempt to return to my "boyish figure." Expecting victory is the essence of Christian hope. The future utopian reality is brought near and makes itself felt in the experience of the believer by the present reality of hope. Abraham, who hoped in God, is the archetype of the Christian believer.[171] Christian hope is clearly based on the finished work of Christ, already accomplished in the past. So Paul argues in Romans: "If the Spirit of him who raised Jesus from the dead is living in you, he who raised Christ Jesus from the dead will give life to your mortal bodies also through his Spirit, who lives in you" (Rom. 8:11). The present work of the Spirit produces hope.

"Faith" is a bold conviction based on a past reality. "Hope" looks optimistically to the future. "Patience" bears up and remains faithful in the present. With this kind of hope for the joy that was set before him, Jesus, the author and perfecter of our faith, as the author of the Book of Hebrews tells us, "endured the cross."[172] In the light of this example from Christ, the biblical author encourages believers to "endure hardship as discipline."[173]

This is certainly the attitude of Paul in the face of suffering, an attitude he proposes for all believers.[174] The term means "patient waiting

for what is not yet manifest." Like every other quality of the Christian
life, this endurance is a gift from God, for God is called "the God of
endurance"[175] or "the God who gives endurance." Faithful endurance
characterizes Paul's work as an apostle,[176] and he is aware that his
endurance serves as an example.[177] Thus generally "endurance" is an
evident sign of true faith[178] and produces hope.[179] It manifests the
believer's deep love for Christ.[180] As biblical scholar Friedrich Hauck
says, "Pious waiting for Jesus is the heart-beat of the faith of the New
Testament community."[181]

Christians understand that their present situation is a patient
wilderness march from Egyptian deliverance to Canaan inheritance,
and the march is to be done "without grumbling."[182] That path leads
from Christ's resurrection (our deliverance) to our own resurrection
(our inheritance). The time in which we now live gives expression
to the unique and simple timeline of the Bible. It is the conjoining
of the age of creation and the age of recreation, which has penetrated
the original creation in anticipatory form. So we know two realities
first-hand:

1. the reality of creation in our flesh and blood, mortal bodies,
    marred by sin but created good, *not yet* transformed;
2. the reality of creation *already* transformed in the resurrection
    of Jesus, which we know in its anticipatory form by the Spirit.

So we live in a tension between the "already" and the "not yet." The
"already" is the foretaste we have through the Spirit of the transformation that awaits us. The "not yet" is our awareness that our earthly body
has not yet been transformed.

The "not yet" keeps us from triumphalism and makes us constantly dependent on God. Paul makes a number of observations that
emphasize the "not yet" aspect of our lives: "Judge nothing before the
appointed time";[183] "we walk by faith and not by sight";[184] "we know
in part. . . ."[185] The present time is a time of weakness, so God's power
is "made perfect in weakness";[186] "we who are alive are always being
given over to death";[187] "though outwardly we are wasting away, yet
inwardly we are being renewed day by day."[188] The great error of certain Christians in Corinth was to believe that they "already were filled,"

that they "already were reigning."[189] They had too much "already" and hardly any "not yet."

However, the right amount of "already" gives us hope and keeps us from despair. Imbued with faith and a foretaste, via the Spirit, of the reality of the new humanity to come, Christians are empowered to carry this treasure in jars of clay, seeking to bring glory to God through the reality of their created bodies, even as they are still marred by the effects of sin. Thus, says Paul, "we are hard pressed . . . but not crushed; perplexed, but not in despair; persecuted, but not abandoned; struck down, but not destroyed. . . . because we know that the one who raised the Lord Jesus from the dead will also raise us with Jesus" (2 Cor. 4:7–14).

A New Way of Relating to the World

ALREADY	NOT YET
Salvation	

ALREADY	NOT YET
Now is the time of salvation . . . 2 Corinthians 6:2 *. . . the time is fulfilled . . .* Ephesians 1:10	*Salvation is nearer than* *when we first believed . . .* Romans 13:11 but salvation is still not here

Justification	
Having been justified Romans 5:1	*By faith we await . . . the justifi-* *cation for which we hope* Galatians 5:5

Redemption	
In him we have redemption Ephesians 1:7	*. . . the Holy Spirit . . . is the* *guarantee . . . until the* *redemption* Ephesians 1:14

Sanctification

To the church of God in Corinth, to those sanctified in Christ Jesus 1 Corinthians 1:2 You have been sanctified 1 Corinthians 6:11[190]	... and called to be holy 1 Corinthians 1:2 May the God of peace sanctify you through and through. 1 Thessalonians 5:23[191] ... so that the Gentiles might become an offering acceptable to God, sanctified by the Holy Spirit. Romans 15:16

Indicative/Imperative
Become (not yet) what you are (already)

You died [past tense] and your life is now hidden in Christ Colossians 3:3 Since we [now] live in the Spirit Galatians 5:25	Put to death [imperative] your earthly nature Colossians 3:5 Walk [imperative referring to the future] by the Spirit Galatians 5:2

Creation/New Creation

If anyone is in Christ he is a new creation 2 Corinthians 5:17 We have this treasure [of the new creation] 2 Corinthians 4:7	we await the setting free of the creation [that is, the new creation] Romans 8:21 ... in earthen vessels [of the old creation]

Jew and Gentile

What counts is neither circumcision nor uncircumcision Galatians 6:15	*What advantage has the Jew? . . . Much in every way!* Romans 3:1–2
In Christ there is neither Jew nor Greek Galatians 3:28	*Has God rejected his people? Certainly not!* Romans 11:1
	to the Jew first Romans 1:16; 2:9

Physical/Spiritual

The kingdom of God is not a matter of eating and drinking, but of righteousness, peace and joy Romans 14:17	*Eat everything that is sold in the market . . . for the earth is the Lord's* 1 Corinthians 10:25–26

The State

Our citizenship is in heaven from whence we await a Savior Philippians 3:20	*Everyone must submit himself to the governing authorities . . . which God has established* Romans 13:1

Work

In Christ there is neither slave nor free Galatians 3:28	*Slaves, obey your earthly masters. . . . Masters, treat your servants in the same way* Ephesians 6:5, 9

The Family

In Christ there is [neither child nor parent] this is a valid inference from what Paul says elsewhere—see opposite: *Children . . . in the Lord* Galatians 3:28 See also the teaching of Jesus: Any disciple following Jesus *must hate his father and mother . . . and children* Luke 14:26	*Children, obey your parents in the Lord* Ephesians 6:1 Jesus repudiates the use of Corban whereby adult children avoided responsibility for their elderly parents Mark 7:11

Male/Female Relationships

In Christ there is neither male nor female Galatians 3:28 See also the teaching of Jesus A disciple must hate his wife Luke 14:26 In heaven there is no marriage Mark 12:25	*Wives, submit yourselves to your husbands* Ephesians 5:22 *I do not permit a woman to teach and have authority over a man, for Adam was formed first* 1 Timothy 2:12 Jesus endorses marriage and cites the Genesis 2:24 passage as normative Matthew 19:4

This particular stance in the world is empowering because it is based on the way things really are, but by this the empowering God intends that the people he calls and refines will engage in witness.

God Empowers His People for Witness

The two great works of God—creation and new creation—are not shown to the world through magical writing in the sky, but through the simple witness of the people God calls. God had always intended his name to be known this way. In the words of Paul: "[God's] intent was that now, *through the church,* the manifold wisdom of God should be made known to the rulers and authorities in heavenly places" (Eph. 3:10).

The clearest evidence of divine wisdom is that godless pagans are included and grafted into the church alongside converted Jews. Only when this great miracle occurs is the *manifold* wisdom of God revealed to the principalities and powers. In this task of reconciliation, the church discovers its cosmic calling. As the new people of the resurrected Christ, who is Lord of the transformed cosmos, the church principally includes people of every race, nation, social position, age, and sex. Such is the wonder of the Gentile inclusion that Paul will grant to the Gentiles the title once exclusive to old Israel, namely God's "treasured possession."[192] This term in the Old Testament was often used of Israel in the context of holy war with the pagan nations,[193] but with the Gentile inclusion the situation is radically altered. The pagans are now part of "God's own possession."

This unity occurs because of God's objective sacrifice of Christ the Creator, through whose blood creation is reconciled to God. Second, the unity occurs because under the power of the Spirit, Paul spent most of his time seeking the pagan lost. This is why Paul will oppose Peter to his face[194] and risk his own life, working tirelessly for the sanctification of the pagans. Reconciliation between antagonistic peoples is God's brilliant, wise achievement through the priceless work of his Son on the cross. A contemporary hymn captures this thought with great insight:

> What wisdom once devised the plan,
> By which our sin and pride
> Was placed upon the perfect Lamb
> Who suffered, bled and died?
> The wisdom of a sovereign God,
> Whose greatness will be shown,

When those who crucified His son

Rejoice around His throne.[195]

The Gnostic autonomous, androgynous, kingless,[196] solitary[197] individual whose spirit will one day lose all identity in the great eternal spirit behind the illusory matter *(maya)* of creation is not an expression of the wisdom of the God of Paul. In a modern apologia for Gnostic Christianity, Abbot George Burke of the Gnostic Orthodox Church, speaks of the "process of evolution into Christhood."[198] But the one new man made according to the image and stature of Christ in Pauline thinking depends upon distinctions and personal uniqueness. When Paul states that "there is neither Jew nor Greek, slave or free, male nor female," he is not speaking of egalitarian sameness. He is explaining spiritual unity—the full inclusion of every kind of person in a rich and diverse ecclesial unity made possible in the covenant bond of Calvary love.[199] Paul is not eradicating distinctions, because difference is the prerequisite of reconciliation. Were there no differences to reconcile, the reality of the gospel would not be evident to the cosmic powers.

The people of God, because they are a community of diverse people, reconciled through Christ, bear this cosmic witness, not only in the future "around the throne," but right now in the world. Believers are reconciled both to one another and to God. Reconciliation with God is necessary because of sin. No matter how sin affects other human beings, it is ultimately committed against God the Creator. Paganism understands redemption as *liberation from* the structures of creation. The Bible speaks of redemption as reconciliation *with* the Creator, and *with* the good structures he made. Christians know they can have it all, both the present joys of submitting to the structures of creation in marriage, family, sexuality, work, and culture, and the future joys of these same things transformed into a magnificence one cannot now imagine.

In his letter to the Ephesian Christians, Paul enunciates this great calling of witness.[200] But in this same letter, he emphasizes both "the riches of God's glorious inheritance" (the future utopia)[201] and present obedience to the will of God the Creator[202] in the various domains of the created order.[203] Because of the ongoing character of the process of reconciliation, Paul, at the end of Ephesians, will describe the Christian life and the situation of the church as militant, a continuous conflict that ultimately has to do with the principalities and powers. The wiles of the devil, like those deployed in the garden, are the subtle temptation to conclude that God is not a good Creator, and that his project will not succeed. In a word, that God is not wise.

A called and tested people, in the image of the faithfulness and character of last Adam, made up of people of all races, genders (male and female), and classes,[204] whose individual and communal life is an earthly, humble anticipation of the utopia to come, will resist those fiery darts. Witnessing to the empowerment of the new life by the Spirit, this people will declare to the principalities and powers, come what may, in season and out of season, whether it be politically correct or incorrect, the wisdom of God, the good news that God's solution works and will prevail.

Prospective

In these pages we have looked at two fundamentally different accounts of utopia. One is based on the power of God—Creator and Redeemer. The other is based on the power of a self-generating and self-transforming cosmos. In biblical terms, the conflict is between Adam in the garden, seeking to bring about utopia on his own human terms, and God's utopian project, which does not depend upon human power. As the apostle Paul so clearly states: "Flesh and blood cannot inherit the kingdom."[205] These two contradictory views of utopia are on an inevitable collision course, destined to clash—perhaps sooner than we imagine.

At the beginning of the third millennium, pagan utopian thinking has gained much attention and has fed the social transformation that has occurred since the 1960s cultural revolution. So-called New Age thinkers during the past generation have spoken of the end of the Age of Pisces and the coming of the Age of Aquarius. Pisces, the fish, represents the Christian era that has come to an end; Aquarius, the goddess or water bearer brings satisfaction for our spiritual thirst and opens up the future for a revival of pagan spirituality. Many now recognize the "necessary stage" of the deconstruction of traditional theory and practice of the bygone Christian era. This other upbeat stage now presses upon us. Just as deconstruction has been real and has taken just one generation, so reconstruction is intended to be as real, brought about with the same amount of intention and dedication. According to world politician Mikhail Gorbachev, we need to reconstruct life on the planet within the next forty years.[206]

Since the 1960s the United States has developed a great interest in earth-based spirituality, and specifically in Native American religion. The white Christian invasion of Columbus and the Pilgrims has finally been beaten back. Sophisticated Americans now put their faith in the prophesies of the Mayan divinity, Quetzalcoatl, and teach in the state schools that Columbus was a villain. The future is read from the ancient Mayan calendar, which foretold the coming of an unprece-dented new age of peace for the entire globe, to begin on August 17, 1987. This is the moment also known as the "harmonic convergence," defined as "the point at which the counter-spin of history finally comes to a momentary halt, and the still imperceptible spin of post-history commences . . . where we enter a new path of spiritual and mental evo-lution in tune with the cycles of the universe, which some call 'Heaven on earth.'"[207]

Such speculative, utopian thinking, in its many pagan versions, also believes that the magnetic field surrounding the planet that has created the illusion of separation between us and the rest of the universe will decrease to zero. This physical oneness with the rest of the cosmos rep-resents a "rare opportunity for collectively repatterning the expression of human consciousness."[208]

A similar vision, couched in other liberationist terms, is to be found everywhere in the academy and in large sections of the modern mainline church. It is difficult to have accurate figures. My judgment has formed after wading through endless scholarly publications on the coming human liberation, after reading scores of semi-scholarly books on spirituality and the culture, and after attending large scholarly annual meetings. It is my impression that thousands of teachers in uni-versity departments of religion and in theological seminaries have accepted some form of this humanist program of ethical, spiritual, and sexual relativism. Their influence on future generations must not be underestimated. The program they espouse is a vast continuum, stretching from the relatively moderate to the most radical extremes. Where someone is on the continuum does not really matter, because the cutting edge of this new agenda is radical paganism. Less radical liberal thinkers are drawn implacably along in its wake, for their relative "conservatism" stands on no solid ground of principle.

To reconstruct the Christian faith according to their own desires, the ancient Gnostics whom Paul encountered actively sought the input of pagan thinking and spirituality. Christianity is undergoing a similar transformation in our day. The seductive program of a unified, liberated humanity enjoying spiritual super-consciousness in deep communion with Earth and with all the religions is sheer paganism. Such a program is nevertheless being promoted as the true goal of Christianity. Contemporary liberal theologians are joining with modern pagans to eliminate Christian theism. Though the language used might be different, there is a convergence of essential beliefs. The end product might have some of the sights and sounds of true faith, but in reality it is nothing more than a diabolical counterfeit.

This worldview is now touted, as we have seen, as an "emerging American wisdom tradition" joining the human potential movement of the West with the age-old spirituality of the pagan East to save the planet as a whole.[209] With this wisdom such visionaries will transform the planet and bring peace on earth.

It seems inevitable that, in the name of human survival and with the help of occult spirituality, global forces will soon arise that will construct an end-time, all-inclusive Tower of Babel as the future hope for the planet. All religions and all sexual permutations will celebrate the glory of the goddess. As Lloyd Geering predicts, Christianity, stripped of its theistic notion of God, will "die but rise again as a facet of a new global religion."[210] But paganism, since it can have no sense of true transcendence, will always construct an earthly utopia, which is limited to this-world power and control. In this future planetary society, there can be no conscientious objectors. The God of theism must go; the old must be eliminated for the new to come. World peace *must* include everyone, otherwise there would be no peace. In order for utopia to work, it must be an all-embracing account of reality. It is the final answer and can accept no rivals.

If the Christian gospel is true, then these human versions of utopia, though enticing, are false hopes at best, and diabolical lies at worst. To keep up appearances of truth, Christianity must be silenced. The fact that opposing versions still exist means that utopia is still in the future. Consistent pagan thinking about the coming political future of peace and love necessarily includes the silencing of rival claims, using politically correct, endlessly malleable definitions of "hate speech."[211] The fact is, Christianity is the only true rival because only its speech is true.

This may well mean a clash with the political powers that are trying to eliminate the Christian voice. Since Christians may not take up the sword, the clash is very one-sided. Their only weapon is the sword of the Spirit, the Word of God. Christians who believe this utopia to be built on the lie must speak out, which will threaten global harmony. As in the Roman Empire, Christians will have no place to run. Whether Christians realize it or not, we are part of a human history that is destined for confrontation and conflict with pagan spirituality and that spirituality is driven, in our time, by a militant homosexual agenda. The average Christian appears to be no match for a small but powerful homosexual elite, imbued by self-preservation, righteous indignation, and a sense of historic destiny. Often highly intelligent and spirit-guided (the meaning of shamanistic), these are formidable people. In particular, the lesbian witches with their own new vocabulary, methodology, ethical system, and righteous rage would leave most heterosexual Christian believers in the dust. They will doubtless stop at nothing to bring in their vision of utopian liberation.

With disarming candor, a gay leader now boasts: "We rule the world these days. Everybody except orthodox religious sects has either been cowed by gay activist intimidation or softened by the politics of victimology and oppression and the doctrines of tolerance, diversity, and inclusion."[212]

The situation of contemporary Christianity resembles and will increasingly resemble that of the early Christians of the first century. With few or no civil rights, those first-generation believers witnessed to Christ with incredible courage and moral power in the context of an antagonistic, all-powerful pagan state. In a real communion of the saints, those fellow believers can now serve as a model of faith for us. It also follows that the gospel Paul preached in the first century, which was the power of God for salvation, and which turned the Roman Empire upside down, is particularly appropriate for preaching in the twenty-first.

As we see the parallels with the past, we realize that in our period of disorienting change, nothing has changed. Paganism is the same. Biblical faith is the same. When in power, paganism will always use its classic methods of political power. Christianity will always use only the power of the gospel.

We do believe that "the earth will be filled with the knowledge of the glory of the Lord as the waters cover the sea,"[213] but we do not know what means God will use to accomplish his purposes. It is easy to cite that verse with careless triumphalism, but it may be that the knowledge of that glory will shine from lighted crosses, as it did in Nero's gardens two millennia ago.

Paul speaks of the mystery of evil and the man of lawlessness who will oppose the truth and the reign of Christ.[214] Peter warns us not to be surprised at the fiery trials the church will face. God's redemptive project and human utopian plans met in a crashing conflict at the beginning of human history. They have been at war ever since, meeting in one great climax at the cross of Jesus, and due for a final showdown at the end of history. This great battle was predicted by God himself at the very moment of the fall.[215]

According to the whole sweep of biblical history, the Lord, as in the days of Babel, will destroy the end-time tower of human arrogance in order to establish his own new construction, a transformed heavens and earth. "Babylon the Great is fallen," says John.[216] The great human construction of economic prosperity and sexual and religious freedom will implode as it flies in the face of creational sanity. As in the Babel/Babylon of old, it will fall. God will intervene. Rabbi Jesus, our glorious Lord, will descend and destroy human pretensions in order to impose his own glorious utopia that no eye has ever seen and of which no ear has ever heard.

Return of the Rabbi

Before that moment arrives, the moment when Christ returns to judge and to save, the church must rediscover and faithfully declare what Paul preached in the pagan empire of his day. The transforming Christian message of the converted Jewish rabbi, apostle of the great rabbi Jesus, eventually brought pagan Rome to its knees. That same message is what the church still needs to believe and what the world still needs to hear. There are no gimmicks or new revelations. In Christ the decisive event has already taken place. The great Rabbi, Christ, will return when the gospel he preached is heard again in its fullness and power. This message is not that all the religions together will help political and spiritual visionaries save the planet, but rather that God, in raising Jesus from the dead, has given the first installment and striking proof that one day he, as the all-powerful Creator, will save and transform the entire cosmos.

Dressed in the armor of God, Christians now must stand with great boldness, wielding the sword of the Spirit, ready to wage spiritual warfare[217] in the name of truth, for the good of the planet and for the glory of its Creator and Redeemer.

O may thy soldiers faithful, true and bold,
Fight as the saints who nobly fought of old,
And win with them the victor's crown of gold.
Alleluia! Alleluia![218]

Endnotes

Preface: The Beast and the Prostitute

1. Malachi Martin, *The Final Conclave* (New York: Stein and Day, 1978), 7.

2. John 21:18–19.

3. Rev. 17:7.

4. Rev. 2:10, 13.

5. Rev. 2:14–15; 2:20–21.

6. Dennis E. Johnson, *The Triumph of the Lamb: A Commentary on Revelation* (Phillipsburg, N.J.: P&R, 2001), 242.

7. Edward Gibbon, *The Decline and Fall of the Roman Empire* (New York: The Modern Library/Random House, originally published between 1776 and 1788).

8. A recent book does the same for the West. See Jacques Barzun, *From Dawn to Decadence: 1500 to the Present: 500 Years of Western Cultural Life* (New York: Harper Collins, 2000).

9. Gen. 2:9.

10. In terms of sheer numbers, Samuel P. Huntington, *The Clash of Civilizations and the Remaking of World Order* (New York: Simon & Schuster, 1996), 65–66, provides the following statistics: "The percentage of Christians in the world peaked at about 30 percent in the 1980s, leveled off, is now declining, and will probably approximate about 25 percent of the world population by 2025." The numbers are declining, but even more is the Christian influence through an obvious rejection of the Christian worldview, even in the so-called Christian West.

11. "Italy's Blood Runs Hot for Ancient Rome," *www.sunday-times.co.uk*, 22 October 2001.

Part One

1. The modern academy now refers to time by the meaningless, politically correct B.C.E. (Before Common Era) and C.E. (Common Era), rejecting any

239

Christian understanding of history and any real direction or meaning to history.

2. Lloyd Geering, *The World to Come: From Christian Past to Global Future* (Santa Rosa, Calif.: Polebridge Press, 1999), 107. Polebridge Press is the publishing arm of the Jesus Seminar.

3. Eph. 2:6; 6:10–20.

4. Gen. 3:15.

5. Rev. 18:1–24.

Chapter 1

1. Samuel Angus, sometime professor of New Testament and historical theology, St. Andrew's College, Sydney, in his book, *The Mystery Religions: A Study in the Religious Background of Early Christianity* (New York: Dover Publications, 1923), 15.

2. Ibid., 16.

3. Pseudo-Plutarch, 1:6, cited ibid.

4. Peter Kreeft, *Ecumenical Jihad: Ecumenism and the Culture War* (San Francisco: Ignatius, 1996), 11.

5. I am following the account of Angus, *Mystery Religions*, 2. He proposes this analysis long before the 1960s and the invasion of Eastern gurus into the West.

6. Marvin W. Meyer, ed., *The Ancient Mysteries: A Source Book* (San Francisco: Harper & Row, 1987), 2.

7. James Jeffers, *The Greco-Roman World of the New Testament Era* (Downers Grove, Ill.: InterVarsity, 1999), 221.

8. Ibid., 78.

9. *Urbs et orbis terrarum.*

10. Florence Dupont, trans. Christopher Woodall, *Daily Life in Ancient Rome* (Oxford: Blackwell, 1992), 76.

11. Ibid.

12. *Gumnos* in Greek means "naked," from which "gymnasium" is derived.

13. Around A.D. 50, the apostle Paul wrote a letter to the Roman church in Greek.

14. Angus, *Mystery Religions*, 36.

15. Juvenal *Satires*, 10, 77–81.

16. Suetonius, *The Lives of the Caesars*, IV: XVIII, translated J. C. Rolfe, (Cambridge, Mass.: The Loeb Classical Library/Harvard University Press, 1970).

17. Dupont, *Daily Life*, 19; Jerome Carcopino, *Daily Life in Ancient Rome: The People and the City at the Height of the Empire* (New Haven: Yale University Press, 1940), ix.

18. Ibid., 54.

19. Albert A. Bell, *Exploring the World of the New Testament: An Illustrated Guide to the World of Jesus and the First Christians* (Nashville: Thomas Nelson, 1998), 212, proposes this equivalency.

20. Michael Grant, *Nero: Emporer in Revolt* (New York: American Heritage Press, 1970), 93.

21. Carcopino, *Daily Life*, 70.

22. Grant, *Nero*, 90.

23. Ibid.

24. As the organizer, he paid for everything, and it was worth every penny.

25. Mary Beard, John North and Simon Price, eds., *Religions of Rome: Volume I: A History* (Cambridge: Cambridge University Press, 1998), 263. See also Carcopino, *Daily Life*, 215.

26. Carcopino, *Daily Life*, 217.

27. According to Dupont, *Daily Life*, 263: "Refinement meant smelling sweet, waging war on bad breath and body odor."

28. C. J. Den Heyer, *Paul: A Man of Two Worlds* (Harrisburg, Pa.: Trinity Press, 2000), 31, notes that throughout the Roman Empire, "much attention was devoted to sport and games and the development of the body had become a real cult." J. P. Toner, *Leisure and Ancient Rome* (Cambridge, UK: Polity Press, 1995), 36, notes how gladiatorial contests acquired "an explicit sexual symbolism." He records how Faustina, the wife of the emperor Antonius (A.D. 138–161) confessed to her husband her passion for one of the gladiators she observed walking by. Her husband had the gladiator killed and forced his wife to bathe in his blood. That seemed to be the end of the matter, though her son, Commodus, "was born a gladiator, 'not really a prince.'"

29. *Mens sana in corpore sano.*

30. Dupont, *Daily Life*, 240.

31. Neal Gabler, *Life, the Movie: How Entertainment Conquered Reality* (New York: Alfred A. Knopf, 1999).

32. Toner, *Leisure*, 40.

33. Carcopino, *Daily Life*, 215. See also Lionel Casson, *Everyday Life in Ancient Rome* (Baltimore: The Johns Hopkins University Press, 1999), 99.

34. Carcopino, *Daily Life*, 221.

35. Ibid., 101.

36. Livy, XLV: XXXIII.

37. According to Grant, *Nero,* 63, Nero used entertainment in the same way, actually building in A.D. 57 a new amphitheater for gladiator and wild beast shows.

38. Carcopino, *Daily Life,* 203.

39. Fronto, *Princip. Hist,* 210, ed. Naber, quoted in Carcopino, *Daily Life,* 212.

40. Dupont, *Daily Life,* 111.

41. Ibid., 112.

42. Carcopino, *Daily Life,* 99.

43. Ibid., 90–92, 260. Carcopino states in 1940: ". . . it is certain that the Roman woman of the epoch we are studying enjoyed a dignity and an independence at least equal if not superior to those claimed by contemporary feminists" (85).

44. Ibid., 90.

45. Ibid., 76.

46. Ibid., 77.

47. Ibid., 84.

48. Ibid., 94.

49. Juvenal, 6, 142–48, cited ibid., 99.

50. Martial, VI, 7, cited ibid., 100.

51. Carcopino, *Daily Life,* 100. See Seneca, *De Beneficiis* III: 16, 2.

52. Caesar had a love affair with Nicomedes (Dupont, *Daily Life,* 163), and Nero was constantly attended by male lovers (Grant, *Nero,* 51). Grant observes: "He was alleged to go to bed not with his wife but with his mother, and with boys younger than himself, and with elder men; and not merely slaves either, which would have been somewhat less disreputable, but free-born citizens. He was also said to have gone through a mock marriage ceremony with a male Greek variously described as one of his ministers, Doryphorus, or a certain Pythagoras, perhaps his cupbearer of that name. Tacitus glumly remarks on the transsexual aspects of the affair. 'In the presence of witnesses, Nero put on the bridal veil! Dowry, marriage bed, wedding torches, all were there. Indeed everything was public which, even at a natural union, is veiled by night'" (43).

53. Tessa Rajak, "Gaius," *The Oxford Classical Dictionary: Third Edition.* Ed. Simon Hornblower and Antony Spawforth (Oxford: Oxford University Press, 1996), 619.

54. Suetonius, *Lives of the Caesars* V: XII, trans. J. C. Rolfe (Cambridge, Mass.: The Loeb Classical Library/Harvard University Press, 1970), 441.

55. Ibid., 461.

56. Dupont, *Daily Life*, 226, 118.

57. Ibid., 226. See also Bell, *Exploring*, 242–44.

58. Will Durant, *Christ and Caesar* (New York: Simon & Schuster, 1944), 666.

59. Ibid. See also Bell, *Exploring*, 240–42.

60. Dupont, *Daily Life*, 127.

61. Ibid., 129.

62. Victor Hanson, *Carnage and Culture: Landmark Battles in the Rise of the West* (New York: Doubleday, 2001), 88.

63. Grant, *Nero*, 109.

64. Cited by Gibbon, *Decline and Fall*, 73. For this reference, I am indebted to William Norman Grigg, *Freedom on the Altar: The UN's Crusade Against God and Family* (Appleton, Wisconsin: American Opinion Publishing, Inc., 1995), 1.

65. Gibbon published his volume in "tyrannical" England in 1776!

66. Gibbon, *Decline and Fall*, 74.

67. Suetonius, *The Lives of the Caesars* XXXIV, says of Caligula that ". . . he took such pleasure in the combats with wild beasts . . . that he would go down to the arena at daybreak."

68. Eusebius, *Ecclesiastical History* v:1:42, trans. Kirsopp Lake (Cambridge, Mass.: Harvard University Press, 1949), 427.

69. Ibid., v:1:56, 431–32. On the general subject of Christian witness in the Roman Empire see Robert L. Wilken, *Remembering the Christian Past* (Grand Rapids: Eerdmans, 1995)

Chapter 2

1. Cited in Robert Turcan, *The Cults of the Roman Empire*, trans. Antonia Nevill (Oxford: Blackwell, 1996), 36.

2. Rom. 1:15–16. The early Christians realized the importance of Rome as the center of the known world. See Acts, which ends with Paul in Rome.

3. Martti Nissinen, *Homoeroticism in the Biblical World: A Historical Perspective* (Minneapolis: Fortress Press, 1998), 28. For this older period, I am indebted to Nissinen's work, which is supported by Helmer Ringgren, *Religions of the Ancient Near East*, trans. John Sturdy (Philadelphia.: Westminster Press, 1973), 25. Ringgren speaks of naked "eunuchs" associated with the cult to the Sumerian goddess Inanna (another name for Istar) that includes a *hieros gamos* rite. These priests "dressed up and wore make-up like a woman, and expressed their 'otherness' via their androgyny. Physically they were men but their appearance either was feminine or had both male and

female characteristics."

4. Neal H. Walls, *The Goddess Anat in Ugaritic Myth: Society of Biblical Literature Dissertation Series* 135 (Atlanta, Ga.: Scholars Press, 1992): 83.

5. See Lucian, *De Syria Dea,* 50–51.

6. For the myth, see Turcan, *Cults,* 78–79.

7. Samuel Angus, *The Mystery Religions: A Study in the Religious Background of Early Christianity* (New York: Dover Publications, 1923), 2.

8. According to Angus, ". . . from the 4th century BC on, Greek rationalism gave way with increasing docility to the mystic and psychic cults of the East. . . . As the Greeks hellenized the East, they became conscious of individual spiritual needs that were more and more met by [the Eastern] mystery religions [of personal redemption]," *Mystery Religions,* 14.

9. Ibid., 8.

10. Turcan, *Cults,* 328.

11. Carcopino, *Daily Life,* 129. This personification of pagan religion does not mean that a "goddess" actually existed.

12. Dupont, *Daily Life,* 216.

13. Ibid., 317.

14. Beard et al., eds., *Religions of Rome,* 115.

15. Ibid., 252.

16. That temples to Isis are built in the first century A.D. on choice pieces of real estate within the sacred boundary of the city is evidence of official public acceptance.

17. Beard, et al., eds. *Religions of Rome,* vol. 1, 317.

18. Like the old Greek gods, they were all too human in their weaknesses, inconsistencies, and even in their immoral lifestyles. See Jack Finegan, *Myth and Mystery: An Introduction to the Pagan Religions of the Biblical World* (Grand Rapids: Baker, 1989), 191–92.

19. Plutarch (A.D. 46–119), *Def. Or.* 421 A.

20. Josephus, *Jewish Antiquities,* XVIII, 256 (Cambridge: Loeb Classical Library/Harvard University Press, 1965), 153.

21. Vespasian, Domitian's father, was reputed to have said on his deathbed, "I think I am becoming a god." See Casson, *Everyday Life,* 84.

22. Dupont, *Daily Life,* 75.

23. Ibid., 222.

24. Ibid., 182.

25. Franz Cumont, *Religions orientales dans le paganisme romain* (Paris, 1909, English translation, Chicago, 1911), 165.

26. Ramsey McMullen, *Paganism in the Roman Empire* (New Haven: Yale University Press, 1981), 70. A magical "science" of control claimed to restore personal power and domination to the powerless.

27. Acts 19:19. See also the excellent work of Clinton E. Arnold, *The Colossian Syncretism: The Interface Between Christianity and Folk Belief at Colossae* (Grand Rapids: Baker, 1997), 15ff.

28. Meyer, ed., *Ancient Mysteries,* 3.

29. Carcopino, *Daily Life,* 121.

30. Ibid., 123.

31. Ibid., 128. Certainly, the pagan gods of the Mystery Religious, like Mithras, brought "deliverance," but this is supremely so in the case of the goddess, the perfect symbol of divinized Nature.

32. From Arnold, *Colossian Syncretism,* 142.

33. Ibid., 124. Angus, *Mystery Religions,* 53, supports this distinction.

34. Arnold, *Colossian Syncretism,* 143.

35. As a second-century A.D. observer stated. See Beard, et al., eds., *Religions of Rome,* vol. 1, 245.

36. Angus, *Mystery Religions,* vii, describes a kind of spirituality rather than a specific Christian heresy. Other examples can be found in Meyer, ed., *Ancient Mysteries,* 131.

37. Walter Burkert, *Ancient Mystery Cults* (Cambridge, Mass.: Harvard Univerity Press, 1987), 11.

38. Ibid., 298. In the mystery cult of Mithras, only men were admitted, but this was an exception, somewhat like the earth-based male spirituality nowadays promoted by Robert Bly.

39. Ibid., 299.

40. Beard, et al., eds. *Religions of Rome,* vol. 1, 300.

41. Liberation from creational norms is the theological meaning of the acceptance and normalization of homosexuality in any culture. See my article, "Androgyny: The Pagan Sexual Ideal," *Journal of the Evangelical Theological Society* (September 2000), 443–69.

42. Augustine, *City of God,* vii:26.

43. Turcan, *Cults,* 58.

44. Augustine, *City of God.*

45. Recent excavations at Catterick, northern England, have discovered the remains of a fourth century young Roman man who dressed as a woman and probably castrated himself. See "Transvestite Ancient Roman Unearthed in Britain" (London: Reuters, 21 May 2002).

46. Angus, *Mystery Religions*, 45.

47. See Burkert, *Ancient Mystery Cults*, 8.

48. Carcopino, *Daily Life*, 54.

49. Col. 2:18, as expertly explained by Arnold, *Colossian Syncretism*, 123, seems to know this reality: "Let no one condemn you by insisting on ascetic practices and invoking angels because he entered the things he had seen." This implies that he based his knowledge/authority on visionary experiences he received during the final stage of his mystery initiation.

50. Cited in Angus, *Mystery Religions*, 70.

51. Ibid., 102. Proclus (A.D. 410–485), *In Remp.* II. 108, 17–30, can still write about this experience in the fifth century: "They . . . assimilate themselves to the holy symbols, leave their own identity, become at home with the gods, and experience divine possession."

52. Burkert, *Ancient Mystery Cults*, 108.

53. Ibid., 112.

54. Ibid., 104.

55. This is the famous passage from Apuleius's *Metamorphoses*, an early second-century A.D. novel, cited in Burkert, *Ancient Mystery Cults*, 97.

56. Cited, ibid.

57. Turcan, *Cults*, 80.

58. Burkert, *Ancient Mystery Cults*, 101.

59. See chapter 4.

60. A cult of witches associated with Mount Ida in Crete who called themselves Dactyls or "Fingers."

61. See H. D. Betz, "Fragments from a Catabasis Ritual in a Greek Magical Papyrus," *HistRel* 19 (1980), 293. These could well be two sides of the goddess, as in the Gnostic text, *Thunder Perfect Mind* VI:13ff, which is a statement by Isis: "I am the whore and the holy one . . . the wife and the virgin . . . I am the one whose wisdom is great in Egypt (Isis) . . . I am sinless and the root of sin derives from me . . . I am the one who is called Truth and iniquity." See *The Nag Hammadi Texts in English* (San Francisco: Harper and Row, 1977), 271–76. According to Robert A. J. Gagnon, *The Bible and Homosexual Practice* (Nashville: Abingdon, 2001), 102, "dog" throughout the ancient world, including the Bible, was a reference to homosexual cult prostitutes, men "'whose masculinity has been transformed into femininity' by a goddess."

62. Turcan, *Cults*, 70, discusses the short period of the repaganization of the now "Christian" empire by the emperor Julian in the middle of the fourth century.

63. Ibid., 130.

64. Ibid., 195–247.

65. Ibid., 87–88.

66. Finegan, *Myth and Mystery,* 196.

67. Ibid., 90.

68. Ibid.

69. Ibid., 91.

70. Ibid., 34.

71. The words of Turcan, *Cults,* 90.

72. The *religious* character of this event is indicated by the *bas relief* details of Titus's arch. The victorious soldiers wearing their laurel wreaths are carrying the seven-branched lampstand, the table of showbread and the sacred trumpets. The value of these spoils was hardly their financial worth but rather their spiritual symbolism as despoiled holy articles, plundered from Jahweh's now-destroyed temple.

73. Josephus, *Wars of the Jews* 6:5:7 in *Josephus: Complete Works,* trans. William Whiston (Grand Rapids: Kregel, 1960), 581. Josephus, who is seeking to win the approval of Rome, argues that Titus had no intention of destroying the Holy of Holies, and sought valiantly to get his men to stop. Josephus makes no mention of the connection between Isis and Titus.

74. Simon Hornblower and Antony Spawforth, eds., *The Oxford Classical Dictionary,* Third Edition (Oxford: Oxford University Press, 1996), 491.

75. Beard, et al., eds., *Religions of Rome,* vol. 1, 253.

76. Ibid.

77. In a particular form, the goddess is present in the church of Thyatira (Rev. 2:20), served by a "Christian" prophetess calling herself Jezebel. The spirituality of the mystery religions is also present in the church at Colossi. See Arnold, *Colossian Syncretism,* 123.

78. Caitlin Matthews, *Sophia: Goddess of Wisdom* (London: The Aquarian Press, 1992), 330.

79. Robin Lane Fox, *Pagans and Christians* (San Francisco: Harper and Row, 1986), 34.

80. Matthews, *Sophia,* 34.

81. Angus, *Mystery Religions,* 191. The term in Greek is πάνθεος. Isis is acclaimed as "panthea." See Fox, *Pagans,* 685–86, note 26.

82. Ramsey McMullen, *Christianity and Paganism in the Fourth to the Eighth Centuries* (New Haven: Yale University Press, 1997), 32–33.

83. Angus, *Mystery Religions,* 19.

84. See Peter Jones, *Spirit Wars: Pagan Revival in Christian America*

(Mukilteo, Wash.: Winepress, 1997), 25–29, reedited as *Pagans in the Pews: How the New Spirituality Is Invading Your Home, Church and Community* (Ventura, Calif.: Regal Books, 2001), 32–37.

85. Angus, *Mystery Religions,* 16.

86. Ibid., 19.

87. Den Heyer, *Paul,* 25, describes the Empire as "a real melting pot of languages, cultures and religions."

88. Ibid., 278. See also Fox, *Pagans,* 34–36.

89. Casson, *Everyday Life,* 85.

90. Angus, *Mystery Religions,* 19–20.

91. Ibid., 11.

92. Angus, *Mystery Religions,* 47.

93. Dupont, *Daily Life,* 162, notes that "the forum was a temple: everything took place under the gaze of the gods. Yet it belonged to no one god in particular, just as it belonged to no single citizen. It was neutral."

94. Fox, *Pagans,* 34. I have slightly modified the translation for the sake of clarity. This syncretism was already the case in Athens in the first century. See Acts 17.

95. Ibid., 278.

96. Turcan, *Cults,* 330.

97. Ibid., 280.

98. Maximus of Tyre, 2:10c-d, cited in Robert Grant, *Paul in the Roman World: The Conflict at Corinth* (Louisville, Ky.: John Knox/Westminster, 2001), 67.

99. Celsus 5:45. Cited in Robert L. Wilken, *Remembering the Christian Past* (Grand Rapids: Eerdmans, 1995), 34.

100. PL 16.1010, cited ibid., 27.

101. Hippolytus of Rome, *Refutation of All Heresies,* 5:7:1–24 cp. 8:31–9:11. See also Meyer, ed., *Ancient Mysteries,* 146–47.

102. For Rome, see Beard, et al., eds., *Religions of Rome,* vol. 1, 249–260, and for the syncretism in general, see the firsthand account in Acts 17.

103. Angus, *Mystery Religions,* 19–20. See also his later work, *Religious Quests of the Graeco-Roman World: A Study in the Historical Background of Early Christianity* (London: Biblo-Moser, 1929), 14.

104. Casson, *Everyday Life,* 84.

105. See Herbert B. Workman, *Persecution in the Early Church* (Cincinnati: Jennings and Graham, 1906), 54, who discusses the charge leveled against Christians, namely "*odium generis humani,* 'hatred against

civilized society,'" or, as we should phrase it today, the crime of anarchism."
Not specific acts of incendiarism or [other crimes], but "the question whether
a man was a Christian became the most essential part of the charge against
him." Workman recalls Christ's prophecy in Matt. 10:22 that his disciples
would be hated by all men "because of the name."

106. McMullen, *Christianity and Paganism*, 32–33, ties the *pax Romana*
and paganism together.

107. Den Heyer, *Paul*, 26, states: "with one exception, Roman tolerance
went so far as to accept the gods of the conquered people and give them a full
place alongside their own religious ideas."

Chapter 3

1. Taken from the text of the *Charter*, posted on the UN Web site, *earth-charter.org*.

2. John O'Leary, "Hope But No Glory at School Prom," *The Los Angeles
Times*, 12 October 2001.

3. A teacher attending my lectures in Milwaukee in October 2001, gave me
this information.

4. Geering, *World to Come*, 95.

5. Alvin and Heidi Toffler, *War and Anti-war: Survival at the Dawn of the
21st Century* (New York: Little, Brown and Co., 1993), 242.

6. William Greider, *One World, Ready or Not* (New York: Simon &
Schuster, 1997), 468.

7. Mikhail Gorbachev, "A Leading Role for the Security Council," *The New
York Times* (21 October 2001).

8. Leo Marx, professor at Amherst College, recently said: "On ecological
grounds, the case for world government is beyond argument." Walter
Williams, "Environmental Radicals' Agenda Red, Not Green," *Human Events*
(5 December 1997), 11. See Samuel L. Blumenfeld, "Mad Madeleine and
WW III," *WorldNetDaily* (2 June 1999).

9. Barry M. Goldwater, *The Architecture of Modern Political Power*
(Cambridge: Cambridge University Press, 1979).

10. "AOL Time Warner to Seek International Dominance," *AFP*, San
Francisco, 3 May 2001.

11. Tim Dearborn, "A Global Future for Local Churches," *The Local
Church in a Global Era: Reflections for a New Century*, eds. Max L. Stackhouse,
Tim Dearborn and Scott Paeth (Grand Rapids: Eerdmans, 2000), 211.

12. James Langton, "Global Trends 2015—Central Intelligence Agency," *Issue 2046,* NewYork, Sunday 31 December 2000.

13. 18 October 2000.

14. Henry Lamb, "U.S. Senate Gives UN Control of 70% of World's Land Mass," *WorldNetDaily,* 9 December 2000.

15. Rex Robinson, "Illinois UN Official Predicts New World Order," *Daily Southtown,* 12 May 2001.

16. This forum brings around two thousand leaders in business to discuss the future of the world's economy.

17. Maurice Strong, *Where on Earth Are We Going?* (New York: Texere, 2001), 2–3.

18. Strobe Talbott, "The Birth of the Global Nation," *Time,* 20 July 1992.

19. Maurice Strong, "Stockholm to Rio: A Journey Down a Generation," see UN Web site. See also Maurice F. Strong, "Preface," International Development Research and Policy Task Force, *Connecting with the World: Priorities for Canadian Internationalism in the 21st Century* (Winnipeg, Manitoba: International Institute for Sustainable Development, in conjunction with the International Development Research Centre and the North-South Institute, November 1996), vi.

20. William F. Jaspers, "Bush and the Council for Revolution," *The New American,* 12 March 2001.

21. *Abcnews.go.com,* 7 February 2001.

22. Geering, *World to Come,* 152.

23. Mihajlo Mesarovic and Eduard Pestel, *Mankind at the Turning Point— The Second Report to the Club of Rome* (New York: E. P. Dutton & Co., Inc./Reader's Digest Press, 1974), 143, 147.

24. Sociologist Wilfred M. McClay, *The Masterless: Self and Society in Modern America* (Chapel Hill: University of North Carolina Press, 1994), 288.

25. Cited in Jaspers, "Bush and the CFR." See also his "Global Gorby," *The New American* (1996), taken from the magazine's Web site.

26. See the thoughtful analysis of Samuel P. Huntingdon, *The Clash of Civilizations and the Remaking of the World Order* (New York: Simon & Schuster, 1996), 40–68.

27. Dearborn, "A Global Future," 211.

28. Ibid., 78–79.

29. Ibid., 84.

30. Richard Kirk, "The Death of Pop Culture?" *North County Times,* 6 November 2001, A8.

31. William F. Buckley Jr., "Porn, Pervasive Presence: The Creepy Wallpaper of Our Daily Lives," *National Review,* 19 November 2001.

32. For these details, see Frank Rich, "Naked Capitalists: There's No Business Like Porn Business," *The New York Times Magazine,* May 2001.

33. Quoted by Buckley, "Porn, Pervasive Presence."

34. See the statement of the author, Toby Young, "Confessions of a Porn Addict," *The Spectator,* 11 October 2001: "They say that in London you're never more than ten feet away from a rat. In modern Britain, it seems, you're never ten seconds away from pornography."

35. Neal Gabler, *Life, the Movie: How Entertainment Conquered Reality* (New York: Vintage, 2000).

36. *Vote.com,* January 2000.

37. Roger Kimball, *The Long March: How the Cultural Revolution of the 1960s Changed America* (San Francisco: Encounter Books, 2000), 5.

38. See Gertrude Himmelfarb, *One Nation, Two Cultures: A Moral Divide* (New York: Knopf, 1999), for an excellent documentation of this phenomenon.

39. In the Bible, patriarchy, literally the rule of the father, or the responsibility of the father for his family, is to be modeled after the loving rule of God the Father. The head of home takes spiritual responsibility for his family and must lead with Christlike service and self-sacrifice—see Eph. 5:22–6:4. In no sense can the Bible's picture of the father/husband be made to look like radical Islamic, "talebanesque" authoritarianism.

40. Liz Trotta, "Museum exhibit puts nude at Last Supper" (Brooklyn Museum confuses vulgarity with art—again!), *The Washington Times ,* 16 February 2001.

41. Melissa Wood, "Book Throws New Grenade into Military Women Debate," *Norfolk Virginian Pilot,* 18 January 2001.

42. Ann Coulter, "Editorial: Title IX defeats male athletes," *Jewish World Review* (31 July 2001).

43. Suzanne Fields, "Feminization of Law," *The Washington Times* 2 April 2001.

44. Taking the whole of Christian history as his subject, Leon J. Podles portrays *The Church Impotent: The Feminization of Christianity* (Dallas: Spence Publishing Company, 1999).

45. Richard Tarnas, *The Passion of the Western Mind* (New York: Harmony Books, 1991), 479.

46. Lionel Tiger, the Charles Darwin Professor of Anthropology at Rutgers University, has a powerful book, *The Decline of Males* (New York:

Golden Books, 1999). See also Christina Hoff Sommers in *The War Against Boys: How Misguided Feminism Is Harming Our Young Men* (New York: Simon & Schuster, 2000), 24ff.

47. Tarnas, *Passion of the Western Mind,* 479.

48. Chris Nutter, "How Gay Men Are Remodeling Regular Guys Post-Straight," *Village Voice,* 8 August 2001.

49. See Larry Crabb Jr., well-known author and psychologist, in the "Foreword," in John Piper and Wayne Grudem, *Fifty Crucial Questions: An Overview of Central Concerns About Manhood and Womanhood* (The Council on Biblical Manhood and Womanhood: Louisville, Ky.: 1992), 9.

50. Judith Lorber, quoted by Germaine Greer, *The Whole Woman* (London: Doubleday, 1999), 324.

51. Wendy Shalit, *A Return to Modesty: Discovering the Lost Virtue* (New York: Touchstone, 2001), 58–60.

52. Anna Quindlen, "Uncle Sam and Aunt Samantha," *Newsweek* , 5 November 2001, 76.

53. Mary Ann Glendon, *The Current State of the Civil Society Debate* (New York: Institute for American Values, 1997).

54. Jean Bethke Elshtain, *Jane Addams and the Dream of American Democracy: A Life* (New York: Basic Books, 2001).

55. Gertrude Himmelfarb, *The De-Moralization of Society: From Victorian Virtues to Modern Values* (New York: Knopf, 1995).

56. Shalit, *Return to Modesty,* 90–98.

57. Elizabeth Fox-Genovese, *Feminism without Illusions: A Critique of Individualism* (Chapel Hill: University of North Carolina Press, 1991).

58. Shalit, *Return to Modesty,* 73.

59. Barbara Dafoe Whitehead, *The Divorce Culture* (New York: Alfred A. Knopf, 1997), 44–65.

60. Cited in Glenn T. Stanton, *Why Marriage Matters: Reasons to Believe in Marriage in a Postmodern Society* (Colorado Springs: Pinon Press, 1997), 20.

61. *Good News, Etc.,* July 2001, 8.

62. *United Press International,* 7 February 2000.

63. Gerard Reed, *Readings* 97 (January 2000): 3.

64. "New State Regulations Mandate Pro-Homosexual Curriculum," *Pacific Justice Institute* (11 April 2001).

65. *Presbyterian Layman* (November–December 2000), 10.

66. Interview with the *Acton Institute* 5(4) July–August 1995.

67. Himmelfarb, *One Nation, Two Cultures.* See also *De-Moralization.*

68. Alison Hornstein, "The Question That We Should Be Asking," *Newsweek* (17 December 2001), 14.

69. "Schoolboy Wins Right to Dress in Drag," *BBC World News,* 16 October 2000.

70. "Survey Finds Ten Partners before Marriage 'Normal'," *Ananova,* 10 December 2001.

71. James B. Twitchell, *For Shame,* (New York: St. Martin's Press, 1998), 60.

72. Ibid., 86.

73. Ibid.

74. Ibid., 35. See William J. Bennett, *The Death of Outrage: Bill Clinton and the Assault on American Ideals* (New York: Free Press, 1998), 129.

75. Shalit, *Return to Modesty.*

76. Cited in McClay, *The Masterless,* 1.

77. Ibid.

78. Joseph Campbell, *The Power of Myth* (New York: Doubleday, 1988), xix.

79. See Jean Houston's web site, *www.jeanhouston.org.* See also Donna Steichen, *Ungodly Rage: The Hidden Face of Catholic Feminism* (San Francisco: Ignatius Press, 1991), 251.

80. Jean Houston, *The Passion of Isis and Osiris: A Gateway to Transcendent Love* (New York: Ballantine, 1995), 2.

81. As an example, at the UN Beijing Conference on Women in September 1995, the Harvard law professor and Vatican observer, Mary Ann Glendon, observed that this global program for the liberation of all women was "more about the ideology of the 1970s than the women's issues of the 1990s." See Joyce Milton, *The First Partner: Hillary Rodham Clinton* (New York: William Morrow and Company, 1999), 355.

82. See Gary Kah, *En Route to Global Occupation* (Lafayette, La.: Huntington House, 1992); Michael S. Coffman, *Saviors of the Earth: The Politics and Religion of the Environmental Movement* (Chicago: Northfield Publishing, 1994); Jaspers, *The United Nations Exposed.*

83. Gorbachev, "A Leading Role for the Security Council," *New York Times,* 21 October, 2001.

84. Geering, *World to Come,* 147.

85. Desmond O'Grady, "Gorbachev Gathers Pals for a New World Order," *smh.com,* 3 April 2001.

86. Strong also authored the *Earth Charter,* a UN document for world ecology, with Mikhail Gorbachev. To see the scope of his influence, see

Strong's autobiography, *Where on Earth?* which includes a foreword by Kofi Annan, General Secretary of the UN.

87. "UN Reform: Restructuring for Global Governance," *Eco-logic: Sovereignty International* (July–August 1998), an Internet Web site.

88. See Strong, *Where on Earth?* 241–42.

89. The editor of *Eco-logic,* ibid.

90. For much of the above, I am indebted to *Eco-logic,* ibid.

91. *The Washington Times,* 9 November 1997, 6.

92. Jaspers, *United Nations Exposed,* 33, 158.

93. Ibid., 38. See also Strong, *Where on Earth?* 382.

94. Jaspers, *United Nations Exposed,* 208–209, 216, 239, 231.

95. Ibid., 268–71.

96. Strong, *Where on Earth?* 384.

97. Ibid., 386.

98. Jaspers, *United Nations Exposed,* 117, 121.

99. *Agenda 21: The Earth Summit Strategy to Save the Planet* (Boulder, Colo.: Earth Press, 1993), 70. Cited ibid.

100. Francis Schaeffer, *The Church at the End of the Twentieth Century; The Complete Works of Francis Schaeffer: A Christian View of the Church,* vol. 4 (Westchester, Ill.: Crossway Books, 1982, originally published in 1970), 79.

101. Ibid., 80, 85.

102. From the information page of Lightworkers, *http.//lightworkers.com,* a channeling group, extremely active at the United Nations. See below.

103. With funds from Turner's UN Foundation, to which he gave a billion dollars. Heading the foundation is Timothy Wirth, a former US undersecretary of state for global affairs in the Clinton administration.

104. Darren Logan from the Family Research Council covered the affair and stated that Turner's speech "was the most blasphemous thing I have ever heard in my life."

105. *Toronto Star,* 19 May 1994, front page.

106. EPI News, September 2000.

107. See John Leo's excellent article, "Stealth Language at The UN Is Dangerously Undemocratic," *Jewish World Review,* 11 September 2001.

108. Discerning The Times website, 7 September 2000.

109. Leo, "Stealth Language."

110. "World Forum 2000: Science, Spirituality, & World Power," *Newsletter of the American Scientific Affiliation & Canadian Scientific & Christian Affiliation* 43 (3) May–June 2001.

111. Cited in Jaspers, *United Nations Exposed*, 30.

112. Strong, *Where on Earth?* 4.

113. Cited in Jaspers, *United Nations Exposed*, 24.

114. Strong, "The Earth as We Know It Has Less Than 30 Years to Survive," *The (Toronto) Globe and Mail*, 22 May 2000.

115. Robinson, "Illinois UN Official."

116. Gorbachev, *"A Leading Role."*

117. Stuart Taylor, *National Journal*, 12 November 2001.

118. Susan Page, "Hillary and Albright," *USA Today*, 16 July 1998. See also the documented evidence by a brilliant woman, Dale O'Leary, *The Gender Agenda: Redefining Equality* (Lafayette, La.: Vital Issues Press, 1997).

119. Strong, *Where on Earth?* 97. Strong boasts of being Wolfensohn's first appointment when the latter took over the bank (287).

120. Ibid., 289.

121. Ibid., 288.

122. When, for instance, Max Padilla, head of the Nicaraguan Ministry for the Family, insisted in defining gender as male and female, the European development agencies, which both share and influence the ideology of the World Bank, demanded the inclusion of gays and transvestites. Nicaragua fired Padilla to get its aid. See Wendy McElroy, "World Bank or World Government?" *Fox News*, 16 April 2002.

123. Ibid.

124. See the Web site, *www.earthcharter.org/draft/charter.htm*.

125. Marilyn Ferguson, "Aquarius Now . . . Making It Through the Confusion Gap," *Visions Magazine* (July 1994): 13, refers to Ilya Progogine's model of dissipative structures.

126. Dianne Knippers, president of the Institute on Religion and Democracy, who was present in Beijing, stated: "The Goddess was everywhere." See her article, "Building a Shrine in Beijing," *Heterodoxy*, 19 October 1995, 7.

127. Tony Schwartz, *What Really Matters: Searching for Wisdom in America* (New York: Bantam Books, 1996), 432.

128. Matthews, *Sophia*, 332.

Chapter 4

1. See Diana L. Eck, *A New Religious America: How a "Christian Country" Has Become the World's Most Religiously Diverse Nation* (San Francisco: Harper, 2001), 352. Eck says: "these enactments have a significance quite beyond the merely ceremonial."

2. Readers will remember that Isis is described as the goddess of a thousand names. Durga is one of her names, one Hindu manifestation of the same, essential spirituality.

3. According to the 1960s musical *Hair*. For some, Aquarius, the water carrier, is the goddess who brings thirst-quenching spiritual fulfillment.

4. David L. Miller, *The New Polytheism: Rebirth of the Gods and Goddesses* (New York: Harper & Row, 1974), 4. Says the once-Christian professor of religion at Syracuse University: "The death of God gave rise to the rebirth of the gods. We are polytheists."

5. In 1979, the publication of the articulate witch Starhawk's *The Spiritual Dance* (San Francisco: Harper and Row) and Margot Adler's *Drawing Down the Moon: Witches, Druids, Goddess-Worshippers, and Other Pagans in America Today* (New York: Viking Press, 1979), set the tone for the Great Goddess Re-Emerging Conference in Santa Cruz, California, and the launching of the Radical Faerie Movement (gay pagans) in Tucson, Arizona, at the same time. In 1993 the Re-Imagining Conference in Minneapolis, where two thousand mainline "Christian" women worshiped the goddess Sophia, signaled her full-blown arrival in the Western Church.

6. See the original citation at the beginning of chapter 2. I am referring here to the World Peace Summit of Religious and Spiritual Leaders that took place from August 28–29, 2000, mentioned in chapter 3.

7. See Eck, *New Religious America*, 383.

8. Richard Grigg, *When God Becomes Goddess: The Transformation of American Religion* (New York: Continuum, 1995).

9. Ibid., 22.

10. Isis is often portrayed with an *ankh* or ancient Egyptian key, symbolizing both authority and the key to life.

11. Mary Daly, *Beyond God the Father: Towards a Philosophy of Women's Liberation* (Boston: Beacon Press, 1973), 96.

12. Houston, *Passion of Isis*, 2.

13. See "First Lady's 'Adviser' Says She's Not a Psychic," *The Providence Journal Bulletin*, 25 June 1996, A3.

14. Houston, *Passion of Isis*, 2.

15. Cynthia Eller, *Living in the Lap of the Goddess: The Feminist Spirituality Movement in America* (Boston: Beacon Press, 1993), 18.

16. See Ben Fenton, *London Telegraph*, 14 May 1999.

17. Campbell, *Power of Myth*, 5.

18. Ibid., 12.

19. Ibid., 4.

20. Wendy Hunter Roberts, *Celebrating Her: Feminist Ritualizing Comes of Age* (Cleveland, Ohio: Pilgrim Press, 1998). See the summer/spring catalog of the Pilgrim Press, the United Church of Christ publishing arm.

21. Sue Monk Kidd, *The Dance of the Dissident Daughter: A Woman's Journey from Christian Tradition to the Sacred Feminine* (San Francisco: Harper, 1996).

22. Deena Metzger, "Revamping the World: On the Return of the Holy Prostitute," *Anima* 12/2 (1986), cited in George Otis, Jr., *The Twilight Labyrinth: Why Does Spiritual Darkness Linger Where It Does?* (Grand Rapids: Chosen Books, 1997), 107.

23. Plutarch (A.D. 46–119), *Def. Or.* 421 A.

24. George Barna, *Virtual America: What Every Church Leader Needs to Know about Ministering in an Age of Spiritual and Technological Revolution* (Ventura, Ca.: Regal Books, 1994), 49.

25. Ibid., 107.

26. Gene Edward Veith, "Unbelieving Politicians," *World*, October 1999, 26.

27. Larry Witham, "What Path for Christianity? Three Theologians, Three Views," *The Washington Times*, 29 February 2000.

28. See Chris Stamper, "Homegrown Paganism," *World*, 24 June 2000, 13.

29. Alan Wolfe, *One Nation after All* (New York: Viking, 1997).

30. Francis Schaeffer, *Pollution and the Death of Man* (Downers Grove, Ill.: InterVarsity, 1970). See also Os Guinness in *Dust of Death* (Downers Grove, Ill.: InterVarsity, 1973), 229, 281.

31. Philip Schaff, *America: A Sketch of Its Political, Social and Religious Character*, ed. Perry Miller (Cambridge, Mass.: 1961), cited in Catherine L. Albanese, "Religion and the American Experience a Century After," *Church History* 57 (September 1988): 337.

32. Eck, *New Religious America*, 4–5.

33. Ibid., 1.

34. Ibid., 376–77.

35. Ibid., 377.

36. See chapter 2.

37. "Oldest Religion in Britain Was Reinvented in the 1960s," *The (London) Times*, 22 June 1998, 11.

38. Winter catalog (HarperSanFrancisco: 1996): 18.

39. Eck, *New Religious America*, 359.

40. Sandi Dolbee, "Harmonic Conversion: Interfaith Unity Raises

Questions about Evangelism," *The San Diego Union Tribune*, 21 April 1998, E1. For an excellent study of the interfaith movement in Great Britain, see Herbert J. Pollitt, *The Inter-Faith Movement: The New Age Enters the Church* (Edinburgh: The Banner of Truth Trust, 1996).

41. Ibid.

42. Ibid., 54. The book is *The Boy Who Cried Abba: A Parable of Trust and Acceptance* (San Francisco: HarperCollins, 1997).

43. John Caddock, "The New Monk of Mystic Protestantism: A Review of Brennan Manning's *The Signature of Jesus*," *Spiritual Counterfeits Project Journal* 21 (4)—22 (1): 46 (1998).

44. Cited, ibid., 53

45. *Presbyterian Layman* (November–December 2000): 2. See also the excellent book by Ray Yungen, *A Time of Departing: How a Universal Spirituality Is Changing the Face of Christianity* (Silverton, OR.: Lighthouse Trails, 2002), 77–92, 131–32.

46. Uwe Siemon-Netto, "Poll shows Protestant collapse," *UPI*, 28 June 2001.

47. *Presbyterian Layman*, November–December 2000, 2.

48. Dan Cohn-Sherbok, *The Jewish Messiah: The Future of a Delusion* (London: Dr. William's Trust, 1999), 3.

49. *Weekly World News*, 13 November 2001, 27.

50. Even serious religious thinkers speak of the transformative power of the Tarot. See Virginia Ramey Mollenkott, *Sensuous Spirituality: Out from Fundamentalism* (New York: Crossroads, 1992), 16.

51. Ibid.

52. Ibid., 128.

53. Matthews, *Sophia*, 330.

54. President Clinton, in a letter to the American Sikh community, said: "Religious pluralism in our nation is bringing us together in new and powerful ways." Cited by Eck, *New Religious America*, 7.

55. Ibid., 77.

56. See Schwartz, *What Really Matters*, 431. See also the end of chapter 3 above.

57. Geering, *World to Come* and *Tomorrow's God: How We Create Our Worlds* (Santa Rosa, Calif.: Polebridge, 2000).

58. Peter Occhiogrosso, *The Joy of Sects: A Spirited Guide to the World's Religious Traditions* (New York: Doubleday, 1996), xvi.

59. Starhawk, "What Would the Goddess Do?" Belief Net Website, September 2001.

60. Kathy Kersten, "A New Heaven & a New Earth," *First Things*, March 1994, 10.

61. Campbell, *Power of Myth*, 121.

62. Judaism and Islam, being Christian heresies, retain something of the structure of biblical theism, though, being heresies, they are more and more unable to stand before the power of paganism.

63. Surya Das, *Awakening the Buddha Within: Tibetan Wisdom for the Western World* (New York: Broadway Books, 1997), 16.

64. Harold Bloom, *The American Religion: The Emergence of a Post-Christian Nation* (New York: Simon & Schuster, 1992), 27. See also his *Omens of Millennium: The Gnosis of Angels, Dreams, and Resurrection* (New York: Riverhead Books, 1996), 165, 171–72. Bloom is a world expert on Shakespeare, Sterling Professor of Humanities at Yale, and Berg Professor of English at New York University.

65. Geering, *Tomorrow's God*, 161.

66. Hans Küng, *A Global Ethic: The Declaration of the Parliament of the World's Religions* (New York: Continuum, 1995).

67. Geering, *Tomorrow's God*, 147.

68. Ibid., 148.

69. Ibid., 158.

70. Ibid., 156–57.

71. This is the view of David Spangler, an ex-Pentecostal New Age teacher, as documented by Ron Rhodes, "The New Age Christ of David Spangler," *Spiritual Counterfeits Project Journal* 23 (2–3): 22–23 (1999).

72. "Global Spirit Library," *The Pilgrim Press: Professional and Academic Books Catalogue 2001–2002* (Cleveland, Ohio: Pilgrim Press, 2001), 9.

73. In 1993 Robert Funk, founder of the Jesus Seminar, published with Roy Hoover *The Five Gospels: The Search for the Authentic Words of Jesus* (New York: Macmillan, 1993), which demonstrated a decided predilection for the "Gnostic" Jesus of the Gospel of Thomas.

74. Larry Witham, "Buddhism Influences American Thought," *The Washington Times National Weekly Edition*, 26 October 1997, 28.

75. Steve Bonta, "New Age Roots," *The New American*, March 1999, 23.

76. Helena Blavatsky, *The Secret Doctrine: The Synthesis of Science, Religion and Philosophy* (Pasadena, Calif.: Theosophical University Press, 1963), xxiv.

77. Ibid., xxxvii.

78. Helena Blavatsky, *Isis Unveiled: A Master-Key to the Mysteries of Ancient and Modern Science and Theology* (Pasadena, Calif.: Theosophical University Press, 1958), 123.

79. Das, *Buddha Within*, 370.

80. Herbert G. McCann, "Dalai Lama Ends Tour of U.S.," *Associated Press/North County Times*, 29 August 1999, A3. Also, Das, *Buddha Within*, 381.

81. Kathleen Alexander-Berghorn, "Isis: The Goddess as Healer," *Women of Power* (winter 1987): 20, cited in Ruth Tucker, *Another Gospel: Alternative Religions and the New Age Movement* (Grand Rapids: Zondervan, 1989), 340–41.

82. See Jones, *Spirit Wars*, 217, or *Pagans in the Pews*, 196.

83. Houston, *Passion of Isis*, 28.

84. Bloom, *Omens of Millennium*, 141.

85. Monica Sjoo and Barbara Mor, *The Great Cosmic Mother: Discovering the Religion of the Earth* (San Francisco: Harper, 1987), 131.

86. Lucian, *Mennipus or Necromancer*, 6, cited in Turcan, *Cults*, 267.

87. Ibid., 2.

88. Houston, *Passion of Isis*, 281.

89. Helen Shucman, *A Course in Miracles* (N.Y.; Foundation for Inner Peace, 1975), 47, 262.

90. Lynn Vincent, "Underestimating Evil?" *World*, 11 March 2000, 29.

91. George Otis, Jr. (Grand Rapids: Fleming H. Revell, Co., 1997) *Twilight Labyrinth*, 22.

92. Ibid.

93. Cited in Lee Penn, "New Age and Global Strategies: Unity, Collectivism and Control," *Spiritual Counterfeits Project Journal* 23 (4)–24 (1): 51 (2000).

94. Matthew Fox, *Cosmic Christ*, 229.

95. Paul Knitter, *No Other Name? A Critical Survey of Christian Attitudes towards the World's Religions* (Maryknoll, N.Y.: Orbis Books, 1986), 224.

96. Ibid., 225–26.

97. Eck, *New Religious America*, 380.

98. Matthew Fox, *Cosmic Christ*, 232.

99. Schwartz, *What Really Matters*.

100. Information taken from the program brochure, on the theme: "Birth of the Planetary Human," tracing the "outlines of a worldwide transformation of the human spirit."

101. Sally McFargue was the keynote speaker at the Sophia Summer Institute at Holy Names College, Oakland, Calif., 28 June—1 July 2001.

102. Willis Harman, in an essay, "Our Hopeful Future: Creating a Sustainable Society," distributed at the State of the World Forum. See Jaspers, "Global Gorby," *The New American* (1996), taken from their Web site, *TheNewAmerican.com.*

103. Ibid., 105.

104. Ibid., 149.

105. "Co-creating Heaven on Earth," *The Light Connection,* July 1992, 11.

106. Wendy Hunter Roberts, "In Her Name: Towards a Feminist Theology of Pagan Ritual," *Women at Worship: Interpretations of North American Diversity,* ed. Majorie Procter-Smith and Janet R. Walton (Louisville, Ky.: Westminster, John Knox Press, 1999), 139, speaking of paganism with the help of a mainline Presbyterian press. See also Geering, *Tomorrow's God,* 160: "There will not be 'only one way' . . . groups must learn to be inclusive."

107. McCann, "Dalai Lama," A3.

108. See UN high-level bureaucrat and New Age spiritualist Robert Mueller's view, cited in Gary H. Kah, *The New World Religion: The Spiritual Roots of Global Religion* (Noblesville, Ind.: Hope International Publishing, 1998), 222.

109. Ibid.

110. Cited on the Internet entry of The Gnostic Society Library, *home.sn.no/home/noetic/nagham/nhlintro.html.* In an ad in the *Los Angeles Times,* 8 August 1988, B5, the "Universal Christian Gnostic Movement: New Order of the U.S.A." offers "knowledge of the truth through direct experience."

111. Schwartz, *What Really Matters,* 32.

112. Ibid., 410, 415.

113. For Wendy Hunter Roberts, tolerance has its limits. In deep prayer, she calls "out for the protection of the Goddess's people from the wrath of right wing fundamentalists and their God." She has no place for the God of the Bible. See *Women at Worship,* 158.

114. *Gnosis Magazine* (fall 1998): 5.

115. Some apparently do not. An example of confusion is Anne Marshall, a Muscogee Creek Indian and executive in the United Methodist Church. She says: "Our Native traditions are not pagan, they are sacramental. They have allowed our people to survive for four hundred years." See Eck, *New Religious America,* 301.

116. Geering, *Tomorrow's God,* 128.

117. Ibid.

118. Ibid.

119. Cited in Lee Penn, "The United Religions: Globalist and New Age Plans," *Spiritual Counterfeits Project Journal* 23 (2–3): 42 (1999).

120. John Shelby Spong, in "A Call for a New Reformation," *The Fourth R* 11 (4): 6–7 (July–August 1998). See also *Why Christianity Must Change or Die: A Bishop Speaks to Believers in Exile* (San Francisco: Harper, 1998).

121. Ibid.

122. Geering, *Tomorrow's God*, 129.

123. Ibid., 154.

124. Charlotte Allen, "The Scholars and the Goddess," *Atlantic Monthly* (January 2001), website version, states that Wiccans who embrace goddess spirituality "tend to be white, middle-class, highly educated and politically involved in liberal and environmental causes." This article debunks many of the historical claims made for feminist/goddess religion.

125. Mikhail Gorbachev, "Environment: Act Globally, Not Nationally," *Los Angeles Times*, 8 May 1997.

126. There seems to be a significant connection between a globalist vision, occult theosophy, and Buddhism, which I cannot develop in this context. Madame Blavatsky, founder of Theosophy, wanted to unite the world through a spirituality of Buddhism; her disciple Annie Besant had a Tibetan/Buddhist spirit guide; Alice Bailey of the Lucis Trust had a Tibetan spirit guide and saw the spirit at work in the UN; Adolf Hitler, with his visions of a this-worldly empire, was also a keen theosophist who brought many Tibetan Buddhists to Berlin; the globalist Gorbachev favors Buddhism and theosophy, declaring the year of Perestroika for the Soviet Union as also the year of Madame Blavatsky; finally, the Buddhist Dalai Lama, who calls the world to spiritual unity, has his own sources of occult spiritual power.

127. An open letter from the Lucis Trust, Wall Street, New York, dated "Three Spiritual Festivals," 2002.

128. *A Spiritual Renaissance* (New York: World Goodwill, 2002), 1–2.

129. Ibid., 2.

130. Eck, *New Religious America*, 377. She singles out for mention the Trappist monastery, Gethsemani, founded by Thomas Merton, where Buddhist and Christian monks pray regularly together. How much this flies in the face of the original Gethsemane, where Jesus prayed the most important prayer ever offered in human history, praying the way he taught his disciples to pray, "not like the pagans" (Matt. 6:7).

131. *Boston Research Center Newsletter* 16 (winter 2000): 14.

132. Ibid., 12.

133. Ibid., 15.

134. Ibid., 12–13.

135. Alice Bailey wrote her autobiography to render a service: "It might be useful to know how a rabid orthodox Christian worker could become a well-known occult teacher." See *The Complete Works of Alice A. Bailey* (New York: Lucis Trust, 2000).

136. Penn, "Coming World Religion": 51.

137. Alice B. Bailey, *Discipleship in the New Age* (New York: Lucis Press, 1955), 35.

138. They also have other posh offices in downtown Geneva and London.

139. Bailey, *A Time of Expectancy* (New York: Lucis Trust, 2001).

140. Ibid., 90.

141. Maurice Strong, *Where on Earth?* 20–21, who knows most of the world's leaders by their first names (how many orthodox Christian leaders could claim that?) imagines the state of the world in 2031. According to Strong, in the midst of a societal meltdown (see his predictions, recounted in chapter 3), his vision includes the appearance of a charismatic figure, Tadi, of Welsh, Armenian, and Morrocan origin, who has "isolated the basic spiritual, ethical and moral values underpinning all the world's religions." After spending ten years as a Christian missionary to Guyana, Tadi "came to reject his narrow, fundamentalist vision of the world" and embrace the idea that "in this Time of Troubles God must call all to a new and transcendent unity. . . . What is new is that people of all faiths [with the exception of Jewish, Moslem, and Christian fundamentalists] have embraced Tadi's formulations." Strong's religious world savior turns out to be an apostate Christian.

142. Strong, *Where on Earth?* 107.

143. See Lee Penn, "The United Religions Initiative—A Bridge Back to Gnosticism," *New Oxford Review* (December 1998). See also Patrick J. Buchanan, *The Death of the West* (New York: St. Martin's Press, 2002), 198.

144. Ted Turner, who gave a billion dollars to the UN, said in 1999: ". . . we're smarter than the opposition, because we're thinking long term. . . . I put my money on a smart minority than on the dumb majority. Wouldn't you?" See Tracey C. Rembert, "Ted Turner: Billionaire, Media Mogul . . . and Environmentalist," *E Magazine*, x (1): 12 (January–February 1999), cited in Penn, "United Religions": 60.

145. Strong, *Where on Earth?* 47, states: "I want to help change the world to enable it to be itself, in all its glorious diversity."

146. See the most insightful book by the Roman Catholic philosopher, Thomas Molnar, *Utopia: The Perennial Heresy* (New York: University Press of America, 1990).

147. Strong, *Where on Earth?* 7, who was once an elder in a Christian church, states: "there is nothing beyond the gates of Planet Earth. . . ."

148. Christopher Lasch, *The True and Only Heaven: Progress and Its Crisis* (New York: Norton, 1991), 36.

149. John H. Adams, "Building Community Reveals a House Divided," *Presbyterian Layman,* March–April 1998, 15.

150. Francis Schaeffer, *Genesis in Space and Time: The Flow of Biblical History* (Downers Grove, Ill.: InterVarsity, 1972), 80.

Part Two

1. In A.D. 312, the Emperor Constantine declared Christianity the official religion of the Empire by naming himself its public champion and defender.

2. Rom. 11:13.

3. Rom. 15:16.

4. Col. 2:8ff, and Eph. 2:11–13; 4:17–19.

Chapter 5

1. Peter Jones, *The Gnostic Empire Strikes Back: An Old Heresy for the New Age* (Phillipsburg, N.J.: P&R, 1992).

2. F. F. Bruce, the much respected classical and New Testament scholar, was of this opinion.

3. 2 Pet. 3:16.

4. 2 Cor. 2:17, 4:1.

5. 1 Cor. 15:8.

6. 1 Cor. 9:1ff.

7. Tertullian, *Adversus Marcion* 3:5, *The Ante-Nicene Fathers,* eds. Alexander Roberts and James Donaldson (Grand Rapids: Eerdmans, 1973), 324.

8. By the third century Neo-platonist, Porphyry.

9. In the nineteenth century, by the French scholar, Renan, and Bernard E. Allo, *Saint Paul: Apôtre de Jésus Christ: Sa vie: sa doctrine* (Paris: Editions du Cerf, 1961), 78.

10. Friedrich Nietzsche, cited in H. D. Betz, *Galatians* (Philadelphia: Fortress Press, 1979), xiv.

11. By the Irish playwright, George Bernard Shaw, cited Betz, *Galatians.*

12. On this, see Betz, *Galatians* and Allo, *Saint Paul.*

13. Osty, cited in Allo, ibid.

14. Allo, *Saint Paul.*

15. Rudolf Bultmann, *New Testament Theology* (New York: Scribner, 1955), 187.

16. Wilhelm Wrede, *Paul* (London: P. Green, 1907), 7.

17. For the sake of brevity, I have not been able to include the various hypotheses, which include psychological disturbance, a mystical experience, underlying paganism, theological doubt, career concerns, ordinary conversion, moral collapse, and a troubled conscience, to name a few.

18. 2 Cor. 4:5.

19. Ibid.

20. 1 Cor. 4:9, cp. 15:8.

21. 2 Cor. 11:30, cp. 12:9.

22. A number of well-known New Testament scholars, realizing the failure of the psychologizing interpretation, accept what Paul says, while honestly admitting they cannot explain it. See A. C. Purdy, "Paul the Apostle," *Interpreter's Dictionary of the Bible* 3 (Nashville: Abingdon, 1962), 681–704; Martin Dibelius and W. G. Kümmel, *Paul* (Philadelphia: Westminster Press, 1953), 46ff; Johannes Munck, *Paul and the Salvation of Mankind* (Louisville, Ky.: John Knox Press, 1977), 11–35; and the Jewish scholar Hans Joachim Schoeps, *Paul: The Theology of the Apostle in the Light of Jewish Religious History* (Philadelphia: Westminster Press, 1961), 53–55.

23. See Munck, *Paul,* 23.

24. 1 Cor. 15:8.

25. Acts 9:1–9; 22:6–11; 26:12–18.

26. Gal. 1:15–16.

27. 1 Cor. 9:1.

28. Exod. 3:1–4:17; Isa. 6:1–6.

29. 1 Cor. 9:1. Munck, *Paul,* 22.

30. Eph. 2:20.

31. George E. Ladd, *A Theology of the New Testament* (Grand Rapids: Eerdmans, 1974).

32. 1 Cor. 3:11.

33. The Latin is more rhetorically impressive: "... *Novum in Vetere lateret et in Novo Vetus pateret"*—see Augustine, *Quaest. in Hept* 3:73.

34. Acts 1:22: "... one of these must become a witness with us of his resurrection." Cp. Acts 10:39–43, and 1 Cor. 15:3–8.

35. Oscar Cullmann, *La Tradition: Cahiers Theologiques* 33 (Neuchâtel/Paris: Delachaux & Niestlé, 1953), 32, states: "the apostolate does not belong to the time of the church but to the time of the incarnation."

36. See Herman Ridderbos, trans. H. De Jongste, *The Authority of the New Testament Scriptures* (Philadelphia: P&R, 1963), 13–51.

37. Cullmann, *La Tradition,* 31.

38. *Apostle* means "someone sent," or "someone who has received a formal commission to represent someone else." This text implies that the aggressive young rabbi sought this commission at his own initiative.

39. Gal. 1:16.

40. Gal. 1:15–16.

41. See Hans Conzelmann, *A Commentary on the First Epistle to the Corinthians* (Philadelphia: Fortress Press, 1975), 251–54.

42. 1 Cor. 15:1–2.

43. ἀρχιτεκτονίας (master-builders). See Exod. 35:35. Cp. 1 Kings 7:14; 2 Chron. 2:12, and Paul's expression, ἀρχιτέκτων (1 Cor. 3:10).

44. Eph. 2:20.

45. 1 Cor. 3:16.

46. 1 Cor. 3:10.

47. Eph. 4:16.

48. Eph. 3:4: "My insight" (τὴν σύνεσίν μου).

49. Exod. 3:6. See Exod. 35:31; 1 Chron. 28:19. The insight comes from knowledge of the divinely-revealed plan, which in some cases is written down, inscripturated (1 Chron. 28:12).

50. 2 Cor. 11:4.

51. Gal. 1:12.

52. In the phrase "the grace that was given to me," we see Paul's typical reference to his divine calling (Rom. 12:3; 15:15; 1 Cor. 3:10; Eph. 3:2; 3:7; Col. 1:25, cp. 1 Cor. 15:10; 2 Cor. 5:18; 13:10; Eph. 4:11).

53. Rom. 2:16; 16:25; 2 Tim. 2:8. Cp. 1 Cor. 15:1; 2 Cor. 4:3;11:7; Gal. 1:7; 2:2; 1 Thess. 1:5; 2:4; 2 Thess. 2:14; 1 Tim. 1:11.

54. R. N. Longenecker, *The Ministry and Message of Paul* (Grand Rapids: Zondervan, 1973), 88.

55. God promises the nations to Messiah as his inheritance (Pss. 2:8; 9:11; 18:43, 49; 67:1–2; 82:8; Isa. 42:1, 6–7; 49:1–6; 52:10).

56. See Joachim Jeremias, *Jesus' Promise to the Nations*: Studies in Biblical Theology 24 (London: SCM Press,1967).

57. Paul's phrase in Col. 1:25. Raymond E. Brown, *The Semitic Background of the Term 'Mystery' in the New Testament* (Philadelphia: Fortress Press, 1968), 53, observes: "Among the new elements [in this letter] is the author's insistence on completing the message of God, in showing the full glory of the mysterious divine plan."

58. See Matt. 24:14; Mark 13:10, cp. Matt. 28:19; Luke 21:24; 24:47; Rom. 16:26; Gal. 3:8; Rev. 15:4.

59. Matt. 24:14; Mark 13:10; Luke 21:24; Rom. 11:25–26.

60. For a detailed treatment of this question, see P. Jones, "1 Corinthians 15:8: Paul, the Last Apostle," *Tyndale Bulletin* 36 (1985), 3–34. See also Anthony C. Thiselton in his monumental commentary, *The First Epistle of Paul to the Corinthians: A Commentary on the Greek Text* (Grand Rapids: Eerdmans, 2000), 1,210, who agrees with the thrust of my argument, and Gordon Fee, *The First Epistle to the Corinthians: The New International Commentary on the New Testament* (Grand Rapids: Eerdmans, 1987), 732.

61. For the use of "last" as the end of a series, see Num. 31:2; Josh. 10:14; Judg. 15:7; Prov. 23:32; 29:21; Matt. 5:26; 12:6; Mark 12:6. Mark 12:22 has the same term "last of all" that we find in Paul.

62. Such is the opinion of Dieter Georgi, *The Opponents of Paul in Second Corinthians* (Edinburgh: T&T Clark, 1986), 36.

63. 1 Cor. 15:7. When Paul states in 15:10 that he "worked harder than *all of them,*" as the context demonstrates, he is speaking of "all the apostles." See 1 Cor. 15:9.

64. 1 Cor. 15:8. The King James, Revised Standard, Phillips, New English Bible, and the New International versions do not show this, but the Greek is quite clear: τῷ ἐκτρώματι "the one untimely born."

65. 1 Cor. 15:9: ὁ ἐλάχιστος τῶν ἀποστόλων A. T. Robertson, *A Grammar of the Greek New Testament* (Nashville: Broadman Press, 1934), 669, maintains that this is "a true superlative . . . one of the few in the New Testament," which thus could be literally translated "the most least."

66. 1 Cor. 15:1–2.

67. 1 Cor. 3:10.

68. Gal. 1:12, 16.

69. See Conzelmann, *First Epistle to the Corinthians*, 251.

70. See Elaine Pagels, *The Gnostic Gospels* (New York: Random House, 1979), 142ff, and *The Origin of Satan* (New York: Random House, 1995); Elizabeth Coleman, "The Good Book: Elaine Pagels Explores the Origins and Omissions of the Christian Bible," *Ford Foundation Report* (winter 2002): 31; Albert Nolan's *Jesus Before Christianity* (Maryknoll: Orbis, 1977), endorsed by Harvey Cox; Stevan Davies, "The Christology and Protology of the Gospel of Thomas," *Journal of Biblical Literature* 3 (4): 663–64 (1992). These and many other titles maintain that the earliest Christianity was not Christian.

71. Matt. 8:17, Luke 22:37, John 12:38, and 1 Pet. 2:22.

72. Not, by the way, the role of the Servant as vicarious sufferer (Rom. 9:3, where Paul wishes he could do it, but recognizes he cannot). See Thomas Schreiner, *Paul, Apostle of God's Glory in Christ: A Pauline Theology* (Leicester: InterVarsity, 2001), 47–49.

73. Rom. 1:1; 2 Cor. 4:5, cp. 6:1–2; Titus 1:1.

74. See 1 Cor. 15:7.

75. Different Bible translations will have different English terms. My argument rests on the Greek original, which uses κοπιάω ("to labor") and κενός ("in vain"). These terms reappear in the Greek text of Isaiah.

76. Isa. 49:4.

77. Isa. 65:2, cited in Rom. 10:21, a passage that further develops this early history of the church. See the brilliant study of the Scandinavian scholar J. Munck, *Christ and Israel: An Interpretation of Romans 9-11* (Philadelphia: Fortress Press, 1967), 89–103.

78. Rom. 1:16 and 2:10.

79. Gal. 2:7.

80. Munck, *Christ and Israel,* notes that Paul is "anxious to teach the Gentiles that *they* are the *late-comers,* the undeserving branches." Matt. 20:1–16 doubtless refers to the Gentiles as the "last [who] will be first." See K. Stendahl, *Paul Among Jews and Gentiles* (London: SCM Press, 1977), 38.

81. Munck, *Christ and Israel,* vii.

82. Acts 13:47, a citation of Isa. 49:6, places in parallel "light to the pagan nations" (φῶς ἐθνῶν) with "ends of the earth" (ἐσχάτου τῆς γῆς).

83. Rom. 11:25, cp. Matt. 24:14 and Luke 21:24.

84. 1 Cor. 15:9; 1 Tim. 1:12, cp. Gal. 1:13.

85. Munck, *Christ and Israel,* 29. For "redemptive history," Munck uses the more technical, German term, *Heilsgeschichte.*

86. Stendahl, "Foreword," in Munck, *Christ and Israel,* viii.

87. See the following for numerous points of contact between the calling and role of both Moses and Paul: Peter Jones, *Paul a Second Moses according to 2 Corinthians 2:14–4:6*: a Ph.D dissertation, Princeton Theological Seminary, 1973; also, "The Apostle Paul: Second Moses to the New Covenant Community," *God's Inerrant Word: An International Symposium on the Trustworthiness of Scripture,* ed. John Warwick Montgomery (Minneapolis: Bethany Fellowship, 1973), 219–41.

88. 2 Cor. 3:1–18.

89. 2 Cor. 3:12.

90. Mark 1:22; 1:27; 11:28.

91. Exod. 20:14.

92. Gen. 2:7. The Greek translation, known as the Septuagint (LXX), reads: ἐνεφύσησεν εἰς τὸ πρόσωπον αὐτοῦ πνοὴν ζωῆς καὶ ἐγένετο ὁ ἄνθρωπος εἰς ψυχὴ ζῶσαν.

93. Deut. 4:2.

94. Conzelmann, *First Epistle to the Corinthians*, 284, states: "Genesis 2:7 ... has been altered, and completely re-interpreted."

95. Earl E. Ellis, *Paul's Use of the Old Testament* (Edinburgh: Oliver and Boyd, 1957), 36, notes that 1 Tim. 5:18 and 1 Cor. 15:45 both contain a citation of the Old Testament plus an addition.

96. Matthew Black, "The Pauline Doctrine of the Second Adam," *Scottish Journal of Theology* 7 (June 1954): 170ff, cited in Ellis, *Paul's Use of the Old Testament*. See also Hans Conzelmann, *First Epistle to the Corinthians*, 284: "Paul adds 45b as if it were a part of the Scripture passage." In support of this, Conzelmann cites a nineteenth-century German commentator, Johannes Weiss.

97. The Greek verb is formed with a preposition, γίνομαι εἰς. The preposition, without the verb, is repeated in the second phrase: ὁ ἔσχατος Ἀδὰμ εἰς πνεῦμα ζῳοποιοῦν. The preposition on its own has no meaning. Without presupposing the verb, the phrase in the Greek ear is gibberish.

98. Lest it be unclear, Paul gladly shares this status with the other apostles (1 Cor. 15: 9–11, cp. Eph. 2:20). The Second Moses ministry is collegial. Christ was the second Moses *par excellence*, and he bequeathed that ministry to his apostles (Mark 3:14–15, Luke 22:29, John 20:17). Paul's particularity lies in his being a Second Mosaic prophet for the nations, that is, his role as "the apostle to the Gentiles" (Rom. 11:13, cp. 1:5 and 16:26. See also 1 Tim. 2:7; 2 Tim. 4:17).

99. 2 Cor. 3:12–13. See Peter Jones, *La deuxième épître de Paul aux Corinthiens* (Paris: Cahiers d'Etudes Bibliques 14, 1992), 56–83. I found support in developing this thesis in an earlier article by Austin Farrer, "The Ministry in the New Testament," in *The Apostolic Ministry: Essays on the History and Doctrine of Episcopacy*, ed. K. E. Kirk (London: Hodder and Stoughton, 1946), 115–82, and the work by Munck, *Christ and Israel*, 12, 29. This thesis was further pursued with great effect by Scott J. Hafemann, *Paul, Moses and the History of Israel: The Letter/Spirit Contrast and the Argument from Scripture in 2 Corinthians 3* (Peabody, Mass.: Hendrickson Publishers, 1995), 33–35, who speaks of "Paul's self conception and ministry as an apostle" as being essentially "compared and contrasted to the ministry of Moses"; and Carol Kern Stockhausen, *Moses' Veil and the Glory of the New Covenant: The Exegetical Substructure of 2 Corinthians 3:1–4:6*, Analecta Biblical 116 (Roma: Editirice Pontificio Istituto Biblico, 1989), 169, n.36, and 172–75,

where she concludes: "In answer to a reproach about his lack of external epis-
tolary recommendations, Paul has proclaimed himself to be the 'new Moses'
of God's covenant in Christ."

100. We note a few of the many examples of Paul's Second Moses ministry. Paul characterizes his teaching of sexual roles in the church as a "command of the Lord" (1 Cor. 14:39), a technical term in the Old Testament for
the commands the Lord gives to Moses, and which He writes down (Exod.
16:28, Lev. 22:31; cp. Exod. 24:12). The "commands of the Lord" given to
Moses are remembered as such by Israel (Josh. 22:3, 5; Judg. 2:17; 1 Kings
11:11; Ps. 19:8; Isa. 48:18; Jer. 19:15. These references are to the exact phrase in
the Greek Old Testament that English translations do not always show).
Stockhausen, *Moses' Veil*, 171–72, notes the parallel between the veil on the
Mosaic covenant and the veil on Paul's gospel (2 Cor. 4:3). A further parallel
can be seen in 2 Tim. 3:1ff where Paul compares the opposition to his teaching by false teachers (v. 10) to the opposition Jannes and Jambres make against
Moses.

101. 2 Cor. 3:13.

102. John Calvin, *The First Epistle of Paul the Apostle to the Corinthians,*
trans. John W. Fraser, ed. David W. and Thomas F. Torrance (Grand Rapids:
Eerdmans, 1960), 338, catches the dynamism of this claim. "It is as if he [Paul]
said: 'Moses states that Adam was given a living soul; but Christ, on the other
hand, is endowed with a life-giving spirit. And it is a far greater thing to be
Life, or the source of life, than just to have life.'"

103. Gal. 1:15–16.

104. Gal. 4:14.

105. John 1:1; Heb. 1:1–2.

106. Schreiner, *Paul*, 39.

107. Rom. 15:9.

108. Eph. 4:11.

109. 1 Cor. 12:2, cp. Rom. 1:18ff and 2 Cor. 6:14ff.

110. Eph. 4:17; cp. Rom. 1:21.

111. Rom. 1:25.

112. Rom. 1:28.

113. Rom. 1:21–22.

114. 1 Cor. 1:23.

115. Rom. 1:24, 26–27.

116. Eph. 2:12.

Chapter 6

1. Rom. 1:25.
2. 1 Cor. 15:45; Eph. 3:9.
3. This is true even of the fine work on Paul by Thomas R. Schreiner, *Paul, Apostle of God's Glory in Christ* (Downers Grove, Ill.: InterVarsity, 2001), which I enthusiastically recommend.
4. Acts 17:29; Rom. 1:19–20.
5. Rom. 3:30; 1 Cor. 8:4.
6. John 14:6–14; 16:15; 17:1; 11:25–26.
7. Matt. 6:26.
8. Eph. 5:20. See also Col. 1:3, 12; 3:17.
9. Rom. 1:21.
10. 1 Cor. 15:24.
11. 1 Cor. 4:6.
12. According to Rudolf Bultmann, *Theology of the New Testament* (New York: Scribner, 1955), 69, God is described as essentially the Creator.
13. John 1:1–3. See also Rev. 3:14: "... the ruler of God's creation": ἡ ἀρχὴ τῆς κρίσεως τοῦ θεοῦ. Cp. Rev. 22:13.
14. Citing Ps. 102:25.
15. See Ps. 89:27.
16. See Job 26:13; 33:4; Ps. 33:6; 104:30.
17. Gen. 1:2, cp. Deut. 32:11 and Jer. 23:9, the only other times the Bible uses this unusual verb.
18. 1 Cor. 2:4; 6:14., cp. Eph. 1:19–21; 3:20.
19. John MacArthur, *The Battle for the Beginning: The Bible on the Creation and the Fall of Adam* (Nashville: W Publishing Group, 2001), 77.
20. Eduard Schweizer, cited in Eduard Lohse, *Colossians and Philemon: Hermeneia—A Critical and Historical Commentary on the Bible* (Philadelphia: Fortress Press, 1971), 50.
21. On creation in general, see Thomas W. Mann, "Stars, Sprouts and Streams: The Creative Redeemer of Second Isaiah," William P. Brown and S. Dean McBride, Jr., eds., *The God Who Creates: Essays in Honor of W. Sibley Towner* (Grand Rapids: Eerdmans, 2002), 135–51.
22. Paul S. Minear, *Christians and the New Creation: Genesis Motifs in the New Testament* (Louisville, Ky.: Westminster John Knox Press, 1994), 74, who argues that in Paul "conversion" is here compared to creation.
23. 1 Tim. 4:10. See Steven M. Baugh, "'Savior of All People': 1 Timothy 4:10 in Context," *Westminster Theological Journal* (1992): 331–40.

24. See Appendix l.

25. Eph. 3:14: πρὸς τὸν πατέρα ("before the Father").

26. Eph. 3:15: πᾶσα πατρία. The close connection between "father" and "family" is easy to grasp in Greek. See Ps. 22:27 and Acts 3:25 citing Gen. 22:18, where the exact same word is used.

27. According to Schrenk in his article *"Patria," Theological Dictionary of the New Testament* (Grand Rapids: Eerdmans, 1968), 104, already in Herodotus, the Greek historian of the fifth century B.C., *"patria"* "means the family as derived from the father ... the father's family tree." Schrenk sees in this verse a reference to God as Creator, but does not pursue the idea, except to refer to Eph. 3:9.

28. Eph. 1:21.

29. Gen. 1:21; 1:24. See also Prov. 8:27.

30. Gen. 1:5, 8, 10.

31. 1 Cor. 8:6; Col. 1:16. On this text, see Larry R. Helyer, "Colossians 1:15–20: Pre-Pauline or Pauline?" *Journal of the Evangelical Theological Society* 26 (1983): 167–79; John F. Balchin, "Colossians 1:15–20: An Early Christian Hymn? The Arguments from Style," *Vox Evangelica* 15 (1985): 65–94; Steven M. Baugh, "The Poetic Form of Colossians 1:15–20," *Westminster Theological Journal* 47 (1985): 227–44; N. T. Wright, "Poetry and Theology in Colossians 1:15–20," *New Testament Studies* 36 (1990): 444–68.

32. As John 1:1–2 makes clear.

33. Col. 1:17.

34. Gen. 1:2.

35. John Calvin in his commentary on Genesis agrees with this interpretation. See also Douglas Kelly, *Creation and Change* (Fearn, UK: Christian Focus, 1997), 85.

36. Gen. 1:3, 6. The verb used here is *diastello* (διαστέλλω) or Hebrew, *badal*, "to distinguish," "to separate." The significance of this will become evident below.

37. Gen. 1:14.

38. διαστέλλω (*diastello*) or Hebrew, *badal*. *Badal* and *qodesh* thus function as synonymous terms.

39. 2 Chron. 23:6.

40. See the well-known Jewish commentator Jacob Milgrom, *Leviticus 1–16: The Anchor Bible* (New York: Doubleday, 1991), 689: "Creation ... was the product of God making distinctions (Gen. 1:4, 6, 7, 14, 18). This divine function is to be continued by Israel: the priests to teach it (Lev. 10:10–11) and the people to practice it (Ezek. 22:26)."

41. λάλησον τοῖς υἱοῖς Ἰσραὴλ καὶ ἐρεῖς πρὸς αὐτούς Αἱ ἑορταὶ κυρίου ἃς καλέσετε αὐτὰς κλητὰς ἁγίας αὗταί εἰσιν ἑορταί μου. See also Lev. 23:21.

42. The apostle Paul shows that making distinctions is essential to everyday life. In 1 Cor. 14:7 he argues: "Even in the case of lifeless things that make sounds, such as the flute or harp, how will anyone know what tune is being played unless there is a distinction in the notes?" The noun, διαστολή, "distinction," comes from the verb used in the Greek Old Testament to translate the key term, "separate," that we have been discussing.

43. Gen. 3:14–16.

44. παντὸς ὀνόματος ὀνομαζομένου . . . καὶ πάντα ὑπέταξεν ὑπὸ τοὺς πόδας αὐτοῦ.

45. See Elaine Pagels, *The Gnostic Paul: Gnostic Exegesis of the Pauline Letters* (Philadelphia: Fortress Press, 1975), 164.

46. Rom. 7:9.

47. Rom. 7:14.

48. Rom. 8:8.

49. Gal. 5:17–18, cp. Eph. 2:3; Rom. 8:4–5, 12–13; 2 Cor. 5:16.

50. The highly-regarded German New Testament scholar Rudolf Bultmann, *Theology of the New Testament,* 201, even observed that, with this terminology, Paul had "come very close to Hellenistic-Gnosticism dualism, not merely in the form of expression . . . but also in the thought itself."

51. This is why Paul can write Gal. 5:17, which Bultmann probably misunderstands.

52. This view of created flesh as "weak," not superhuman, is reflected in 1 Corinthians 15:42–44. If "natural" and "spiritual" describe two kinds of bodies without sin, then this is doubtless true for everything else Paul has said about these two comparable but different bodies. On this, see Scott Brodeur, *The Holy Spirit's Agency in the Resurrection of the Dead: An Exegetical-Theological Study of 1 Corinthians 15:44b–49 and Romans 8:9–13* (Rome: Editirice Pontificia Università Gregoriana, 1996), 77, who says "it is God who gives the natural body." F. Altermath, *Du corps psychique au corps spirituel: Interprétation de 1 Corinthiens 15:35–49 par les auteurs chrétiens des quatre premiers siècles* (Tubingen: J. C. B. Mohr, 1977).

53. Rom. 1:4 and 1 Tim. 3:16.

54. Rom. 9:3, 5.

55. Rom. 2:28.

56. Matt. 16:17; 1 Cor. 15:50; Gal. 1:16.

57. 1 Tim. 4:1, 6: see the use of "teaching."

58. 1 Tim. 1:10.

59. 1 Tim. 4:16.

60. 1 Tim. 4:4.

61. Gen. 1:4, cp. Gen. 1:31.

62. πᾶν κτίσμα θεοῦ καλόν.

63. Occhiogrosso, *Joy of Sects*, xvi, states that behind the many antagonistic expressions of the world's religions, there is a deep level of agreement "which is not spoken of by their mainstream purveyors," and which he identifies as the "Perennial Philosophy."

64. Harold Bloom, *Omens of Millennium*, 165, 171–72.

65. Ibid., 27.

66. 1 Tim. 4:1–6.

67. 1 Cor. 15:45a. It is also to be implied in his use of Ps. 8:6 in 1 Cor. 15:27 and Eph. 1:22; cp. Rom. 16:20; 1 Cor. 15:25; cp. Heb. 12:13; 10:13.

68. 1 Cor. 6:1–3.

69. Exod. 3:13–14; Isa. 40:10.

70. Ps. 102:26; Mal. 3:6.

71. 2 Pet. 3:8.

72. Isa. 46:9–11; Rom. 1:19–20; 8:28; Eph. 1:11.

73. Ps. 19:7.

74. 1 Cor. 15:28; Acts 17:28.

75. Deborah Blum, "The Gender Blur," *Utne Reader* (September–October 1998): 45.

76. Katherine Raymond, "Homosexual Pioneer," ibid.: 57.

77. Andy Steiner, "Glam I Am: This Time the Revolution Will Be Absolutely Fabulous," ibid.: 60.

78. Gen. 6:2, cp. Ps. 81:6 in Greek: ἐστε καὶ υἱοὶ ὑψίστου πάντες and Ps. 29:1. See also Ps. 80:15.

79. Exod. 4:22–23, cp. Ps. 80:15, above. See also Deut. 1:31; 8:5; Prov. 3:12.

80. 2 Sam. 7:14.

81. 2 Cor. 6:18; Rom. 8:14; 8:21; Gal. 4:6–7.

82. Luke 3:37.

83. 1 Cor. 15:45–47; 1 Tim. 2:13. Note that the term "physical" in verse 46 is used in the previous verse to designate Adam.

84. This is an obvious reprise of Gen. 2:7, since it includes two of the most significant words: τί γάρ μὴ πρῶτος ἀνθρώπων ἐγενήθης . . . cp. Gen. 2:7b: ἐγένετο ὁ ἄνθρωπος εἰς ψυχὴν ζῶσαν.

85. "Living being" is the New International Version rendering of the Greek, which I transliterate as *psuche zosa*.

86. Here they translate the Genesis text to mean that Adam became physically alive. Why not translate the exact same phrase in 1 Cor. 15:45 in the exact same way? There seems to be some inconsistency between the Contemporary English Version Old and New Testaments.

87. This psalm uses the same verb, "rule," as does Gen. 1:28.

88. Num. 32:29.

89. Phil. 2:10.

90. See Rosemary Radford Ruether, *Women-Church: Theology and Practice* (San Francisco: Harper and Row, 1985), 57.

91. See the discussion of 1 Cor. 15:45 above, "First in Time," and the discussion in chapter 5, "Messing with Genesis."

92. See the same phrase in Gen. 2:8: "the man which God made." Paul is clearly commenting on this text because he employs the unusual verb πλάσσω which occurs in the New Testament only to refer to the creation of Adam (1 Tim. 2:13) and in the Old Testament only for the creation of man in Gen. 2:7 and 2:8 (though see Zech. 12:1 for a general reference).

93. Αδὰμ γὰρ πρῶτος ἐπλάσθη, εἶτα Εὔα.

94. 1 Tim. 2:13.

95. Uses the same verb καλέω.

96. Gen. 1:26.

97. Gen. 1:27; 5:2.

98. αὕτη κληθήσεται γυνή ὅτι ἐκ τοῦ ἀνδρὸς αὐτῆς ἐλήμφθη αὕτη.

99. Gen. 1:28: "God blessed them . . ." See Marsha M. Wilfong, "Human Creation in Canonical Context: Genesis 1:26–31 and Beyond," Brown and McBride, eds., *God Who Creates*, 44.

100. καὶ ἐκάλεσεν Αδαμ τὸ ὄνομα τῆς γυναικὸς αὐτοῦ Ζωή.

101. 1 Tim. 2:15. See Baugh, "'Savior of all People.'"

102. 1 Tim. 2:13.

103. See Ken Carey's channeled message, *Starseed: The Third Millennium: Living in the Posthistoric World* (HarperSanFrancisco, 1991), ix. The book is endorsed by Jean Houston.

104. John Calvin, *Commentary on Genesis*, trans. John King (Edinburgh: Calvin Translation Society, 1847; repr., Grand Rapids: Baker Book House, 1984), 112–13.

105. 1 Cor. 15:45a. Below we will deal with the second element of the verse.

106. Geerhardus Vos, *The Pauline Theology* (Phillipsburg, N.J.: P&R, 1991, first published in 1930 by Princeton University Press), 44–45, saw that eschatology precedes soteriology, meaning that prior to sin, in the plan of God from the outset, provision was made for a higher kind of body. See also Richard B. Gaffin, Jr., *Resurrection and Redemption: A Study in Paul's Soteriology* (Phillipsburg, N.J.: P&R, 1978), 82–83.

107. See Meredith G. Kline, *Kingdom Prologue* (self-published manuscript, 1991), 57, for reflections on the Sabbatic structure of Genesis, anticipating end time consummation.

108. James D. G. Dunn, *The Theology of Paul the Apostle* (Grand Rapids: Eerdmans, 1998), 262, in his erudite 808-page tome, states that 1 Cor. 15:45 "is unique in the Pauline writings," but he fails to give it any significant place in his theology, considering it "highly mythological or symbolical language" (242).

109. Rom. 8:18ff.

110. 1 Cor. 15:26, cp. Eph. 1:10 and Col. 1:20.

111. John Shelby Spong, *Why Christianity Must Change or Die: A Bishop Speaks to Believers in Exile* (HarperSanFrancisco, 1998). See Witham, "What Path for Christianity?"

Chapter 7

1. Between 70 and 92 percent. Rich Bordner, "Society Disregards Abortion's Aftermath," *Ohio State University's Lantern*, 27 April 2001.

2. Richard C. Paddock, *Los Angeles Times*, 30 April 2001.

3. According to Shucman, *Course in Miracles*, 262, 57, 78, "Jesus" comes with the incredible message: "Your only calling here is to devote yourself . . . to the denial of guilt in all its forms."

4. According to New Age guru and author, Neale Donald Walsch, *Conversations with God*, cited by Penn, "United Religions": 45.

5. 1 Cor. 6:9–10.

6. Ps. 14:1–3; 53:1–3.

7. 1 Cor. 6:12; 10:23.

8. Rom. 2:17ff; 13:8–10; Gal. 5:14.

9. See Gal. 4:21; Rom. 3:19.

10. Rom. 7:2, 22.

11. Rom. 2:15.

12. Rom. 7:12.

13. Rom. 10:5.

14. For food, see verse 3.

15. See Jones, *Spirit Wars*, 166. See also MacArthur, *The Battle for the Beginning: The Bible on Creation and the Fall of Man* (Nashville: W Publishing Group, 2001), 206.

16. In the twentieth century, theories of determinism came in tension with a robust belief in "choice." We blamed our problems on biological/genetic, chemical, economic, and social forces, but then made political and moral decisions on pro-choice arguments.

17. Rom. 2:15.

18. Rom. 3:23. See also Rom. 5:12, and the excellent book by Henri Blocher, *Original Sin: Illuminating the Riddle* (Grand Rapids: Eerdmans, 1997), 76–81.

19. Rom. 1:19–20.

20. Robert Funk, "The Coming Radical Reformation," *The Fourth R*, July–August 1998, 3.

21. Ps. 72:8. This psalm uses the same verb, "rule," as does Gen. 1:28.

22. Though this text is applied immediately to the king of Babylon (14:4), it is often taken as pointing beyond a human figure to the fallen angel, Lucifer (see v. 12). On this, see MacArthur, *Battle for the Beginning*, 100. See also Ezek. 28:11–19.

23. Gen. 2:17.

24. This is a phrase from the occult leader Alice Bailey of the Lucis Trust, cited in Penn, "United Religions Initiative": 56.

25. Gen. 1:27.

26. See John Frame, *Cornelius Van Til: An Analysis of His Thought* (Phillipsburg, N.J.: P&R, 1995), 231–38.

27. Rom. 1:25.

28. Ps. 106:20, doubtless commenting on the pagan reversal of Psalm 8, uses the exact terms Paul will pick up in Rom. 1:23: καὶ ἠλλάξαντο τὴν δόξαν αὐτῶν ἐν ὁμοιώματι μόσχου ἔσθοντος χόρον.

29. Turcan, *Cults*, 7.

30. "Twenty-One Theses," *The Fourth R*, 11 (4): 8 (July–August 1999).

31. Cited with approbation by Robert W. Funk, founder of the Jesus Seminar, in his article: "Radical Revolution": 3.

32. Spong, *Why Christianity Must Change*, xviii.

33. Geering, *World to Come*, 157. See also *Tomorrow's God*.

34. Ibid., 158.

35. Ibid., 157.

36. Houston, *Passion of Isis*, 2.

37. Ibid., 7.

38. See chapter 2.

39. Ibid., 174–76.

40. Images of the goddess Sophia are much in evidence at the Re-Imagining Conferences. Art critic and writer Suzi Gablik, "Altar States," *Ions: Noetic Science Review* (June–August 2000), 24, 27, purchased a carved wooden female Santos from the Philippines because the statuette "seemed to house the spirit of the Black Madonna" and because the idol might help her find a lover. "What if . . . the Black Madonna . . . had the power to make this happen . . . ?" Gablik did not stop with a statue. She built an altar which has become "unendingly alive."

41. Oliver O'Donovan, *Resurrection and the Moral Order: An Outline for Evangelical Ethics* (Grand Rapids: Eerdmans, 1994), 63.

42. This is the approach of Gerald R. McDermott, *Can Evangelicals Learn from World Religions? Jesus, Revelation and Religious Traditions* (Downers Grove, Ill.: InterVarsity, 2000), who tells us we can learn from other religions, even though practices in Christianity derive from reasons that contradict those offered by non-Christian religions.

43. Acts 17:22.

44. 1 Cor. 10:20.

45. 2 Cor. 6:16.

46. 1 Cor. 10:14.

47. Gen. 3:20.

48. Eph. 5:25.

49. Gen. 3:12.

50. Gen. 2:5. Eden means "abundance."

51. Gen. 3:17–18.

52. Rom. 5:12.

53. Danna N. Fewell and David M. Gunn, *Gender, Power and Promise: The Subject of the Bible's First Story* (Nashville: Abingdon, 1993), 30.

54. Ibid., 31.

55. Gen. 3:2–3. She even adds her own embellishment to the command: "nor touch it."

56. Gen. 3:6.

57. Gen. 3:6.

58. Gen. 3:16.

59. Francis Watson, "Strategies for Recovery and Resistance: Hermeneutical Reflections on Genesis 1–3 and its Pauline Reception," *Journal for the Study of the New Testament* 45 (19912), 90–91.

60. Bell Hooks, *Teaching to Transgress: Education as the Practice of Freedom* (New York: Routledge, 1994).

61. Otis, *Twilight Labyrinth*, 107.

62. Cited in R. Bayer, *Homosexuality and American Psychiatry* (New York: Basic Books, 1981), 140. See also the important book by Joseph and Linda Ames Nicolosi, *A Parents' Guide to Preventing Homosexuality* (Downers Grove, Ill.: InterVarsity Press, 2002).

63. Rom. 1:18–27.

64. Heresy takes an element of truth and misuses it. Apostasy overturns every truth in a complete and systematic denial of the truth. Semi-Pelagianism is a heresy; Gnosticism is an apostasy.

65. Khalid Duran, "Homosexuality and Islam," *Homosexuality and World Religions*, ed. Arlene Swidler (Valley Forge, Pa.: Trinity Press International, 1993), 196.

66. Michael J. Clark, "Gay Spirituality," *Spirituality and the Secular Quest*, ed. Peter H. Van Ness (New York: Crossroads/Herder, 1996), 337.

67. Ibid., 342.

68. Ibid. Readers will remember that the great vocation of Anakin, the hero of the Star Wars series, is to be a balancer of the two sides of the force. Such a notion has sexual implication, as the gay philosopher Clark indicates.

69. Those interested in the sexual implications of paganism can consult my book *God and Sex: How Our View of God Affects Our Sexual Practice and Vice Versa*, (working title) to appear shortly.

70. See also, Peter Jones, "Androgyny: The Pagan Sexual Ideal," *Journal of the Evangelical Society* 43/3 (September 2000), 443–69.

71. *A Course in Miracles*, 187, 220–1.

72. Acts 17:23.

73. 1 Tim. 4:10.

74. See the fascinating material written from the perspective of Intelligent Design, such as William Dembski, *Intelligent Design: The Bridge Between Science and Theology* (Downers Grove, Ill.: InterVarsity, 1999), Michael Behe, *Darwin's Black Box: A Biochemical Challenge* to *Evolution* (New York: Free Press, 1996); Phillip E. Johnson, *Darwin on Trial* (Lanham, Md.: Regnery Gateway, 1991), and others.

75. Rom. 1:20.

76. Ibid.

77. Rom. 1:32.

78. *North County Times*, 15 August 2000, A-7.

79. See James B. Twitchell, *For Shame: The Loss of Common Decency in American Culture* (New York: St. Martins Press, 1997).

80. Peter Kreeft, *Christianity for Modern Pagans* (San Francisco: Ignatius Press, 1993), 69.

81. Rom. 1:27.

82. 2 Cor. 3:6.

83. 2 Cor. 3:7.

84. 2 Cor. 3:9.

85. Gen. 2:17, alluded to in Rom. 5:17.

86. Rom. 7:12.

87. Rom. 6:16.

88. Rom. 7:3.

89. Eph. 2:1.

90. 1 Cor. 15:50.

91. 1 Cor. 15:26.

92. Eph. 2:1.

93. Rom. 8:8.

94. Isa. 64:6; cp. Rom. 3:9–18.

Chapter 8

1. Gen. 1:2; Luke 1:35.

2. Gen. 3:20.

3. 1 Cor. 15:21.

4. See O'Donovan, *Resurrection*, 85. This Oxford professor asserts: "We are asserting that true knowledge is to be had in this place [the Word made flesh] and no other; it is an exclusive claim which must disallow some pretensions to knowledge as well as allow others."

5. Phil. 2:11.

6. Sarah MacFarland Taylor, "Songs of Sacred Ecology: Interspecies Ecumenism in Paul Winter's Missa Gaia and Solstice Celebrations, *New Religions Seminar* (American Academy of Religion, 2000).

7. Craig McMillan, "Poor, White Stupids: A Review of Theodore Dalrymple's book, *Life at the Bottom: The Worldview that Makes the Underclass*," WorldNetDaily.com, 28 March 2002.

8. Col. 1:15.

9. Col. 1:16.

10. Phil. 2:6.

11. Rom. 8:3. This is a phrase of special possession: τὸν ἑαυτοῦ υἱὸν, "his own Son." See Rom. 5:8; 1 Cor. 7:2, 37;10:24.

12. Gal. 4:4: ἐξαπέσετειλεν ὁ θεὸς τὸν υἱὸν αὐτοῦ.

13. Rom. 1:2.

14. Gal. 4:7; Rom. 8:14; 9:26; Gal. 3:26.

15. Cp. Luke 3:37.

16. Gen. 6:2; 2 Sam. 7:14; Pss. 2:6–7; 28:19 (note: both Hebrew and Greek have "sons," though the text is often translated "mighty ones"); Ps. 82:6; Isa. 9:6; 43:6; Jer. 31:9; Hos. 1:10.

17. Exod. 4:22; Hos. 11:1.

18. For other texts where "son" bears this meaning, see Rom. 1:9; 5:10; Gal. 2:20; Col. 1:13; 1 Thess. 1:10.

19. As the Gospels do. See Matt. 1:18–25; Luke 1:26–56; 2:1–20. Paul's approach is more like that of the Gospels of Mark and John which have no birth narratives either.

20. Rom. 8:3.

21. 1 Tim. 1:15.

22. 2 Tim. 1:10. This is his first "appearing" as opposed to his second; see 2 Tim. 4:1; Titus 2:13.

23. O'Donovan, *Resurrection*, 158, 15.

24. Gal. 4:4.

25. Rudolf Bultmann, *Theology of the New Testament* (New York: Scribner, 1999, first published, 1955), 238.

26. See Rom. 15:1–4; Phil. 2:5ff; 2 Cor. 4:7–15; 8:9; and everywhere where the name Jesus alone is used. On this subject, see the important work of G. N. Stanton, *Jesus of Nazareth in New Testament Preaching* (Cambridge: Cambridge University Press, 1974).

27. Rom. 5:15; 5:17; 1 Tim. 2:5.

28. 1 Cor. 11:23ff.

29. 2 Cor. 8:9.

30. Gal. 6:17; 1 Thess. 4:14.

31. 1 Cor. 15:4.

32. 1 Cor. 12:3. Fee, *First Epistle to the Corinthians*, 580, calls the "proto-Gnostic" explanation "more ingenious than realistic," though he does cite a number of scholars who favor it. For support of this not mentioned by Fee, see J. D. G. Dunn, *Jesus and the* Spirit (London: SCM, 1975), 234. The commentary by Anthony C. Thiselton, *The First Epistle to the Corinthans: A Commentary on the Greek Text* (Grand Rapids: Eerdmans, 2000), 922, is much more open to this "Gnostic" interpretation. Such an explanation consistently fits with the rejection of the *physical* resurrection in 1 Cor. 15:12, which is a rejection of resurrection "from the dead." One must reckon with the presence of proto-Gnostic pagan spiritualistic thinking at Corinth, especially since Paul introduces the subject by reminding the Corinthians of their spiritual pagan

past (v. 2) and connects that past and the cursing of Jesus with the word *therefore*.

33. 1 Cor. 15:45.

34. 1 Cor. 15:46.

35. 1 Cor. 15:49.

36. Rom. 8:3. The NIV actually translated two different words for "likeness," so these texts are not exact parallels.

37. Phil. 3:21.

38. Rom. 2:12.

39. Rom. 10:5.

40. Rom. 7:12.

41. Rom. 7:10.

42. See Mark 1:12–13; Matt. 4:1–11; Luke 4:1–13.

43. Mark 3:20–30.

44. Gal. 3:24.

45. Rom. 7.

46. Rom. 7:13.

47. Rom. 8:4.

48. Rom. 10:5.

49. Rom. 10:4.

50. Gal. 6:2, cp. 1 Cor. 9:21.

51. Rom. 8:3.

52. Rom. 8:3.

53. Rom. 6:19.

54. Rom. 8:3.

55. Phil. 3:21.

56. Rom. 7:24.

57. See Rom. 5:14; Phil. 2:7; cp. Rom. 6:5. I maintain this interpretation against Schreiner, *Paul*, 142.

58. 2 Cor. 5:21.

59. Isa. 53:4.

60. Rom. 6:23.

61. Rom. 8:6.

62. See Kurt Rudolf, *Gnosis: The Nature and History of an Ancient Religion* (Edinburgh: T&T Clark, 1977), 157.

63. Apocalypse of Peter 81:15–25.

64. Apocalypse of James 31:14–21. Interestingly, the Koran of the Muslims maintains that the death of Jesus was only apparent.

65. Marcus Borg, *Jesus: A New Vision: Spirit, Culture, and the Life of Discipleship* (HarperSanFrancisco, 1991), 114, 178, 183.

66. Marcus Borg, ed. *The Complete Gospels* (HarperSanFrancisco, 1995), 251.

67. Shucman, *Course in Miracles,* 47, 262.

68. Transcript of tapes of the RE-Imagining Conference, published by *GoodNews,* January 1994, 11.

69. *Presbyterian Layman* 27 (1) (January–February 1994): 3.

70. See Hans Conzelmann, *First Epistle to the Corinthians,* 252ff. See also Anthony C. Thiselton, *Corinthians,* 1189, who also defends the creedal structure and the early Aramaic origin of this confession, and claims it goes back, through Luke, to Jesus himself.

71. 1 Cor. 15:2: "... by which you are being saved."

72. See also Rom. 8:34; 2 Cor. 5:15; 1 Thess. 5:10.

73. 2 Cor. 3:6.

74. 2 Cor. 3:7.

75. 2 Cor. 3:9.

76. Gen. 2:17; cp. Rom. 5:17.

77. Rom. 7:12.

78. Rom. 7:10.

79. Rom. 6:16.

80. Rom. 7:3.

81. Eph. 1:23.

82. Rom. 1:20.

83. 2 Cor. 5:10.

84. 1 Cor. 15:26.

85. 1 Cor. 15:50.

86. Rom. 5:6.

87. Cited in Marvin Olasky, *World* (March–April 2002): 46.

88. 2 Cor. 5:15; cp. 4:10.

89. Gal. 3:13.

90. 2 Cor. 5:21.

91. 1 Cor. 5:7.

92. Program brochure for a spiritual transformation conference at Holy Names College (Oakland, Calif., summer, 2000).

93. Rom. 5:6.

94. Rom. 5:8.

95. Borg, *Jesus, A New Vision,* 114, 178, and 183.

96. Isa. 28:5.

97. Isa. 53:10.

98. Isa. 53:5.

99. Isa. 53:12: ἁμαρτίας πολλῶν ἀνήνεγκεν.

100. Ps. 130:4: ὅτι παρὰ σοὶ ὁ ἱλασμός ἐστιν.

101. Rom. 3:25: ὃν προέθετο ὁ θεὸς ἱλαστήριον.

102. Exod. 25; Lev. 16; cp. also Ezek. 43:13ff. See especially Lev. 16:15. See J. D. G. Dunn, *Romans 1–8: Word Biblical Commentary* 38A (Dallas: Word, 1988), 170.

103. Paul's language concerning the death of Christ is very close to other New Testament formulations. See 1 John 2:2; "He is the atoning sacrifice for our sins," cp. 1 John 4:10: "he [God] loved us and sent his Son as an atoning sacrifice for our sins"; Heb. 2:17: "As high priest Christ made atonement for the sins of the people."

104. Rom. 5:9; 3:25; 1 Cor. 11:25; Eph. 1:7; 2:13; Col. 1:20.

105. Cp. 1 Cor. 1:17–18; Gal. 6:12–14; Eph. 2:16; Phil. 2:8; Col. 1:20.

106. Rom. 8:3.

107. 1 Cor. 15:52.

108. 1 Cor. 15:26.

109. Rom. 1:18; 2:8; 2:19; Eph. 5:6; Col. 3:6. See this theme elsewhere in Scripture: Exod. 4:14; 32:10; Num. 11:1; 25:4; 2 Chron. 24:18; Ps. 2:5; John 3:36.

110. Rom. 5:10.

111. Rom. 8:7.

112. Eph. 2:14.

113. Rom. 15:33; 16:20; 1 Cor. 14:33; 2 Cor. 13:11; Phil. 4:9; 1 Thess. 5:23.

114. 2 Thess. 3:16.

115. Eph. 6:15.

116. Eph. 2:14.

117. Col. 1:20.

118. Eph. 2:14.

119. This dividing wall is the one that kept Gentiles out of the temple in Jerusalem, a sign of a much deeper hostility.

120. Eph. 2:17: "He came and preached peace to you who were far away and peace to those who were near."

121. Eph. 2:14.

122. See Rom. 1:7; 2:10; 5:1; 12:18; 14:17; 1 Cor. 7:15; 2 Cor. 13:11; Gal. 5:22; 1 Thess. 5:13; Col. 3:15; Eph. 4:3; Tim. 2:22.

123. Rom. 3:26.

124. Rom. 5:1.

125. Rom. 10:3.

126. Rom. 5:15–16. This gift is described both as the gift that came by Jesus Christ and as "the gift of God," cp. John 4:10.

127. Eph. 2:18. See also Eph. 3:12, 1 John 5:14.

128. 2 Cor. 5:21.

Chapter 9

1. 1 Cor. 2:9.

2. 1 Cor. 9:1; 15:8.

3. 1 Cor. 2:10.

4. Acts 17:31.

5. See E. Kasemann, *Commentary on Romans* (Grand Rapids: Eerdmans, 1994), 6–10.

6. 1 Cor. 15:5–8.

7. Richard Grigg, *When God Becomes Goddess,* 20, 22. He is doubtless correct in saying that ". . . [traditional] religion contributes little to the cognitive framework through which educated Westerners view the world."

8. Geerhardus Vos, in a sermon preached in Princeton Chapel, 23 April 1905, reprinted in *Modern Reformation* 9 (3): 6 (May–June 2000).

9. 1 Cor. 2:8.

10. See also Exod. 20:11; Job 10:8; Ps. 95:5; Isa. 37:16; 44:24; 45:12.

11. Rom. 1:20.

12. Gen. 1:2; Job 33:4; Ps. 33:6. See M. Kline, *Images of the Spirit* (Grand Rapids: Baker Book House, 1980), 13–14.

13. Rom. 6:4.

14. 1 Cor. 6:14; Rom. 8:11.

15. G. Vos, *Pauline Eschatology* (Phillipsburg, N.J.: P&R, 1992), 34, fn. 42, notes that Paul describes the necessity of the second stage without reference to sin.

16. O'Donovan, *Resurrection,* 14, 19.

17. Geerhardus Vos, "The Eschatological Aspect of the Pauline Conception of the Spirit," *Biblical and Theological Studies* by members of the Faculty of Princeton Theological Seminary (New York: Scribner, 1912), 231, argues that Paul, by this term *natural,* refers to "the order of things established in creation" prior to sin.

18. See Gaffin, *Resurrection and Redemption: A Study in Paul's Soteriology* (Phillipsburg, N.J.: P&R, 1993), 82. See also M. Kline, *Kingdom Prologue* (South Hamilton, Mass.: M. G. Kline, 1991), 57.

19. Matt. 4:1–11; Luke 4:1–13.

20. Eph. 5:31–32. See also, O'Donovan, *Resurrection*, 53.

21. Gen. 1:20, 24; 9:12, 15–16; Lev. 11:10. Already Calvin saw this, see *1 Corinthians*, 338.

22. ψυχή cp. ψυχικόν.

23. The same verbal form is used in Exod. 2:10—"And the child grew, and she brought him unto Pharaoh's daughter, *and he became* her son."

24. This option is found in French, Catalan and Italian translations of the New Testament, and also in The Contemporary English Version of 1995, and The New Living Translation of 1996.

25. This is an inceptive aorist, that is, a past tense, emphasizing entrance into a state; see Daniel Wallace, *Greek Grammar Beyond the Basics* (Grand Rapids: Zondervan, 1996), 576.

26. 1 Cor. 15:46.

27. Rudolf Bultmann, *Theology of the New Testament* (New York: Scribner, 1951), 295.

28. Thomas Sheehan, "The Resurrection: An Obstacle to Faith," *The Fourth R*, March–April 1998, 7.

29. The argument was made by the German scholar Gerd Luedemann. See his book, *The Resurrection of Jesus: History, Experience, Theology* (Minneapolis: Fortress, 1994). Since that time, Luedemann has renounced the Christian faith.

30. Col. 1:22.

31. W. Pannenberg, *Jesus, God and Man* (1964), 100, argues that Paul does not mention the empty tomb because his teaching on the resurrection seeks to show the parallelism between the resurrection of Jesus and that of the believer.

32. 1 Cor. 15:42–44.

33. 1 Cor. 15:37–38.

34. 1 Cor. 15:53.

35. Ibid.

36. Wolfhart Pannenberg, *Jesus, God and Man*, trans. by Stanley J. Grenz (Louisville, Ky.: Westminster/John Knox, 1983), 76.

37. 1 Cor. 15:46.

38. Much of what I say is dependent upon the excellent work of Gaffin, *Resurrection and Redemption*, who seeks to show the soteriological implications of the resurrection for the last Adam. I have merely sought to restate his thesis in some fresh ways and to add one or two points of my own.

39. Eph. 1:3.

40. Eph. 1:20 and 2:6.

41. Rom. 1:4.

42. Luke 3:38.

43. Gen. 3:24.

44. Jer. 31:1, 9.

45. 2 Cor. 6:16.

46. Rom. 8:23. In Paul adoption is often a juridical/forensic term. See Gal. 4:5; Eph. 1:5; cp. Rom. 8:15.

47. Luke 3:22. Clearly Luke sees this sonship as human, since he immediately develops the genealogy of Jesus that ends with the sonship of Adam. See Luke 3:23–38.

48. Murray Harris, *Raised Immortal: Resurrection and Immortality in the New Testament* (Grand Rapids: Eerdmans, 1983) 74, sees the deep connection between "sonship" and resurrection in this text, though he does not use adoption terminology.

49. See Exod. 4:22.

50. In Rom. 1:1–4, for example.

51. See Rom. 1:1; Phil. 2:6.

52. Our present dating is inaccurate by three or four years.

53. Gal. 4:4.

54. Rom. 1:3.

55. Luke 2:1.

56. 1 Cor. 15:3. Hans Conzelmann, *1 Corinthians: Hermeneia* (Philadelphia: Fortress Press, 1975), 252, notes that there are two major affirmations: "he died" and "he was raised," confirmed by verifying information: "he was buried" and "he was seen."

57. 1 Cor. 15:45.

58. Rom. 8:29.

59. Described in 2 Cor. 5:17, cited above.

60. On this, see H. Ridderbos, *Paul: An Outline of His Theology* (Grand Rapids: Eerdmans, 1975).

61. Gal. 6:15.

62. The new birth/new creation theme can be seen in all that Paul says about the Spirit who is the *Spiritus Creator* and the agent of the resurrection (Rom. 1:4 and especially 8:11); his use of the adjectives νέος and καινός (both meaning "new") can be seen in his use of "new batch of yeast" (1 Cor. 5:7); the "new man" who is renewed according to the image of its creator, ὁ κτίσαντος (Col. 3:10 cp. Eph. 2:15 and 4:24); the "new covenant" (1 Cor. 11:25 cp. 2 Cor. 3:5); as well as the theme of "renewal of the inner man" (2 Cor. 4:16), of "the mind" (Rom. 12:2);

all these theological *topoi* bear witness to the extent of this new creation theme.

63. See Rom. 3:24; 1 Cor. 6:20; 7:23; Gal. 3:13; 4:15; Eph. 1:17; 1 Tim. 2:6; Titus 2:14.

64. O'Donovan, *Resurrection,* 55.

65. Eph. 4:30.

66. Rom. 8:23; cp. Eph. 1:14; 4:30. The common term is ἀπολύτρωσις.

67. Col. 1:18.

68. Rom. 6:19; 8:3.

69. Rom. 7:18.

70. Rom. 7:25.

71. Rom. 8:8.

72. The two past tenses, "appeared," and "justified," point to specific events in the history of redemption, and to the humiliation/exaltation schema of Phil. 2:5–11.

73. 1 Tim. 3:16. Older commentators tended to see this verse as an expression of Paul's doctrine of the two natures joined in the earthly Jesus, where the human flesh would represent the humanity of Jesus, and the justified spirit as an expression of his divinity. This, however, does not work.

74. ὑμεῖς ἔσεσθέ μοι δίκαιοι λέγει κύριος.

75. This is surely how we must understand the soteriological statements of Rom. 4:25: and 1 Cor. 15:17. See Harris, *Raised Immortal,* 76.

76. 2 Cor. 5:21.

77. Col. 1:18.

78. O'Donovan, *Resurrection,* 148.

79. Rom. 3:25–26.

80. Phil. 2:7.

81. Luke 15:32; 19:10.

82. Eph. 2:17.

83. Eph. 2:3.

84. Rom. 2:5; 3:5; 9:22; Eph. 5:6; 1 Thess. 5:9. See especially Rom. 5:9.

85. Matt. 27:46.

86. Eph. 2:18.

87. Phil. 1:23.

88. Eph. 1:20.

89. Eph. 2:6.

90. Eph. 3:12, sometimes translated "freedom and confidence," but still describing access.

91. Col. 1:20.

92. Gen. 1:2; cp. Rom. 8:11; 1 Pet. 3:18.

93. His present manifestation is called the "down-payment" (upfront money against a future full payment; 2 Cor. 5:5), or the "first fruits" (the first crop of the future harvest—Rom. 8:23). Also, in Eph. 1:13–14 the Spirit is called "the Holy Spirit of promise," and the promise concerns the future inheritance.

94. See Vos, "The Eschatological Aspect," 229.

95. See Rom. 1:3–4. Notice the parallelism in the Greek:

περὶ τοῦ υἱοῦ αὐτοῦ [concerning his Son]:

τοῦ γενομένου [who was born]; τοῦ ὁρισθέντο υἱοῦ θεοῦ ἐν δυνάμει [who was declared Son of God in power]

ἐκ σπέρματο Δαυὶδ [out of the seed of David]; ἐξ ἀναστάσεως νεκρῶν [out of the resurrection from the dead]

κατὰ σάρκα [according to the flesh]; κατὰ πνεῦμα ἁγιωσύνης [according to the spirit of holiness]

96. Gaffin, *Resurrection*, 112, speaks of "two successive modes of incarnate existence."

97. 1 Tim. 3:16. Note another perfect parallelism: ὃ ἐφανερώθη ἐν σαρκί ("manifest in the flesh") ἐδικαιώθη ἐν πνεύματι ("justified in the spirit"). In support of this is another text of Paul we have already examined, which speaks of Christ as the one: "who was manifested in the flesh, vindicated [or justified] in the spirit."

98. τὸ πνευμάτικον.

99. τὸ ψυχικόν.

100. Rom. 8:4–5.

101. Used 20 times by Paul—see Rom. 8:4–5, 12–13; 2 Cor. 5:16; Gal. 4:29; 5:18.

102. 1 Cor. 15:45.

103. Rom. 12:2.

104. Eph. 4:23.

105. Eph. 5:8.

106. Rom. 1:4.

107. 2 Cor. 5:21; Heb. 4:15; 1 Pet. 1:17–19.

108. Mark 1:24.

109. Acts 20:32; note the perfect tense, which in Greek signifies an specific occasion in the past that continues to be true in the present. See also 1 Cor. 1:2; 2 Cor. 1:2; Eph. 1:2; Phil. 1:1; Col. 1:2; Rev. 5:8.

110. 1 Cor. 6:11; note again the past tense of the verb.

111. 1 Cor. 1:30.

112. For a similar view, see O'Donovan, *Resurrection*, 15.

113. Ps. 8:6.

114. This was Jesus' hope as Messiah while he was on earth. See Luke 20:39; Acts 2:32.

115. This psalm is also cited in the same vein in Heb. 2:5–9, cp. 1:13. For a third use in Paul, see Phil. 3:21, and see below.

116. Gen. 1:26. cp. 1:28.

117. Acts 17:31.

118. 2 Cor. 5:10; Rom. 2:16, cp. John 12:48.

119. 1 Cor. 6:3.

120. Again the verb is *hupotasso*. See also Rev. 3:9. See also O'Donovan, *Resurrection*, 54.

121. 1 Cor. 15:24.

122. Col. 1:19.

123. Col. 1:20.

124. Eph. 3:9.

125. Gen. 1:1.

126. Eph. 4:13.

127. Jer. 8:16.

128. Ibid., 5–6.

129. The verb in Greek is ὑποτάσσω, "to set under," and is a compound of τάσσω, "to set or place."

130. Rom. 8:20.

131. Gal. 3:13.

132. Gal. 4:4.

133. O'Donovan, *Resurrection*, 55. "When we ask what it is that was given and lost, and must now be recovered," observes O'Donovan, "the answer is not just 'mankind', but mankind in his context as the ruler of the ordered creation that God has made; for the created order, too, cannot be itself while it lacks the authoritative and beneficent rule that man was to give it."

134. A new theory of the Trinity has appeared in our day, under the pressure of egalitarian ideology, according to which the Trinity is marked by *mutual* submission, so that while the Son submits to the Father, the Father also submits to the Son, etc. Further, it is alleged that subordination is only for the sake of redemption, so that when Christ's redemptive work is done, any notion of subordination is forever banished from the universe. As a corollary, complimentarian Christians are being accused of the heretical doctrine of subordinationism. See Gilbert Bilezekian, "Hermeneutical Bungee Jumping: Subordination in the Godhead," a paper delivered at the Annual Meeting of the Evangelical Theological Society, 18 November 1994;

Stanley Grenz and Denise Muir Kjebo, *Women in the Church* (Downers Grove, Ill.: InterVarsity, 1995), 153; and Kevin Giles, *The Trinity and Subordinationism* (Downers Grove, Ill.: InterVarsity, 2002). See also Stephen D. Kovach, "Egalitarians Revamp the Doctrine of the Trinity," *CBMWNEWS* (December 1996). This debate may be superfluous, at least as far as this text is concerned, if Paul is speaking of this final act of the Son as the act of the last Adam, in which case the text is not addressing the subject of the Trinity, but it is affirming the abiding subordination implicit in the Creator/creature distinction.

135. 1 Cor. 15:43.

136. Rom. 6:4.

137. 2 Cor. 4:6.

138. 1 Cor. 15:42–44.

139. Phil. 3:21.

140. 1 Cor. 15:40.

141. Rom. 8:17. "If we suffer with him, that we may also be glorified with him" indicates that the final state of resurrection will be glorious.

142. Mark 9:1.

143. Rom. 1:4.

144. Rom. 8:21.

145. Rom. 1:21.

146. Eph. 1:17.

147. See O'Donovan, *Resurrection*, 150, who shows the unavoidable exclusivity wrapped up in the resurrection event. "Since Jesus is the only one in whom the restored and renewed creation has come into being, only he can be the unique teacher about the nature of the cosmos. The Buddha has only said things about what is inherent in fallen human nature."

Chapter 10

1. Eph. 6:13.

2. 2 Tim. 3:1–9.

3. 1 Cor. 15:19.

4. 1 Cor. 1:18.

5. Certain liberal theologians describe the present time of the church as a theological embarrassment. According to Bultmann, Jesus was a prophet who expected the end of the world. When the end did not come, the age of Christian theology and ecclesiology was born. The so-called "delay of the *parousia*" created the Lucan history of redemption, according to H.

Conzelmann in *The Theology of Saint Luke* (New York: Harper and Row, 1961), 95–97; and early Catholicism, according to E. Kasemann in "The Beginnings of Christian Theology," *New Testament Questions of Today* (Philadelphia: Fortress Press, 1969): 82–107, 236–51.

6. Rom. 8:29; Col. 1:18, cp. Rev. 1:5.

7. Heb. 2:10.

8. Heb. 5:9.

9. Luke 19:10.

10. Rom. 15:19.

11. Acts 17:18.

12. Rom. 1:11; 15:24.

13. Rom. 15:24, 28.

14. Rom. 15:20.

15. Rom. 11:13.

16. As Jesus prophesied. See Matt. 28:19; Rom. 10:18.

17. Rom. 2:4.

18. Matt. 28:20.

19. Eph. 6:15. My translation, justified by the fact that Paul is quoting language from Isa. 52:7: messengers "who *bring* good tidings, who *proclaim* salvation, who *say* to Zion: 'Your God reigns.'"

20. 1 Cor. 9:16; cp. the word of Jesus in Matt. 10:19.

21. Acts 2:47. See Acts 2:41; 5:12–16; 6:7; 9:31.

22. Rom. 1:5; 16:26.

23. 1 Thess. 4:3.

24. Rom. 1:16; 2:9; Acts 13:46; cp. Matt. 10:6.

25. Eph. 2:12.

26. Rom. 1:24ff; 1 Thess. 4:7.

27. Acts 13:47.

28. Gal. 2:7.

29. Rom. 15:16. The offering is apparently not the collection for the Jerusalem saints, mentioned in 2 Cor. 8–9, but the offering that Paul "the priest," serving the gospel (ἱερουργοῦντα τὸ εὐαγγέλιον τοῦ θεοῦ) offers to God. It must mean either the offering which *is* the Gentiles [James D. G. Dunn, *Romans: Word Biblical Commentary* (Dallas, Tex.: Word Books, 1988), 860: "a genitive of apposition"], or the offering the Gentiles give of their obedience, which would still be the result of Paul's ministry, setting the Gentile believers apart for God through their obedience.

30. Gentiles are grafted into Israel, the "holy root" (Rom. 11:16), learning to be a biblical "people."

31. 2 Cor. 10:8; Jas. 1:12.

32. Eph. 4:3; Col. 1:28.

33. 1 Cor. 14:20; cp. Eph. 4:14.

34. Eph. 4:15.

35. 1 Cor. 9:24–27.

36. Phil. 3:11–14.

37. Eph. 4:16.

38. Phil. 1:29; 1 Thess. 2:14; cp. 1 Pet. 2:21.

39. 1 Cor. 3:12–15. Christians also test themselves. See 2 Cor. 13:5; cp. Rom. 12:2; 1 Cor. 11:28; Eph. 5:10.

40. Schreiner, *Paul*, 87. See his discussion of suffering (87–102). See Scott J. Hafemann, *Suffering and Ministry in the Spirit: Paul's Defense of His Ministry in 2 Corinthians 2:14–3:3* (Grand Rapids: Eerdmans, 1990).

41. Phil. 3; cp. Rom. 8:18; Col. 1:24.

42. 2 Cor. 1:3–11.

43. Rom. 5:4.

44. Eugene Peterson, *A Long Obedience in the Same Direction: Discipleship in an Instant Society* (Downers Grove, Ill.: InterVarsity, 1980).

45. See Greg L Bahnsen, Walter C. Kaiser Jr., Douglas J. Moo, Wayne G. Strickland, and Willem A. Van Gemeren, *Five Views on the Law and Gospel* (Grand Rapids: Zondervan, 1996).

46. Rom. 7:6.

47. Rom. 3:20; 5:20; 7:7; Gal. 3:17.

48. Rom. 6:14–15.

49. Rom. 6:19.

50. Gal. 6:2; 1 Cor. 9:21.

51. Matt. 5:17.

52. Rom. 10:4. See R. Badenas, "Christ: The End of the Law: Romans 10:4 in Pauline Perspective," *Journal for the Study of the Old Testament* (1985), who shows that until the Enlightenment, this text and the noun "end" (τέλος) were understood to mean "goal" or *scopus* (Latin, "culminating point").

53. Gal. 5:17.

54. Gal. 5:23.

55. Rom. 13:8.

56. Rom. 3:31.

57. Eph. 6:2.

58. Deut. 5:16.

59. Rom. 1:21. What the pagans do not do, Christians do.

60. Eph. 2:12.

61. Rom. 1:20.

62. Rom. 1:5; 16:25.

63. 2 Cor. 11:2; Col. 1:22; Eph. 5:27.

64. 1 Cor. 6:9–11; cp. Rom. 1:20–32.

65. Rom. 1:25.

66. 1 Thess. 4:5.

67. Rom. 8:21.

68. 2 Cor. 5:10. We will be judged for what we have done "in the body."

69. 1 Tim. 4:3–4.

70. 1 Cor. 14:34.

71. 1 Cor. 11:8–9; 15:45; Eph. 5:31; 1 Tim. 2:12–15.

72. 1 Cor. 11:14. David Blattenberger, *Rethinking 1 Corinthians 11:2–16 through Archeological and Moral-Rhetorical Analysis* (Lewiston: The Edwin Mellen Press, 1997), 38–42, argues against Fee, *First Epistle to the Corinthians,* 527, who maintains that the reference is merely to social custom. Battenberger shows that Paul's appeal to nature buttresses an appeal already made to social custom in vv. 6 and 13. For other appeals to nature which have nothing to do with custom, see Rom. 1:26 (lesbianism is "against nature"); 2:14; 2:27; 11:21, 24; Gal. 2:15; 4:8; Eph. 2:3.

73. This structure is evident in Greek.

74. Rom. 13:1–7.

75. Rom. 1:19–20.

76. Ps. 8:6, using ὑποτάσσω.

77. Ps. 47:3, cp. Ps. 18:47; 1 Chron. 22:18.

78. Rom. 8:20.

79. The curses of Gen. 3:14–19 reconfirm, in a fallen world, the structures of creation for family, marriage and work, and thus limit the progress of evil.

80. 1 Cor. 15:27; Eph. 1:22; Phil. 3:21.

81. 1 Cor. 15:23. The term is ἐν τῷ ἰδίῳ τάγματι, a form derived from *tass.*

82. Rom. 13:2: ἐν τῷ ἰδίῳ τάγματι, from the root, *tass.*

83. ὑποτάσσω.

84. 1 Cor. 16:16.

85. 1 Cor. 16:15.

86. Titus 2:9: δούλους ἰδίοις δεσπόταις ὑποτάσσεσθαι ἐν πᾶσιν.

87. 1 Tim. 3:4: τέκνα ἔχοντα ἐν ὑποταγῇ; Eph. 6:1–4.

88. Eph. 5:24: αἱ γυναῖκες ὑποτάσσεται τοῖς ἀνδράσιν ἐν παντί cp. 1 Cor. 14:34: ὑποτασσεάσθωσαν, καθὼς καὶ νόμος λέγει.

89. Rom. 13:2: διαταγη.

90. 1 Thess. 4:2–7.

91. 1 Cor. 7:17; 9:14; 11:34; 16:1; Titus 1:5: διατάσσομαι cp. "the law which was commanded [διαταγείς] through angels." See Gal. 3:19.

92. 1 Cor. 11:16; 14:33b.

93. 1 Cor. 7:25; 14:37: ἐπιταγή.

94. Rom. 16:26.

95. 1 Tim. 1:1.

96. 1 Tim. 1:1: ἐπιταγὴν θεοῦ; 1 Cor. 7:25: ἐπιταγὴν κυρίου; Titus 1:3, Rom. 16:26: ἐπιταγὴν τοῦ θεοῦ.

97. Rom. 8:7: τῷ γὰρ νόμῳ τοῦ θεοῦ οὐχ ὑποτάσσεται.

98. Rom. 10:3: οὐχ ὑπετάγησαν.

99. Rom. 13:2: ἀντιτασσόμενος.

100. Rom. 13:2: διαταγῇ.

101. 1 Thess. 5:14: ἀνάκτους.

102. 1 Tim. 1:9: ἀνυπότακτοις; Titus 1:6: ἀνυπότακτα; Titus 1:10: ἀνυπότακτοι.

103. Luke 2:51: ὑποτασσόμενος.

104. 1 Cor. 15:28: ὑποταγήσεται

105. 2 Cor. 9:13: ἐπὶ τῇ ὑποταγῇ τῆς ὁμολογίας ὑμῶν εἰς τὸ εὐαγγέλιον τοῦ Χριστοῦ.

106. Eph. 5:21.

107. 1 Cor. 14:32: καὶ πνεύματα προφητῶν προφήταις ὑποτάσσεται, οὐ γάρ ἐστιν ἀκαταστασίας ὁ θεὸς ἀλλὰ εἰρήνης. Note how disorder is placed in antithetical parallelism with ὑποτάσσω and with the character of God.

108. 1 Cor. 14:33, 40: κατὰ τάξιν.

109. Col. 2:5: ὑμῶν τὴν τάξιν.

110. Heb. 3:11; 4:1–11.

111. 1 Cor. 10:1–13; Phil. 2:14–16; cp. Heb. 3:6–19.

112. 1 Cor. 10:11; Rom. 15:4.

113. Ibid.

114. Deut. 6–8; see Matt. 4:1–11.

115. 1 Thess. 2:4; cp. Deut. 8:2.

116. 2 Tim. 4:8.

117. 1 Cor. 9:25.

118. Heb. 12:1.

119. Rom. 8:18.

120. Heb. 6:5.

121. Acts 1:4.

122. 1 Cor. 15:45; John 15:26; 20:21.

123. On the general subject of the Spirit, see H. B. Swete, *The Holy Spirit in the New Testament* (1910; repr. Ed. Grand Rapids: Baker, 1964); J. D. G. Dunn, *Jesus and the Spirit* (London: SCM, 1975); Scott J. Hafemann, *Suffering and Ministry in the Spirit: Paul's Defense of His Ministry in 2 Corinthians 2:14–3:3* (Grand Rapids: Eerdmans, 1990); D. A. Carson, *A Call to Spiritual Reformation: Priorities from Paul and His Prayers* (Grand Rapids: Baker, 1992); G. Fee, *Paul, the Spirit and the People of God* (Peabody, Mass: Hendricksen, 1996).

124. See on this subject B. M. Metzger, "Paul's Vision of the Church," *Theology Today* (1949); J. A. T. Robinson, *The Body: A Study in Pauline Theology* (London: SCM, 1952); L. Cerfaux, *L'Eglise dans la théologie de Saint Paul* (Unam Sanctam, 10, Paris, 1951); B. Gaertner, *The Temple and Community in Qumran and the New Testament* (Cambridge: Cambridge University Press, 1965); R. Batey, "MIA SARX: Union of Christ and the Church," *NTS* 66 (1967); M. J. McKelvey, *The New Temple* (Oxford: Oxford University Press, 1969); E. P. Clowney, *The Doctrine of the Church* (Phillipsburg, N.J.: P&R, 1974); G. L. O. R. York, *The Church As the Body of Christ in the Pauline Corpus: A Re-examination* (Lanham, Md.: University Press of America, 1991).

125. Jesus predicts the *coming* of the Spirit in John 4:23; 14:15, 26; 15:26; 16:7, 13. Clowney, *The Church* (Leicester, UK: InterVarsity, 1995), 53, rightly points out that at Pentecost God does not create the people of God but renews them, inasmuch as the origin of the church is to be found in the Old Testament.

126. See Elaine Pagels, *Gnostic Gospels,* (New York: Random House, 1979), 35–36.

127. 1 Cor. 15:22: "as in Adam all die."

128. 1 Cor. 15:22: "in Christ all will be made alive."

129. Greek, ἐκκλησία.

130. Col. 1:24.

131. Eph. 2:11–22.

132. Rom. 12:3ff; 1 Cor. 12–14. On the much-debated issue of the continuance of "supernatural" gifts, see the excellent discussion of Clowney, *The Church*, 237–54.

133. Eph. 4:11.

134. Col. 3:16.

135. Col. 3:16; cp. John 4:23.

136. Eph. 4:15–16.

137. Eph. 6:17.

138. Col. 1:5.

139. Col. 1:25; cp. Titus 1:3. For the argument that Paul is claiming to bring the final version of the original apostolic gospel, see P. Jones, "1 Corinthians 15:8: Paul, the Last Apostle," *Tyndale Bulletin* 36 (1985), 28–29 and in chapter 5.

140. Rom. 1:16.

141. 1 Cor. 2:4; 1 Thess. 1:5–6.

142. Rom. 8:37.

143. Eph. 1:3.

144. Eph. 1:5.

145. Rom. 8:15.

146. 2 Cor. 4:16.

147. 2 Cor. 3:18.

148. Rom. 8:23.

149. Eph. 6:18.

150. Eph. 6:12ff.

151. Gal. 5:22–23.

152. Clowney, *The Church*, 52: "But while the Spirit does not incarnate the Son in the church, the Spirit does bring him to the church in a union that only the Spirit can accomplish."

153. Rom. 8:9.

154. Gal. 4:6.

155. Eph. 1:13.

156. Gal. 2:20; 2 Cor. 13:5; Eph. 3:17.

157. Rom. 8:11; 2 Tim. 1:14.

158. Phil. 3:10.

159. Phil. 1:21.

160. Phil. 3:10.

161. Eph. 2:8.

162. Gal. 2:20; 2 Cor. 1:24; 5:17; Rom. 11:20; 1 Cor. 16:13.

163. Gal. 3:25.

164. Rom. 10:8; Gal. 3:2.

165. Christopher Reardon, "Islam and the Modern World," *Ford Foundation Report,* winter 2002, 22.

166. Pagels, *Gnostic Gospels,* and *The Origin of Satan* (New York: Random House, 1995)

167. This is not a convincing explanation of the origin of Christianity, or any religion for that matter. Religions catch hold because they have a specific, clear message. Pagels wants us to believe that religious confusion between Gnosticism and orthodoxy marked the earliest expressions of Christianity.

168. Ibid., though she sentimentally prefers the same reality dressed in Christian terminology.

169. Elizabeth Coleman, "The Good Book: Elaine Pagels Explores the Origins and Omissions of the Christian Bible," Ford Foundation Report (winter 2002): 31. When Pagels says "became," indicating a long process, is she taking into account the "set of beliefs" we find in the earliest creed of Christianity, cited by Paul in 1 Cor. 15:3–5, and dated to the late thirties or early forties. See Murray Harris, *Raised Immortal,* 13, who argues that this tradition could have been circulating "as early as A.D. 33." This is clearly what Christianity *is.* See the discussion of this subject in chapter 5.

170. Matt. 10:34.

171. Rom. 4:11.

172. Heb. 12:2.

173. The term for patience is ὑπομονῆς (Heb. 12:1). The verb used here (Heb. 12:7), translated "endure," is from ὑπομένω.

174. Rom. 8:18; 12:12; cp. 5:3; 2 Cor. 1:4–7.

175. Rom. 15:5.

176. 2 Cor. 6:4; 12:12.

177. 2 Tim. 2:10.

178. Rom. 2:7; 2 Thess. 1:4.

179. 1 Thess. 1:3; Rom. 5:3–4.

180. Eph. 2:17.

181. F. Hauck, "Μένω," *Theological Dictionary of the New Testament* 4 (Grand Rapids: Eerdmans, 1967), 586.

182. 1 Cor. 10:10; Phil. 2:14.

183. 1 Cor. 4:5.

184. 2 Cor. 5:7.

185. 1 Cor. 13:9.

186. 1 Cor. 4:10; 2 Cor. 12:10.

187. 2 Cor. 4:11.

188. 2 Cor. 4:6.

189. 1 Cor. 4:8.

190. Cp. Heb. 10:10: "And by that will, we have been made holy through the sacrifice of the body of Jesus Christ once for all."

191. Cp. Rev. 22:11.

192. See Titus 2:14 which quotes Deut. 14:2; 26:8.

193. Jerome D. Quinn, *The Letter to Titus: Anchor Bible* (New York: Doubleday, 1990), 160. See Ps. 130:8; Exod. 19:5, three texts in Deut., and Ezek. 37:23.

194. Gal. 2:11–15.

195. Bob Kauflin, "The Glory of the Cross."

196. ἀβασίλευτός.

197. μόναχος.

198. Abbot George Burke, *Gnostic Christianity: An Introduction* (Geneva, Neb.: Saint George Press, 1994), 41.

199. See Richard Hove, *Equality in Christ: Galatians 3:28 and the Gender Dispute* (Wheaton, Ill.: Crossway, 1999).

200. Eph. 3:10.

201. Eph. 1:18.

202. Eph. 3:14.

203. Eph. 5:21–6:9.

204. Gal. 3:28.

205. 1 Cor. 15:50.

206. See Jaspers, "Global Gorby," (*The New American,* 1996)

207. A statement by Jose Arquelles, a leading New Age thinker, cited on *thewildrose.net*, a web site run by a number of women with PhDs, who practice North American native Indian spirituality.

208. Ibid.

209. Schwartz, *What Really Matters: Searching for Wisdom in America* (New York: Bantam Books, 1996), 431.

210. Geering, *World to Come: From Christian Past to Global Future* (Santa Rosa, Calif.: Polebridge Press, 1999), 154.

211. Randal Baer in his book, *Inside the New Age Nightmare* (Lafayette: Huntingdon House, 1989) has collected chilling prophecies from New Age purveyors of universal peace and love: Maharishi Mahesh Yogi of Transcendental Meditation fame: "there has not been and there will not be a place for the unfit. The fit will lead, and if the unfit are not coming along there is no place for them . . . non-existence of the unfit has been the law of nature" (160); Ken Carey, a New Age channel and author, uses the biblical image of the sifting of wheat: "The Great Day of Purification has begun, a short but essential cycle of division that will gather those who promote fear and violence and separate them from this season of the world as chaff is separated from wheat at threshing" (168); J. Randolph Price, through his spirit guide, Asher, reveals

that all those who deny the divinity of all men are of Antichrist, and that "nature will soon enter her cleansing cycle during which those of 'lower vibratory rates' will be purified off the planet" (Baer, 169).

Already the level of rhetoric is rising in contemporary society among radical feminists: "We are going to stop all confinement of women. WITCH calls down destruction on Babylon. Oppressors: the curse of women is on you. Death to male chauvinism." ["WITCH documents, 1969," *Sisterhood Is Powerfull: An Anthology of Writings from the Women's Liberation Movement*, ed. by Robin Morgan (New York: Random House, 1970), 53, cited in Mary Daly and Jane Caputi, *Webster's First New Intergalactic Wickedary of the English Language* (Boston: Beacon Press, 1987), 117.] This may mean a clash that attempts to eliminate the Christian voice by the use of political power. Since Christians may not take up the sword, the clash is very one-sided.

212. Tom Hoopes, "Can Same-Sex Marriage Be Stopped?" *Crisis*, 2 July 2002, citing John McKellar, president of the homosexual movement, HOPE.

213. Hab. 2:14.

214. 2 Thess. 2:3, 7.

215. Gen. 3:16.

216. Rev. 18:2.

217. Eph. 6:10–20.

218. William Walsham How, "For All the Saints," *Trinity Hymnal* (Atlanta/Philadelphia: Great Commissions Publications, 1990), 350, stanza three.

Index